FLYING SOUTH

FLYING SOUTH
A Pilot's Inner Journey

BARBARA CUSHMAN ROWELL

PHOTOGRAPHS BY GALEN ROWELL AND
BARBARA CUSHMAN ROWELL

A MOUNTAIN LIGHT PRESS BOOK PUBLISHED BY

TEN SPEED PRESS
BERKELEY · TORONTO

Flying above the clouds through the Patagonian Andes.

Passing the Mayan ruins of Palenque.

Flying past the Ecuadorian volcanoes, Cotopaxi and Chimborazo.

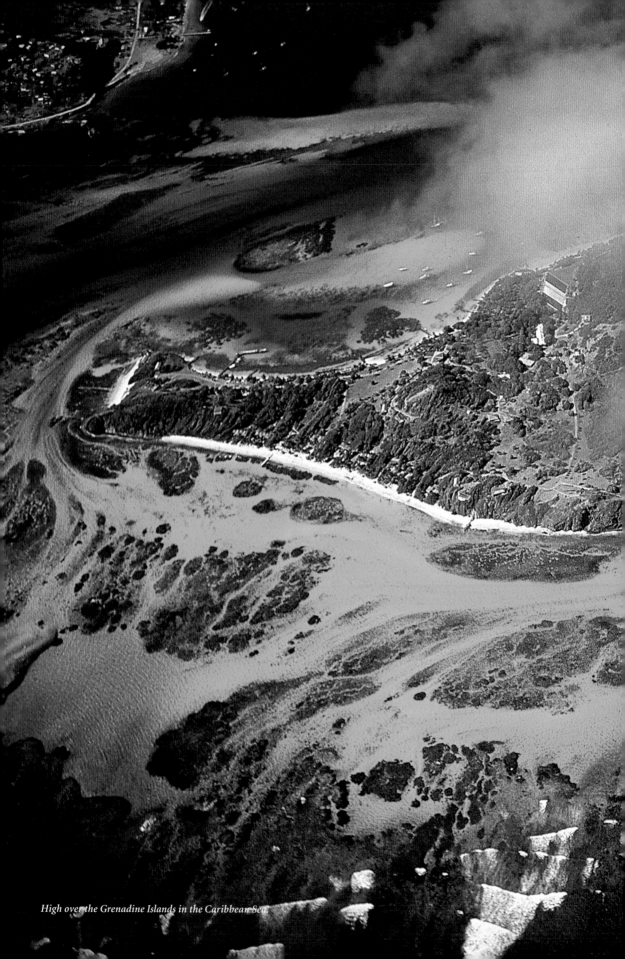

High over the Grenadine Islands in the Caribbean Sea

CONTENTS

There comes a time—it is the beginning of manhood or womanhood—

when one realizes that adventure is as humdrum as routine

unless one assimilates it, unless one relates it to a central core which

grows within and gives it contour and significance.

—LEWIS MUMFORD

Machu Picchu, Peru (left).

TAKEOFF

I

*I*n the hour before dawn, I passed through the metal security gate at Oakland Airport and drove out toward a dimly lit Cessna sitting alone on the tarmac. Even on this moonless night, I could make out my airplane's freshly painted call sign N735LY in twelve-inch-high letters, a requirement for crossing international borders.

The pressure to be ready for takeoff was palpable. As I thought about preparing myself and my single-engine airplane for the most serious flight of my life, the apprehension that had been temporarily held at bay by easy conversation on the way to the airport now rushed in to fill my soul. I dared not let it linger a moment too long for fear that it might overpower me, so I quickly slid out of the car and unlocked the plane.

My husband, Galen, backed up our old Chevy Suburban to the right wing near the cargo doors, careful not to hit the strut. He jumped out and began unloading a large number of duffels while my younger brother, Robert, set out to the terminal building to get ice for our plastic food chest.

Our friend Doug Tompkins would soon be flying over the Oakland Airport in his own Cessna 206. Doug was flying from Gnoss Field in Marin, 30 nautical miles north, to meet us in the air just before sunrise. He wasn't someone who would wait well, if at all, and I wasn't someone who liked to make people wait, or be left behind, so I scurried over to the terminal building to check for messages and make a final pit stop—my last chance to use a real bathroom for the next five hours.

As I jogged across the tarmac, my body tingled in the cool, dense air. The wind brushed against my face and hands. I welcomed the cold air as the chill would keep me on my toes. This was the kind of air that an airplane likes, too—cold and thick, something its propeller can bite into and pull itself skyward.

When I returned, I was unprepared for the way the plane looked after Galen had loaded it with all our gear. Its tail was now very low to the ground in a way I'd

N735LY, my Cessna 206.

heard stories about but had never actually seen, so I asked Galen if he could shift more things forward.

"Everything is fine the way it is," Galen replied with unabashed confidence.

"But the plane is so heavily loaded that it worries me," I replied.

"Bush pilots fly with a lot more weight than this all the time," he said.

"I'm not a bush pilot, remember?" I said.

Though Galen is not a pilot himself, he'd spent many hours flying in and out of rugged mountains with some of Alaska's best bush pilots. He'd been witness to hair-raising landings on glaciers and riverbanks that I had never considered doing. Nevertheless, he kept trying to convince me to fly like a bush pilot.

As he headed off to park the car, I double-checked his packing job. I was not convinced that he had believed me when I explained just how unforgiving an airplane can be with too much weight placed toward the rear. Since I would be the only pilot on board, it was my responsibility to ensure that the airplane was loaded correctly.

It may be demanding to fly a heavily loaded plane, but it can be deadly when the center of balance is moved too far aft. The weight in the tail can act like a fat kid on one end of a teeter-totter, forcing a comparatively lighter kid (the nose) ever higher. The angle at which the wing meets the air can become so steep that the airflow over the wing is interrupted. Then the wing stops providing lift and stalls, and the plane drops out of the sky like a rock.

Galen had indeed put the majority of light things, such as sleeping bags and parkas, in the rear, and the heavy things—his tripod, climbing hardware, and bottled water—toward the front, but he'd also left some open spaces. Before leaving home, I'd weighed each item and mapped out exactly where we'd put them based purely on weight, but I'd clearly underestimated the volume. At this point, to change the airplane's center of gravity significantly, I would have to take everything out, consider what to leave behind, and repack. That would delay takeoff, and Doug was the kind of guy who just might head south without me.

My calculations showed our final load to be 720 pounds of fuel, 500 pounds of luggage, plus 420 pounds of flesh and bones among the three of us. Combined with the empty weight of the aircraft, the total added up to exactly the airplane's maximum allowable takeoff weight of 3,800 pounds.

Flying a plane at its maximum weight is disquieting for a number of reasons: It takes longer to get off the ground, longer to clear any obstacles at the end of the runway, and longer to climb to a safe altitude. It also increases the speed at which the plane stalls. Emergency situations become more serious. If the engine were to quit, the plane would come down quicker and need more distance to stop. The pilot would have fewer choices about where to put down.

It is legal to fly a small plane this heavy but not a great idea, especially where we were heading. Flying 20,000-plus miles to Patagonia and back would take me over endless miles of remote rainforests and high Andean peaks, where airports are few and far between. Mountainous terrain and unruly drug lords are common enough that initially no one would insure me except Lloyd's of London, which wanted nearly $6,000 for this trip alone. Due to my lack of overall accumulated flight hours (less than 600 before departure) I was considered inexperienced. I would need 150 hours more flight time before I could even rent the type of airplane that I already owned.

I didn't need an insurance company to tell me that the chance of an emergency situation in the upcoming trip was painfully real. I'd already lost many a night's sleep contemplating it. This was a trip that I needed to make for reasons that I couldn't explain to friends who seemed happier in the safety of their own homes. After spending nine years of marriage supporting my husband's passions and desires while putting my own on hold, I was feeling desperate for an adventure that was my own.

Not long after I'd married Galen, a world-renowned climber, I felt as if I were being carried along in a whirlwind as I traveled the world with him on his assignments to write about and photograph his real-life adventures for magazine and book publishers. I resigned as director of public relations for The North Face and managed the business side of his photography. But, over time, I grew ever more disenchanted with my life as merely a support person.

There was no question that I had lots of fascinating stories to tell when I returned home from my husband's expeditions in Pakistan and Tibet on assignment for the likes of *National Geographic* and *Sports Illustrated,* but waiting around reading in base camp while he challenged unclimbed routes on Mount Everest and other peaks made it ever so clear to me that this was not *my* life's adventure.

Though I was not a climber and had no desire to be, I began to envy adventurers and wanted to know what it was like to be out on the edge, to experience the rush of one's own passions. My desire to fly arose from this deep longing to do something rewarding in life. I wanted to know what it felt like to be on my own expedition and in control of my own destiny. I was seeking to wake up in the morning challenged to my core. I wasn't going to let life pass me by without experiencing something like this just once.

This morning, reckoning by the turmoil roiling in my stomach, I had already accomplished part of what I'd set out to do. I was feeling so emotional that all I could manage was to keep moving, follow my to-do list, and begin to preflight my airplane. I enjoy the ritualistic inspection because it brings me face to face with my craft, refamiliarizes me with all its parts, and readies me to fly.

I walked around the airplane and scanned everything from the tail to the propeller. I'd waited for this moment for over a year, and now, despite my nervousness about our cargo, I was ready to go, but we still hadn't heard from Doug. Galen headed off to the terminal to check for messages one last time. He ran back to report, "Doug called and said he would be here in a few minutes."

I suggested that my brother, Robert, climb into the back seat first. Galen took a photograph of me, then scrambled in to take his place in the copilot's seat. Even though no one else appeared to be stirring at this hour of the morning, six years of habit had me opening the window and yelling "clear!" to alert anyone who might be standing nearby before I started the engine.

As I eased in the throttle, the plane reacted slowly. I felt as if I were trying to steer a giant slug. When I gave it a little more throttle and stepped hard on the right rudder pedal to help initiate a turn, nothing happened. Only when I gave it more throttle and stepped so hard on the pedal that it touched the floor did the plane begin a very slow arc. I added right brake to help pivot it along.

"I can't believe this! I can barely get the plane to go." My words resonated loud and clear into Galen's and Robert's ears through the voice-activated David Clark headsets we all wore to be able to hear one another over the drone of the engine.

"Robert and I can get out and push," Galen offered.

"It's worth a try, but stay clear of the propeller," I cautioned. As the two of them climbed out behind me in the dark, the butterflies in my stomach began to feel like ravens. My nerves, which normally calm down once I'm behind the controls, started to fray. Galen and Robert pushed on the wing struts, and the plane finally turned. After they clambered back in, I steered with the rudder pedals, using a string of blue lights to guide me to the engine run-up area. The active runway paralleled my path and could easily be identified in the dark by the long row of pearly white lights.

I held the plane in place using the brake pedals and tested my engine by pushing the throttle in until it reached 1,700 rpm. The engine sounded powerful and the instruments confirmed what my ears heard. When I was assured that everything looked good, I brought the power back to idle, looked over at my husband and brother, and smiled. I was ready for takeoff.

A moment later, Ground Control radioed: "Five Lima Yankee, are you expecting someone? I have a Cessna north of the field inquiring about you over the radio."

"Yes sir," I replied.

Switching frequencies, I told the tower that I was ready for departure.

"Five Lima Yankee cleared for takeoff. Climb and maintain two thousand feet until advised," the controller instructed.

I slowly maneuvered onto the runway and aimed down the centerline. With dawn still almost an hour away, we began slowly rolling down the strip as I asked Galen to start a timer. I could feel the extra weight in my hands and it didn't feel good. Instead of responding like a sports car, the plane felt more like an overloaded Volkswagen bus. When we passed the point where I normally lift off, the airspeed wasn't high enough for the airplane to fly, but the nose wheel popped up off the runway anyway. Immediately, the stall-warning buzzer blared with a screech, which so startled me that I put both hands on the control yoke and pushed as hard as possible to pitch the nose back down and build up airspeed. I could barely get the yoke to move. The weight in the tail was counteracting my efforts. The stall-warning continued to blare on and off. Now adrenaline pumped through my every cell. I tried desperately to keep the nose from rising up in such a steep manner, terrified the plane might stall, drop back down to the ground, and crash on takeoff.

"What's going on?" someone asked.

"Quiet!" I yelled. My ears were glued to the roar of the engine and the blare of the stall-warning buzzer. I knew I'd screwed up badly, and my heart pounded so hard it hurt. I needed to devote every ounce of concentration to fly us out of this situation.

"Five Lima Yankee radar contact. Say altitude."

I heard the controller call me but I was too busy to answer. I could not allow this flight configuration to continue even a few more seconds. I grabbed the base of the trim wheel beside my right leg and spun it forward a few inches to counteract the rearward shift of the plane's weight and balance and help release the weight in my hands. It was still no good, so I spun the trim wheel once again, this time all the way to its maximum position where it could go no farther. Finally, the nose began to lower. I glanced at the airspeed indicator and confirmed that it had increased enough to fly. As the plane crawled skyward, my legs were shaking uncontrollably and my hands were trembling.

Before takeoff, I'd set the nose trim where I always set it, but it should have been trimmed even more nose-low to accommodate the additional load in the rear. It was one of several mistakes I'd made this morning. A more experienced pilot might have caught this error, but I had missed it.

The white runway lights blurred against the black sky as the airport disappeared behind me and the plane headed into a dark void, which I knew to be the Oakland Hills. I said a private good-bye to everyone I was leaving behind. Shaken, I wondered if I would return alive.

"Everything is okay," I announced, as much to calm myself as my passengers. Now that we were out of imminent danger, I took a deep breath and answered the tower's call, "Five Lima Yankee is climbing through five hundred feet, sir."

I was upset that I had not trusted my own instincts about the weight and balance, resulting in a near disaster. After losing the argument with Galen over weight, I let myself be cornered into a classic aviation have-to-go-right-now trap. This trip was already stacking up to be more of an adventure than I'd bargained for.

At 600 feet the tower called again: "Five Lima Yankee; turn right zero niner zero degrees, vector to Niner One One Delta Juliett. Contact Bay Approach on one two seven decimal zero; advise them when you have the traffic in sight and tell them you are a flight of two."

I spotted the blinking white strobe lights of Doug's airplane against the black silhouette of Mount Diablo rising into the predawn glow of the eastern sky. Then I made the required radio call. Before I could say that we were a formation flight of two, Doug cut in and requested a radio frequency change and canceled radar flight following. I followed suit, switching frequencies to a prearranged air-to-air channel for talking discreetly. I heard Doug say, "Five Lima Yankee, are you there?" His gravelly voice was a welcome sound.

"Yeah Doug, I've got you in sight. I'm at your four o'clock position."

"Hey. Good morning, Barbara. How's it going?"

"I'm feeling a little tail-heavy. We look like Toys "Я" Us goes to South America," I said, trying to make light of the situation. I wanted to sound calm even though I was holding back tears. I'd nearly blown my first takeoff on the most important adventure of my life.

*Doug flying beside me at sunrise
after takeoff from Oakland (right).*

FLYING SOUTH

II

"*W*e're off like a herd of turtles!" I blurted out, repeating a phrase that my father always uttered as he pulled out of the driveway with our Pontiac station wagon stuffed to the ceiling for a summer vacation. Now I was at the controls of the aircraft version of that vehicle, a Cessna 206 Stationair, filled with family and possessions.

With everything finally under control, I took a moment to check on my passengers. Galen was looking out the window at the predawn glow and fidgeting with his camera gear. He seemed to be quite content, so I glanced over my shoulder to check on Robert. He was sitting absolutely motionless, staring out the window. When he noticed me turning around, he looked up with pale blue eyes that appeared to question me. He seemed painfully uncomfortable. I suspected that the stall warning had scared him as much as it had me. I reflected on how I would never forgive myself if anything happened to him during this adventure.

With the plane flying level for now, I wondered how much my weight and balance would change for the worse as 100 pounds of fuel an hour burned off from the tanks in the wings. From the difficulty I had had during takeoff, it was apparent that my plane was at its aft limit of balance. I felt I had no choice but to ask Robert to move whatever he could forward. Without a word, he unbuckled his seat belt, reached behind him, and moved several things up front. I felt the nose of the plane drop as the cubbyhole that remained for Robert virtually disappeared.

As the morning sun was about to poke into view from the east, the sky turned pinkish gold, lighting up a line of stratus clouds clinging to the coastal mountains to the west. The beauty of the morning sky from our bird's-eye view reminded me why I loved to fly. Galen's gasp of excitement showed he appreciated the scene, too. Moments later, he asked if I could slow the plane so that he could take a photograph of Doug's aircraft against the golden glow with the window open. All I could think about for the moment was going forward, not slowing down. But the sunrise was truly a splendid sight, and I knew that we would all appreciate his pictures later on.

"Oh my God. That's gorgeous!" Galen broke in over the intercom. "Ask Doug

Sunrise over the Coast Range,
south of San Francisco Bay (left).

to make a 360-degree turn so that I can get a closer silhouette of his plane against the sky."

"I'm not doing that," I stated.

"Why not?"

"I'm just not! If *you* want him to make a circle then you call him," I said.

I could not imagine asking Doug Tompkins to go out of his way to do something like that. I'd never flown tandem with another plane, so I had no idea what protocol was for two aircraft traveling together. But more important, I found Doug intimidating. Doug was the co-owner of Esprit, a billion-dollar clothing empire, and I was still a little in awe of him from my college days as a textiles student. It was a big deal for me to be following Doug at all, so asking him to change course for a photograph was simply out of the question.

"Push this button down on the yoke when you want to talk," I said, pointing out the radio switch on the copilot's yoke.

"No honey, you do it. Please?" Galen pleaded. He had never made a radio call before so I suspected that he had stage fright.

I didn't want to make Galen uncomfortable so I took a deep breath to gather courage and radioed Doug. He listened to my request and replied in a nonchalant voice, "Okay," seeming not to be the least bit disturbed by the inconvenience.

As he arced back around through his circle, I watched carefully in order to anticipate the moment Galen would need me to lift the right wing out of view. Just when N911DJ lined up against the muted reds, golds, and blues in the sky, looking like it was flying beside a Japanese tapestry, I gently lifted my right wing up and out of sight. Over the roar of cold air rushing into the cockpit from Galen's open window, I could hear the motordrive of his camera clicking away. When Galen put his camera down and closed the window, I asked, "Did you get it?"

"Yeah, I sure did. That was fantastic!" he exclaimed, as if he were seeing a sunrise from the air for the first time. From his response, I was pretty sure that he'd gotten a really fine photograph of publishable quality. He's still as passionate about seeing unusual light and form come together in the landscape as he was the day we met. I love that about Galen. His pursuit of photography has led me to see so many wonderful things in the natural world that I never would have seen if we weren't together. It also adds a dimension to flying that gives me great joy.

After I lowered the wing, I immediately called Doug to thank him for modeling. As we continued down the San Joaquin Valley, Doug and I flew side by side, less than a mile apart, trying to keep each other in sight, which was much harder to do than I had imagined. Thirty minutes into the flight I asked Galen, "Do you still see Doug?"

Both of us leaned forward and scanned the sky. If we didn't keep an eye on Doug every minute, we easily lost sight of him. It was imperative to maintain visual contact or stay well separated by altitude or distance.

"I've got him," I said.

My plane tended to overtake Doug's, even though his was the same model Cessna 206. His aerodynamics were different because of larger tires for landing on rough fields, plus a Robertson STOL (short takeoff and landing) conversion that altered his wings. The conversion was the main thing about his plane that I coveted; it allowed him to fly at slower speeds before inducing a stall, which might have been comforting this morning. Wind resistance on his larger tires combined with the STOL modification lowered Doug's cruising speed by several knots.

I flew down the right side of the lush farm-filled valley spreading nearly 100 miles to our east and 250 miles south. From 5,500 feet above the ground, I could see cattle huddled together in a field, but could only imagine their sounds and smells, which was fine with me. To my right was the vast California Coast Range, here and there veiled in mist as it appeared to vanish in the distance.

Gliding effortlessly over the land always gives me a rush. I feel like a visitor to Mother Nature's museum, where the show is never the same. Landforms, both natural and man-made, constantly entertain my eyes. There is always more than enough to look at, both within the cockpit and without. Besides the sheer beauty of the earth from above, I'm constantly checking engine gauges and cross-checking landmarks against my map and navigational instruments.

I'm never bored in flight. When I am at the controls, time flies with me. That sense of flow is how I know that flying is truly my passion. When I'm in the air on a clear day, I don't want it to end. When I'm on the ground, I can't wait to be back up in the sky. It's a feeling that is all-encompassing. The alternating sensations of feeling vulnerable and exhilarated are much like falling in love.

As the sun rose well above the horizon and bathed each nook and cranny of my cockpit with light, I felt comforted by its warmth. I thought that Robert must be feeling better, too, until I glanced back to see how he was doing. He looked terrible. His face was pale and tense. I didn't have to be his sister to know something was wrong.

"What's up, Robert?"

"I don't feel so good. I'm feeling kind of claustrophobic," he groaned.

"There is an air vent next to your head. Open it and let some cool air blow on your face."

There was nothing more I could do except to try to take his mind off his discomfort. He was too old for the kids' games we used to play in the backseat of our parents' car, but I knew that he loves music and I had just installed a brand new CD player for such occasions. For Robert, some upbeat music might be just what the doctor ordered.

"Let's listen to music! Galen, can you find my new Gipsy Kings disc to play?"

My husband reached between our seats for the binder that held the compact discs and found it. This would be the inaugural session for the new CD player. Doug had one in his plane. When I heard how glorious his sounded, I wanted one, too. Music would be great for long flights. It would help reduce the annoying drone of engine noise.

Galen carefully placed the Gipsy Kings CD in the player and hit the play button. "Nothing is happening," he said with obvious frustration. He kept tapping on the play button and finally asked, "What should I do?"

I had no idea. The player was to Galen's right, difficult to see from my position. Its amber lights glowed, but no music came out. He kept tapping on the player and reinserting the CD, but nothing happened.

I'd spent a lot of money and time having an Oakland avionics shop specially adapt the CD player to the voltage of my plane and install it in time for our flight. I'd gone to great lengths to put together an assortment of one hundred discs in a binder, with emphasis on Latin music to help me study Spanish during our airtime. Galen bent forward to look closer with his reading glasses. "There is definitely power to it, but it isn't playing."

I let out a big sigh. Not having music for the entire trip was so upsetting to contemplate that I focused my attention on the distant horizon of snow-covered peaks 100 miles to the east. We were just coming abeam Mount Whitney, the highest peak in the contiguous United States and one of the few mountains that I have climbed. Even at 14,496 feet, the white hulk is barely distinguishable from its tall neighbors at the southern end of the high peaks of the Sierra Nevada ("snowy range" in Spanish). From my aerial vantage point I could see almost 200 miles of white-capped summits.

I appreciated the rugged mountains from a distance, but I was happy that we were flying over a level valley dotted with small airports that were within gliding distance in the event that my engine quit. This was a feeling that Galen did not share with me. He prefers me to fly low over the mountains so he can scout places to climb and photograph. He's comfort-able in the wildest landscape because he's been climbing since he was a child. I see mountains as beautiful but hazardous. I find them fascinating, yet intimidating when I'm flying over them.

Though I was flying in clear condi-tions where filing a flight plan is not re-quired, a special flight plan must be filed to cross an international border. I had wanted to file one before departure, but Doug wanted to do it in flight. Since he was the one with more border-crossing experience, I deferred to him, but I was not com-pletely comfortable with the idea.

I come from a family where my father saluted men and stood at attention in their presence based purely on little stripes sewn onto their clothing. I still remem-ber visiting my father's office when he was stationed in the navy as a lieutenant commander. I thought he was in charge of everyone, until I watched him stand at attention, click his heels together, and salute a man simply because that person wore more glitter. I had come to believe in a defined hierarchy of power based purely on one's rank, and no matter how hard I've tried, I've been unable to shake my child-hood beliefs completely.

Although Doug wasn't in uniform, I felt he outranked me in many ways: he was older, he had a hundred times my flight experience, he'd flown to South America before, and he was a self-made multimillionaire. It made sense to me to defer to him when in doubt.

Central Valley farmland (left); eye to eye with Mount Whitney (on an earlier flight) (above).

Somewhere over the Central Valley, Doug called to say he was changing radio frequencies. I changed too and overheard him filing a DVFR (defense visual flight rules) flight plan to Mexicali with the FAA's Los Angeles Flight Service. The *D* in DVFR indicated we would be penetrating our country's Air Defense Identification Zone as we crossed the U.S.–Mexico border. If a pilot fails to call prior to crossing the border, he or she can be intercepted and forced to land—or worse. VFR (visual flight rules) signifies navigation by sight as opposed to IFR (instrument flight rules), which refers to navigation by instruments, usually in weather conditions too poor for VFR flight.

As soon as Doug was finished with his radio call, I filed my flight plan, too. Now anyone who was listening in on the same frequency knew my name, phone number, where I'd departed from, where I was headed, how many passengers were traveling with me, how much fuel I had on board, the color of my airplane, my route of flight, my altitude, and my estimated time to my destination. By adding ADCUS (advise customs) to the list, Flight Service was required to advise Mexican customs of my arrival.

As we crossed the Tehachapi Mountains at the northern edge of the Mojave Desert, I contemplated whether we would be able to find adequate service in Mexico to have the CD player repaired or whether we should land and fix it while we were still in the United States. I radioed Doug and asked him what he thought. Since Palm Springs was the closest airport from our position and my pilot's guide indicated that avionics repairs were available on the field, we agreed to change heading and fly directly toward the airport, which was not far off our course. Doug called Flight Service to amend both of our flight plans. He seemed genuinely flexible. I began to feel a little more comfortable communicating with him over the radio.

Above Joshua Tree National Park, I started my descent over a contorted desert landscape of strange trees and eroded rocks. I'd been here many times, both on the ground and in the air, but it never ceased to amaze me how insignificant this wild and beautiful desert looked from thousands of feet above. Some landscapes look wilder from the air, while others fade into a kind of monotony with each increment of altitude. The desert looks more dramatic the closer I am. I try to balance flying high enough to be as safe as possible and low enough to experience the earth moving beneath me and with me.

As I descended toward Palm Springs, the landscape continued to gain visual power and speed as veritable Stonehenges of eroded rocks passed beneath my wings. Once we landed, a tanned, young line-service fellow arrived in an oversize golf cart and tied my plane down before I could explain that we weren't staying. He insisted that we ride with him the short distance to the terminal building, even though we assured him that we were physically fit enough to make the walk. We hopped in and were whisked toward a fancy flight office surrounded by private jets. Once we entered the waiting room, we each grabbed an apple from a bowl sitting on the counter and began to nibble as we waited for a young woman to finish talking to a pilot over the radio about securing a rental car. When it was my turn, I inquired about the nearest avionics shop. She looked past me, directly at Galen, and said, "There isn't one anymore. There used to be."

I wanted to forget about trying to get the CD player fixed but Galen called the avionics shop in Oakland for advice. Since he had once owned an auto-repair service, he wanted to see if he could repair it himself. They gave him some things to look for, so he caught a ride back out to the plane. While he fiddled with the player, I made a few phone calls to various friends to say we were really on our way. Fifteen minutes later, he returned to share the bad news: he couldn't get it to work and concluded that the unit had burned out due to an improper voltage conversion. The display no longer lit up when turned on, as it had in the first minute or two. I felt a surge of frustration toward my avionics shop but decided to forget about it and move on. Perhaps we'd find a mechanic along the way who could fix it.

As we walked back to the plane, Robert put his arm around me and asked, "Do you think I can get a commercial flight out of here?"

"Why?"

"I don't know. I just feel uncomfortable. Maybe if I weren't here with all my luggage, you wouldn't be having all these problems."

It had been a challenge for Robert to leave work for the entire month of December to join us. The timing couldn't have been worse. As assistant director of the Squaw Valley Ski Patrol, he risked losing his job by being gone during the busy weeks of Thanksgiving and Christmas. It's common wisdom that no one dares ask for time off during the heart of the ski season. ("Thousands of skiers would love to have your job.") Besides risking his job, he was also worried about leaving behind his girlfriend of seventeen years to celebrate her fortieth birthday alone. Yet the opportunity to fly to Patagonia with your sister comes only once.

Knowing all this, it was difficult for me to watch him consider giving up so soon. Even more than wanting him to stay, I wanted him to have a good time. I had traveled by car through both the Chilean and Argentine sides of Patagonia five years earlier, and I wanted him to experience this incredible part of the world with me.

"Why don't you change places with Galen? You can help me navigate," I suggested, trying to keep him involved in the process of our adventure together. I needed him on this trip. Having Robert along meant more than he could possibly understand. Whenever my brother is around, I perform better in everything I do, from tennis to skiing. Though he has been a competitive athlete in ice hockey, swimming, tennis, and table tennis, he has always avoided directly competing with me and somehow brings me along toward his level of expertise. His contagious positive attitude inspires me to greater personal accomplishments than I would normally achieve alone. I didn't want to give him the opportunity to leave this trip.

To complete the flight, I needed more than piloting skills. Most of all, I needed to believe in myself. Robert's very presence would help me do that. Crossing the border to Mexico and flying on into the unknown loomed large in my mind. I looked to his unspoken trust to help balance my apprehension.

Overhearing us discuss our weight problems, Doug offered to take some of our load, but I didn't respond soon enough. While I was still sorting out having Robert and Galen switch places, Doug started his engine and began taxiing toward the runway. He hadn't said a word about departing.

I had flown into Palm Springs beneath Mount San Jacinto many times before (right).

WEIGHT AND BALANCE

III

When I asked Galen to switch places with Robert, he did so without complaint. Being crowded in the backseat of a plane was nothing to Galen compared to being in countless hanging bivouacs on vertical cliffs thousands of feet above the ground. Climbing huge rock walls both for fun and on assignment left Galen well prepared for more ordinary physical hardships. Sometimes I wondered if he were really human or if I'd married an animal, especially when I listened to him tell stories about the time he'd skied 285 miles across the Karakoram Himalaya with 120 pounds— 60 pounds on his back plus 60 more in a sled behind him. He ran out of food well before reaching the only cache, from where he continued on for weeks and lost 30 pounds. He clearly had exceptional capabilities for handling hardship. I could count on him to handle being crowded.

As Robert climbed back into the airplane and settled into the copilot's seat, his face relaxed and his smile returned. I thought this new arrangement might work out perfectly. Robert could help navigate, which would keep him from feeling like a burden to me, while Galen could photograph through the little hinged window port on the left side behind my seat without my having to slow the plane to open the entire large window on the right and blow a sudden rush of cold air throughout the cockpit. When I glanced back, Galen was smiling amid the tightly stacked piles of luggage.

Robert's only previous experience navigating an airplane had been a few days earlier on my flight simulator. I tried to explain navigating to a VOR (very high frequency omnidirectional radio) by comparing the invisible magnetic headings, which we needed to follow, to the spokes of a bicycle wheel aimed at a central hub from an outside circle. We needed to use compass readings to navigate toward the fixed central point where a VOR station on the ground emitted signals.

Within an hour of simulator time on my home computer, Robert had been able to pinpoint exactly where a virtual aircraft that I had hidden on my computer screen

Before leaving for South America, I'd flown only briefly with another
plane to get photographs, but never on an extended flight (left).

was located on a map. It was obvious that he had a talent for navigation and that would come in handy when I was busy at the controls.

As a safety precaution, I had called my flight instructor and said, "I know this is a bit unusual, but I want you to take my husband and my brother flying and have them land an airplane even though they don't know how to take off. Let them feel what it's like to put the tires on the runway. I want them to have that experience just in case."

I set up an appointment for Galen to practice landings that week. On the morning he was scheduled to fly, he looked out our bedroom window and said, "It's too windy today."

"That's funny!" I commented. "You never think it's too windy for *me* to fly."

Normally, nothing seems to scare Galen, so I was amused that he postponed his flight lesson twice, due to the wind. He justified his decision by adding that he was tired from a many-city press tour for his current book.

Three days before departure, Robert arrived in Berkeley from his home at Lake Tahoe to hang out with me and prepare for the trip. I rescheduled the flight lesson so that Robert and Galen could go together.

I thought Galen might make a perfect landing on the first try since he had been sitting at my side during so many of my landings, both good and bad. I honestly expected flying to have rubbed off on him, though I secretly hoped he'd find it difficult. When Galen returned from the airport, I asked him how it went.

With a sheepish grin he admitted, "I bounced it a bit. I had no idea how hard it is to land. I have a lot more respect for flying now."

That was exactly what I'd hoped to hear.

Robert arrived in his own car an hour later and asked, "Were you trying to kill me?"

I called the flight instructor to get an objective opinion.

"Galen porpoised down the runway, but that was to be expected. For the most part, it went all right," Aaron said. "Having Galen at the controls scared Robert, and he wanted out of the plane. Landing was easier for Robert. He's a real natural."

I was relieved that they both had an idea of what it really felt like to put an airplane down on a runway, just in case something happened to me. I didn't expect that would be the case, but the chances were greater traveling through foreign countries and eating foreign foods just before spending hours behind the controls.

As I was about to enter Mexico in my own plane, I wanted everything to go just right. Even though I knew all the pretakeoff procedures by heart, I began my ritual-istic reading and complete follow-through of every item on the checklist. After the engine was purring, I flipped the avionics switch that powered up the radios and brought the red instrument lights to life. To ascertain local airport conditions, I dialed in ATIS (automatic terminal information service), the recording available at most airports with control towers.

A male voice droned, "Palm Springs Airport ATIS information Whiskey, eighteen forty-five Zulu observation: skies clear, visibility two zero, temperature seven two, dew point not available, wind two five zero at five, altimeter two niner niner zero, ILS Three Zero in use. All arriving aircraft contact Approach on one two six point seven. All departing aircraft contact Clearance Delivery on one two one point niner and say direction of flight and VFR cruising altitude. Advise on initial contact that you have ATIS information Whiskey."

Non-pilots seem amazed that anyone can make heads or tails out of this strange gobbledygook. But once a pilot has been trained to understand the basic formula, the jargon is nowhere near as complicated as it sounds.

After noting the relevant information in my own version of shorthand, I dialed in the new altimeter setting and double-checked that my gauge now indicated 448 feet to match the field elevation indicated on my map. Then I called Clearance Delivery: "Palm Springs Clearance, November Seven Three Five Lima Yankee, Cessna two zero six for Mexicali four thousand five hundred with Whiskey." I said only what was required: nothing more, nothing less.

A controller responded, "November Seven Three Five Lima Yankee, Roger, climb and maintain runway heading at or below two thousand feet, contact Departure on one one eight decimal five, squawk three two seven eight, contact Ground before taxi on one two one decimal niner."

I enjoy talking on the radio. It's so straight to the point and unemotional. When a pilot says "Stand by," it's so much more clear and simple than saying: "Sorry, I'm busy; I can't talk right now; I'll call you back later. "Stand by" says it all and no one gets his or her feelings hurt.

"Roger" is great, too. In aviation it simply means: I understand what you have said. And "Wilco" goes a step further to say I *will* *com*ply with what I heard you say. Only dorks say, "Roger, Wilco, over and out," as in the B movies. A little goes a long way, and I love the challenge of making my radio communications as clear and concise as possible.

On the other hand, I love hearing all the radio chatter of other pilots and controllers. I get a kick out of overhearing airline pilots talking to my same flight controllers. Even though flying is not my career and I am not an airline pilot, participating in the same procedures in the same way they do makes me feel as if I'm one of them.

After completing a short round of controller-speak/pilot-speak, I began rolling down the taxiway toward Doug, who was parked doing his engine run-up. My feelings were a little bruised by his taxiing off without helping me unload some of my gear after saying he would.

As I pulled alongside Doug, I nosed Lima Yankee into the wind to keep the engine cooler during the run-up. I remembered my takeoff earlier this morning and shuddered, but even without transferring any of our gear into Doug's plane, Lima Yankee was 320 pounds lighter, having flown 3 hours and burned off 53 gallons of fuel. My weight-and-balance situation had also improved after Robert moved things toward the front. Nevertheless, I still didn't like flying my plane so heavy.

Doug's plane held comparatively little. He was carrying his own gear and only one passenger, Peter Buckley, a business partner from Marin County, who had brought only an overnight bag and planned to return on a commercial flight as soon as we arrived in Santiago. Peter was in the process of getting his pilot's license and wanted to join Doug mainly for the flight experience.

When I had peeked inside Doug's plane, it looked empty. How he was able to travel so light, I couldn't fathom. When he had come over to ours, he had commented on how ridiculous we looked stuffed to the ceiling. His blue-and-white plane sat on the tarmac with its tail held high like a proud bird poised to take flight. My plane still sagged in the rear like a dog with its tail between its legs.

Weeks before departure, Galen and I had discussed at length what each of us would bring on this extraordinary journey. We'd had more than a few unpleasant exchanges. When I'd assert that he'd have to limit all his climbing and adventure gear, he'd counter by pointing out the 40 pounds of bottled water and all the Costco food I'd stockpiled.

My packing list was extensive, too. But I felt justified in what I was taking because I was planning to fly over parts of the Atacama Desert of Chile, where it hadn't rained for a hundred years and over the Andes, right where a Uruguayan rugby team had crashed and the survivors ended up eating their teammates. I'd be much happier eating Costco bulk food than my brother or husband.

Although Doug had provided the opportunity to fly our planes together on the way down, flight and survival preparations were entirely my responsibility. I needed to prepare for the fact that even though he'd be nearby during flight, I'd be on my own if my engine failed. I'm a perfectionist, so I began obsessing over every detail. This came as no surprise to family or friends, who know me to be a worrywart. It's hard work that runs in my family. I get it from my mother, who inherited if from her mother, but until I came along, nobody was better at it than my grandmother.

To be a truly great worrier, one must have a good imagination. I'm strong in that category, too. Before departure, my daydreams went wild. I envisioned every conceivable remote location where we might crash. I could see the headline in the *San Francisco Chronicle:* BERKELEY FAMILY DISASTER MAKES DONNER PARTY TRAGEDY LOOK TAME.

My way of dealing with my personal fears is to prepare myself thoroughly for as many eventualities as possible. Much of what I packed was for surviving in a desert or in open water. Besides food and drink, I included 3 life jackets, several emergency flares, 4 quarts of engine oil, 6 spark plugs, a small tool kit, 40 pounds of flight maps and guidebooks, plus a light step stool to check fuel in my tip tanks. I was not taking a lot of clothing, but I did pack a few dress clothes as well as a raincoat, down parka, gloves, and hiking shoes.

As I watched the pile of gear grow in the garage, it was clear that Galen and I had different agendas. I thought he understood that we were finally heading off together on my adventure—a flying adventure, not a climbing adventure or a photographic adventure. For me, the essence of this trip would be the challenge of flying through foreign countries and seeing them from above. It was all about the mode of getting there, rather than the there itself.

But while Doug had invited me to fly with him, he'd also invited Galen to climb with him. By the time we left, Galen had packed for three separate adventures. To climb an unscaled Andean peak with Doug, he brought heavy ropes, carabiners, mountain boots, ice axes, and a whole assortment of mountaineering gear. He also brought lots of photographic gear, including a big telephoto lens for wildlife.

Galen also planned to photograph endangered alerce trees in a remote part of southern Chile for *National Geographic.* The idea came from Rick Klein, an environmental activist for Ancient Forest International, who had heard about Doug's forest activism and arranged to meet us in Chile for a multiday trek into the heart of an old-growth alerce forest. Galen said this endeavor wouldn't add much additional weight, since he was already bringing his camera equipment, but he did add his heavy-duty, 6-pound tripod to photograph in the deep forest, plus a lighter Gitzo tripod to take climbing. Every little pound added up.

The third adventure also revolved around Doug. He wanted all of us to spend Christmas week descending Chile's Bio Bio River, renowned for its extreme whitewater rapids. A world-class kayaker, Doug had been down it before. He thought we would get a thrill out of rafting it while he kayaked along beside us. I wasn't keen on this idea. Though I'd been a competitive swimmer and wasn't afraid of water per se, I was extremely afraid of wild whitewater. Even the two mild rafting trips I'd been on had scared me enough not to want to do more. When I mentioned my concern to Doug, he replied that he and his ex-wife, Susie, had rafted the Bio Bio with their two girls when they were very young and had had no problems. Hearing that, I agreed to give it a try.

Galen was adamant about bringing most of what he needed because we might not be able to get proper supplies in South America. I was sure there were things he could leave behind, so I hovered nearby as he organized his gear in the garage. Every pound that he added to the heap sparked the already combustible atmosphere at home. We were both on edge. Even though our life was normally fast paced and we were accustomed to doing many things at once, we had reached our limits. After several years without enough fun or quiet time, neither of us was handling the increased workload very well.

From the outside, I appeared to have everything I could possibly want: a wonderful, loving husband; a successful and exciting business; interesting friends; and the opportunity to travel around the world to photograph glorious landscapes, wild creatures, and vanishing cultures. What I was missing was something that I couldn't quite define at first.

Our trips were not vacations. We didn't lie around on beaches, go on picnics, play games, go to concerts, or take easy neighborhood strolls. Instead, our marriage had become a parallel work machine, seven days a week from early morning into the wee hours of the night.

The more I worked with Galen, the more my emotions became stirred up like unsettled dust caught in a tornado. His untempered enthusiasm for jumping into new projects without time to recover in between left me feeling empty. When I hounded him to slow down and make room for me, he repeatedly promised to do so. But with each passing month, a new book or assignment would find its way into our lives and take over any hope of unstructured time together.

Employees and friends vied for his attention, competing with journalists requesting interviews, photographers wanting technical advice, publishers setting deadlines, climbers asking for help planning expeditions, plus fans from all over the world asking for just a moment of his time.

I tried to match his work ethic, hoping this would bring us closer together. Our mutual high energy was something that had brought us together in the first place, but no matter how hard I worked, he managed to work harder. He would accept impossible deadlines from publishers and set himself up for a time crunch in which I was always the loser. Week after week I would hear him say, "This is the worst week ever. As soon as it's over, things will calm down."

I did take personal pride in watching Galen's career skyrocket. We complemented each other in business: his writing and photography paid our bills, and my organizational skills and vision took us to higher levels.

Still, it was a rude awakening when a man at a party given in Galen's honor cornered me and asked, "How does it feel to be living in someone's shadow?" I looked around the room hoping to wave Galen over to step in and defend my honor by saying, "You've got it all wrong! She isn't in my shadow. She's largely responsible for my success." But Galen, surrounded by a crowd of people, was oblivious to my discomfort.

"I don't see it like that," I said. "His success is my success, too."

The gentleman raised his eyebrows and stared at me in disbelief. Financially, I was telling the truth. Emotionally, I was beginning to feel bankrupt, but I hadn't admitted that to anyone—not even to myself. Having a total stranger approach me with a question like that was paralyzing.

For a long time after the party, the man's question burned inside me. It made all my hard work seem like years of doing dishes. Nobody cared about all the hours I'd contributed to Galen's career. I was a nobody. I didn't have my own life experiences from which I could produce books and lectures for adoring fans. All I had were the secondary experiences of tagging along on someone else's coattails. Everywhere we went, his fans looked around me, over me, past me, and through me. They wanted to see Galen Rowell, not his wife. I was invisible.

I had to accept that Galen's career had become our way of life. I struggled between helping my husband reach his goals and pursuing goals of my own, which admittedly I had yet to define.

By the late eighties, I was attending personal growth workshops and going to counseling in order to gain insight on how to correct my growing sense of loneliness. Everywhere I turned, I was told to search for my own fulfillment. Outside of work, I began taking horseback-riding lessons, tennis lessons, and classical-guitar lessons, while working on a novel, hosting Spanish study groups, and going out to dinners and movies with friends. Though I was casting about for anything that

would stir my passions, all along I secretly hoped to land on an activity that we could share together. But Galen would always excuse himself because he was overbooked.

While I loved my husband, the more I did without him, the more I wondered why I was staying married. When inner despair turned to depression, I began suggesting a divorce. Each time the subject came up, Galen pleaded with me not to leave, still promising a better relationship someday soon. But days turned to months, and then years, without my needs for companionship being met. My self-esteem hit bottom. By the time we left for South America, Galen's and my world had begun to move apart. Beneath all the turmoil, I still held onto a vision of everything working out for us in the long run. If our marriage and dreams were to survive, both of us would have to change. I would need to establish an inner and outer respect. He would need to change his priorities to put us first.

Flying my own plane to South America was the beginning of my quest for a new self. I was counting on this trip to be very different from our past travels done on Galen's terms. I viewed the stall warning that had sounded this morning as a signal to listen to my own intuition. Our lives depended on it.

In urban Pakistan, where women's faces are publicly invisible, I wore a veil (above), but in the privacy of a Karakoram hut, an Islamic mother let me capture an unveiled moment (right) that became the lead photograph in a National Geographic *story.*

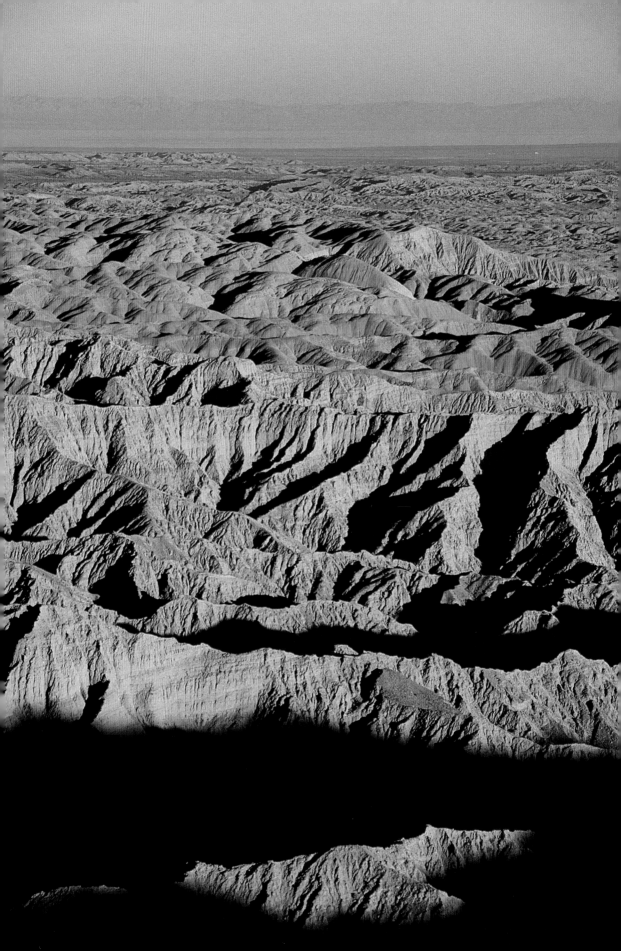

BORDER CROSSING

IV

*A*fter Doug and I flew over the Anza-Borrego Desert along the western rim of the Salton Sea, I could see the Imperial Valley gradually flattening in the distance into a patchwork of farmland that stretched toward the border. For the moment, my attention was on flying the shoreline to avoid piercing restricted military airspace immediately to the west. As soon as we passed the salty inland sea, I dialed in Mexicali Tower on my second frequency and pushed in a communications switch that allows me to monitor two radio frequencies at the same time. The voice of a Mexican pilot reporting his position to the tower in Spanish made me tingle with expectation: "Mexicali Torre. Piper Seneca Dos Siete Nueve Oscar Papa diez millas al sur para Mexicali. Cambio."

Spanish! My adventure was beginning to feel real. I was finally flying south into my childhood dreams of fuzzy llamas and lofty volcanoes, steamy green rainforests and cool damp cloud forests, Andean peaks and Quechua Indians. I would see it all, from reed boats sailing on Lake Titicaca in the Altiplano of Peru to the arid Atacama Desert of Chile, up close and personal from the best seat in the house.

"Mexicali Tower, November Seven Three Five Lima Yankee, twenty miles north, landing Mexicali," I announced over the radio, using my full call sign as required on initial contact. The letter N in the call sign, which I signified by saying "November," identified my airplane as registered in the United States of America, not the month of my flight, although that happened to be true, too.

"November Seven Three Five Lima Yankee," the controller said slowly with a heavy Spanish accent. "This is Mexicali Tower. What is your departure airport and type aircraft?"

After I responded with the appropriate information he called again and said, "Five Lima Yankee report crossing the border."

English is the international language of flight. The Mexicali tower controller was doing just fine in my mother tongue, making the procedures seem quite easy to follow. Moments later, I heard him switch easily between the English instructions he had given me to Spanish instructions for another pilot who was reporting inbound within Mexico. I'd spent years trying to make Spanish my second language and I

Badlands of Anza-Borrego (left).

was looking forward to using it on this trip, but I contained my urge to join in and try my hand at Spanish.

All the sleepless nights that I'd spent worrying about this very border crossing faded away. Even the stories I'd heard of American airplanes being confiscated by Mexican officials or appropriated by drug smugglers seemed as unreal as a scene out of a B movie.

Doug had told me that he'd never had any such problem, and he'd flown to South America in his single-engine Cessna several times before. The first time was in 1971, shortly after he had received his pilot's license. As Doug told the story, he simply piled Susie and their two daughters, Quincy and Summer, into his Cessna 182 and flew to Chile. The flight itself did not seem as remarkable to me as the fact that he did it with almost no experience as pilot-in-command. That was impressive. Hopping into an airplane with your family to fly around Latin America right after becoming a pilot seemed like the opening scene of an episode of *The Twilight Zone*. It was also a clear illustration of the difference between Doug's adventurous personality and my own.

I recalled the day Galen introduced me to Doug in 1982, soon after we were married. When Galen first mentioned that he was friends with a climber named Doug Tompkins, I didn't believe he was the same Doug Tompkins that I'd heard stories about long before I'd ever heard of Galen Rowell. The Doug I knew had become famous after he and his wife started a women's clothing company out of their garage in 1968. Their San Francisco–based Esprit de Corps skyrocketed to worldwide success during the seventies. Doug and Susie became extremely wealthy overnight. The storybook rags-to-riches couple began raking in hundreds of millions of dollars as everything Esprit touched turned to gold.

Galen could not be talking about the same man. He described a regular guy who fit right in with the grubby climbing crowd in Yosemite and the Grand Tetons. I had imagined that the Doug Tompkins who owned Esprit most certainly spent his time with the jet set and surrounded himself with gorgeous models and high-powered fashion moguls, such as Bill Blass or Calvin Klein. Although I could not imagine this Doug Tompkins hanging out with climbers, the possibility became real when Galen mentioned that Doug had sometimes shown up in Yosemite Valley in a Ferrari.

Galen first met Doug in Yosemite in the sixties. They were both rock climbers who spent time in Camp Four and loved to scale big granite rock walls. After their

Camp Four days, they each headed off into different worlds, but stayed in touch. Doug frequently invited Galen to his lavish San Francisco parties.

One day Galen invited me to join Doug for lunch at the Esprit cafeteria. Doug was polite and said hello to me when we first arrived, but directed his conversation at Galen, rarely looking me in the eye. I began to feel invisible in Doug's presence and remained speechless throughout the lunch hour, listening intently to Doug carry on about kayaking uncharted rivers in Chile and climbing peaks in the Antarctic with some of America's most legendary adventurers. He frequently dropped Yvon Chouinard's and Royal Robbins's names like pennies in a pond. Not by coincidence, both Robbins and Chouinard had founded their own clothing companies. In fact, Chouinard named his company Patagonia at Doug's suggestion while climbing there with him.

As Doug told stories, Galen rarely got a word in edgewise, unusual for someone who normally holds his own in conversations. I scanned the trendy corporate dining room and tried to conjure up what it might be like to work for Doug.

I'd been in the clothing business too, but on a much smaller scale. My career, which began on my mother's sewing machine at the age of eight, was launched when I made an adorable fire-engine-red cotton skirt that went well with my white buck shoes. Of course that first skirt didn't hold a candle to the designs in the Esprit line, but it was quite high fashion for a third grader. Sewing the seemingly endless hem of a circle skirt challenged my young patience, but by high school, I was making most of my wardrobe. By college, I was sewing everything in my closet, from swimsuits to jumpsuits.

Although making clothes started out as a hobby, it eventually turned into a livelihood when I left my first husband after seven years. Once we agreed that we weren't compatible, I moved from Sacramento to Lake Tahoe to start a new life in the mountain resort near where my brother lived. With forty dollars to my name and no college degree or family money to fall back on, I turned to the skill I knew best: sewing. I began designing Western shirts for men. Some of my unique patterns attracted the attention of a young woman from Los Angeles who invited me to design skiwear with her. My experience was limited, but she didn't seem to care. With her experience as a clothing designer for Walt Disney, plus funding from a friend, we opened a small factory in the ice-skating rink at Squaw Valley and named our company Space Cowboy. From scratch, we produced downhill ski parkas, ski pants, and one-piece warm-up suits.

Not wanting to be sewing in my old age, I left the mountains and enrolled at Sacramento State College. I also applied to enter the highly respected textiles program at the University of California at Davis with hopes of becoming a clothing designer. In my enthusiasm, I told everyone about my plan to make something of my life, including an attorney who frequented the restaurant where I'd worked and had asked me out. When I mentioned UC Davis on our first and last date, he said, "Davis? That's where I got my law degree. You'll never get accepted there. If you do, you'll never make it through."

Gripping my chair to restrain myself from strangling him, I asked, "Are you serious?"

He was.

How was he judging me? By my petiteness or my blonde hair? Certainly, my language skills were up to snuff. Did he know something about me that I hadn't told him? That neither of my parents finished college did not mean my family wasn't smart. Perhaps he suffered from the belief that "once a waitress, always a waitress."

Though this guy knew me only superficially, I took his words as a challenge. What right did he have to throw cold dishwater on my dreams?

Within the year, UC Davis accepted my application. I worked every spare minute patching together a variety of part-time jobs to pay for books, tuition, food, and rent. I moved to an apartment near school, sold my car for a bike, and attended a full load of classes during the day. My main income came from waiting tables at lunch, but I also worked two afternoons a week setting up student internships for the university. On the weekends, I designed and sewed custom skiwear for students.

Before attending UC Davis, I imagined distinguished, mature students strolling gracefully across the campus, perhaps intellectualizing over the effects of chaos on the making of fine wines. Instead, I found students who looked barely out of high school, sporting farmer-johns and dashing about on cheap bicycles. Nearing the ripe old age of thirty, I felt out of place. But my age worked to my advantage. While many classmates partied at night, I studied. With a late start on my career, I didn't want to waste even a moment on frivolous activities. I made out a weekly to-do list and followed it religiously.

To keep up with skiwear design, I hitched a ride to an outdoor retailer's trade show in Oakland, where I bumped into a ski-racer friend from Squaw Valley. He introduced me to Klaus Obermeyer, owner of Sport-Obermeyer, a skiwear manufacturer in Aspen. Klaus invited me to take a summer off and come to Colorado to work as a liaison between his factory production staff and his wife, who designed their skiwear line.

I accepted his invitation, packed my worldly possessions into two cardboard boxes and flew to Colorado with my trusty bike. By the end of summer, Klaus was still paying me minimum wage, but having me sketch out parka and sweater designs for his wife. The university agreed to give me college credit to continue working in Colorado during the fall quarter.

My forte was creating patterns that looked good in motion from a distance, but Mrs. Obermeyer immediately dismissed my drawings as too complicated. Strangely, however, she banned me from wearing my own personally designed and handcrafted parkas on the streets of Aspen, saying that other designers might copy my work. Like a ghost, I worked invisibly in the back room, producing a broad range of ideas that seemed to vanish after I turned them over.

I could not draw as well as I could sew. For the next several weeks, I worked around the clock, making patterns and sewing shells of most of my designs. When Klaus returned from Europe, he discovered my original work hidden in my tiny workspace at the back of the warehouse. He told his wife that it looked better than anything they had planned to copy from European designers. They incorporated most of my work into their new line of skiwear.

Life at Lake Tahoe had not prepared me for the harder, faster pace of Aspen. At the end of the year, I'd had enough of its glitz, so I returned to Davis to finish school. The following year, I graduated with highest honors, but more important, when I stepped up to the podium to receive my diploma, I was a changed person.

After graduation, I moved to San Francisco to be nearer to the heart of the West Coast clothing industry and make my mark. Starting at the top, I applied for a job at the hottest company in town, Esprit de Corps. Before going to the interview, I drove by Esprit to check it out, see how people dressed, and get a feel for the company. Esprit far exceeded my expectations. Doug and Susie Tompkins's unusual work ethic was on the cutting edge of corporate leadership. Their employees were allowed to exercise during the middle of the day in the corporate gymnasium and could wear their gym clothes for the remainder of the day, if they so desired. Their benefits package included rafting trips to foreign countries and cruises on the company sailboat. Esprit also looked like paradise—big glass windows, bountiful natural light, handmade desks, and a beautiful collection of Amish quilts on the walls. As I watched earnest young designer-types dashing about, I felt a stomachache coming on.

I prepared for the interview by giving myself a pep talk. "I have a degree in textiles; I have experience; I am perfect for this job!" The advertised position was in human resources, not design, but I didn't care. I just wanted a foot in the door and a chance to prove myself. The director of personnel said that I was well qualified, perhaps overqualified, but not a perfect fit. When he turned me down in favor of a younger classmate of mine, his words stung. How could all my years of hard work not have landed me the job?

Years later, as Galen and I sat talking to Doug in the Esprit cafeteria, I reflected on how profoundly my life had changed since then. He had no idea how nearly our

paths had crossed. At that time, I had wanted to work for Doug Tompkins more than anything in the world. Doug embodied success. And now I was sitting in Esprit, having lunch with him. In that moment, the fact that he barely talked to me didn't matter. That I didn't have the courage to talk to him did.

A year after that lunch at Esprit, Galen and I decided to have a going-away party before Galen left for Tibet to climb the West Ridge of Mount Everest. After he made out the invitation list, I got on the phone to call everyone personally. When I came to Doug's name, I froze and was unable to make the call. I told myself, "He is too busy to come to a party at our house. It's better not to bother him." I was certain Galen would never notice Doug's absence.

Hours before the party started, Galen asked, "Is Doug coming?"

"Doug who?"

"Doug Tompkins."

"Ummm. I don't know."

"Didn't you call him?"

I wanted to crawl into a hole. How could I admit feeling intimidated around one of Galen's climbing friends? A regular guy. Could Galen ever understand? It would be hard to explain, especially since we had just spent a month in Nepal trekking with Robert Redford, and I hadn't shown signs of being intimidated around him. Redford was much more famous than Doug. So what was going on with me?

Galen felt that I was so irrepressible that he could count on me to handle any difficult call or meeting. He seemed to believe that I was capable of moving mountains. But I didn't see myself that way, and I couldn't bring myself to call Doug, even when I pondered my mother's gem of advice about the rich and famous: "When they're sitting on the toilet, they're no different than you or me."

For years, Galen and Doug had stayed loosely in touch. Then in 1985, Galen was assigned to do a major climb of his choice for the books division of *National Geographic*. He chose Fitz Roy, a wild rock spire in Argentine Patagonia that is considered to be one of the world's hardest peaks to climb. Doug had made the first American ascent of Fitz Roy in 1968 and offered to come to our house to help Galen plan his expedition.

Doug's quick, dry wit and display of intelligence had an edge to it. He didn't suffer fools and he was openly opinionated. I liked that. But I still couldn't bring myself to talk to him. Before Doug arrived, Galen reminded me that there was no good reason for me to be afraid of him. Doug was a down-to-earth kind of guy to people who were straight with him. But Galen's nervous twitches and stuttering in Doug's presence had not escaped my notice. Galen said that Doug was a pilot and suggested that I try breaking the ice by talking to him about flying. At that time, I had been flying all of five months.

"I got my pilot's license this year," I ventured.

"That's great!" Doug responded, before quickly changing the subject back to climbing.

Two years later, Galen and I coincidentally ended up on the same flight to Tokyo with Doug while we were en route to Pakistan on an assignment for National Geographic. Though we flew first class, paid for by National Geographic, Doug, a multimillionaire, was in coach. He didn't believe in wasting thousands of dollars for a few hours of comfort. Doug was going to Tokyo on business, and he invited us to spend the night in a beautifully appointed apartment owned by Esprit. We accepted and shared a cab into town. During the 40-minute ride, I tentatively tried to strike up a conversation by asking, "Do you still fly?"

The granite spire of Fitz Roy rises 10,000 feet above the plains of Argentine Patagonia (left); Doug Tompkins (above).

"Yeah. When I can."

"What do you fly?"

"A Cessna 210."

"Oh really? That's a nice plane."

Doug look surprised at my response. Was he wondering how I knew which planes were nice planes? Galen jumped in and mentioned something about my planning a flight to Alaska later that summer.

"What do you fly, Barbara?" Doug asked.

"I have a turbocharged Cessna 206." I was proud of my plane. It was a bush pilot's plane, a plane even a multimillionaire could appreciate.

"Really? That's the airplane I want to get," Doug said. Finally he was looking me straight in the eye. "How do you like it?"

"I love it. There is no better plane for what I do," I replied confidently. Doug and I talked all the way into town about flying. When we arrived at his apartment in Tokyo, Doug offered to carry in my luggage. I felt there was a mutual regard for the first time since we'd met.

A few years later, in 1989, Doug invited us to his annual chile pepper party in San Francisco. When we arrived at his exquisite home, perched amid a huge garden high over Lombard Street, he greeted both of us warmly and blurted out, "Hey guys, I bought a Cessna 206 on floats!" He beamed like a little kid.

"Wow!" I said, truly impressed. Owning a float plane is a real luxury. The insurance alone costs a fortune.

"Come flying with me," he said as he went off to greet arriving guests. While Galen and I wandered around the vast garden, making small talk with people we didn't know, I got a different feeling about Doug. I was fascinated by his eclectic collection of guests, who consisted of the fashion crowd peppered with a few river guides and aging climber types like my husband. Doug moved in and out of the crowd like the skilled kayaker he is, stopping to dance on tiny waves as he worked his way through the rapids. He looked elegant in his crisp white shirt and jeans. In spite of the fact that he was in the midst of a divorce from Susie, he seemed confident and fully in control. He appeared to have the world in the palm of his hand.

On another pass a little later, he casually asked, "Barbara, why don't you and Galen fly to Patagonia with me this winter? You could copilot my plane."

"On floats?"

"I'll have the floats taken off for the trip," Doug said.

When I turned to Galen, he was smiling broadly. His bright eyes danced with the knowing look that Doug's invitation fit my passion for the Spanish language, flying, and traveling in South America. I turned toward Doug and said, "I'd love to!"

"Great. Let's do it!" Doug said. "Then perhaps you could bring my plane back home for me afterward."

That last comment made my stomach feel like an alien had invaded it. Was he serious? He'd take a jet home and leave me to fly his plane through Peru, dodging bullets from guerrilla terrorists? I had agreed to be his copilot, but I had not considered being pilot-in-command.

A short time after Doug invited me to be his copilot, Galen shared a story about watching him land on Highway 101 in the early 1970s.

"Did he have an emergency?" I asked.

"No. He wanted to drop off a few friends at a party at Malinda and Yvon Chouinard's beach house in Ventura."

"What about the cars?" I asked. I'd heard of airplanes successfully landing on roads, but a busy route like Highway 101 sounded like the wrong place to put down.

"A section of new highway was under construction and closed to traffic. Nobody else at the party seemed to notice Doug make a low approach and land about 100 yards from the house after buzzing it, so I ran out to say hello and ended up going with Doug on a short flight to the nearest airport."

Galen began to laugh out loud as he described how the funniest part was the look on Yvon's face. As previously arranged, Yvon had jumped in his car to pick up Doug at the airport as soon as he saw him circle overhead. Yvon missed seeing Doug land on the highway. When Galen got out of Doug's plane at the airport with a plate of food from the party, Yvon was dumbfounded.

The more I heard about Doug's antics, the more concerned I felt about having said that I would be his copilot. Galen told me about Doug's reputation for pushing the envelope in everything he does, from climbing to kayaking to business to flying, but what most worried me was his comment that Doug has a habit of sandbagging people.

"What does that mean?" I asked.

"Suggesting that a person do something extremely difficult that he portrays as not a big deal."

"That sounds mean!"

"I wouldn't say that. Doug knows *his* limits, pushes himself, and doesn't think twice about pushing other people into things he believes they can do. They rarely get hurt and usually come back the better for it."

This was confirmed by a story I'd already heard about Doug that suddenly took on new meaning after I had agreed to be his copilot. An old friend of Galen's and Doug's, Pat O'Donnell, had joined us in 1988 while we were hiking the John Muir Trail and photographing it for *National Geographic*. Pat loved the trail so much that he took a week off his job to accompany us hiking over 13,200-foot Forester Pass along the last section of the trail that ends on top of 14,496-foot Mount Whitney. As we walked along together, he filled us in on how he'd first done the trail in 1966 at the suggestion of Doug Tompkins.

When he was twenty-six years old, Pat had been loitering around the original North Face store in San Francisco to rub shoulders with climbing gurus like Doug Tompkins and Yvon Chouinard, with obvious hopes of being a great climber, too. One day, Doug taunted Pat by saying, "There are walkers and climbers. You're a walker. If you are going to be a walker, at least go out and be a *good* walker."

Doug suggested that Pat set out to walk the John Muir Trail by himself. Taking the bait, Pat made out a list of equipment and showed it to Doug. "Tents are for babies," Doug said, "and you don't need to carry a stove or pot either. There's plenty of downed firewood and a Folgers' coffee can over a campfire will do."

Doug disdained nearly every item on the list, saying that traveling light is always better. Even a ground cloth and sleeping bag were not really necessary on a summer walk, he said. Wanting to be accepted by the inner sanctum of the climbing elite, like Tompkins and Chouinard, young Pat set off for 23 days to hike 211 roadless miles from Mount Whitney to Yosemite with what looked like a day pack.

"I've never been that cold in my life, not even at 20,000 feet on Mount McKinley in Alaska," he told us decades later, as we were walking the same trail with full camp gear. "It rained for days, and I was afraid to go to sleep at night because I would shiver until dawn. I kept on going because I was too proud to quit. Damned if I was going to come back early and whimper to Doug Tompkins!"

Pat not only completed the entire trail but also returned home with a newfound sense of accomplishment and personal empowerment. He'd experienced a self-taught Outward Bound course by pushing himself out of his comfort zone and extending his personal limits on a solo adventure. When he returned, he played the whole thing down and told Doug matter-of-factly that he had a great time. On the inside, he was grinning from ear to ear.

"It was the finest walk I've ever been on," Pat confided as we walked the same route with him. "It had a great bearing on my life. I went on to climb on Annapurna in Nepal and reach the summit of Nun Kun in Ladakh with Galen in 1977."

Pat's walk became his pathway to a career revolving around the outdoors. Thirty years later, he had moved through a stint as president of Patagonia for Chouinard, to president of Whistler Mountain in Canada, and on up the ladder to his present position of president of the Aspen Skiing Company in Colorado. Remembering his roots, he has returned twice to walk the entire John Muir Trail since that first trip in 1966. He never forgets to pack a warm sleeping bag, tent, and Gore-Tex rainshell.

Doug files a nick off his propeller with a rock (left); I sit atop my plane while other members of our flying trip stand below: from left to right, Robert Cushman, Doug Tompkins, Galen Rowell, and Peter Buckley (above).

At the time, Pat's story gave us a good laugh. When we later talked about it, shortly before we set off for South America, Galen said, "That's classic Doug. All his friends have similar stories about him."

Galen pulled out a copy of a new book, *First Descents: In Search of Wild Rivers,* with a chapter about a radical first descent of the San Joaquin River Gorge written by Royal Robbins, who had been America's greatest rock climber before taking up kayaking. Both Galen and Doug had climbed with Royal in the sixties. Doug had become a world-class kayaker and had lured Royal into the water and the outdoor-apparel business. Galen read aloud a description of Doug on a river in the eighties, written by Royal, that mirrored Pat's assessment from the sixties:

> Doug was the engine. His life has been filled with adventurous under-takings, from making important first ascents, running a guide's service, snorkeling in the Red Sea, winning Class A ski races, and flying a small plane several times between California and the tip of South America, to kayaking the wild waters of Chile and California. Doug's intense drive leads him to, but never over, the verge of recklessness. He is at home on the fine edge, and possesses a certain ineffable quality that enables him to get away with what, for someone else, would have been bad judgment.

As early as 1962, when he ventured onto the 4,500-foot north face of Mount Temple in the Canadian Rockies with Yvon Chouinard, Doug seemed to know exactly when to quit. The unclimbed face was regarded as the Eiger of North America. After bivouacking on a snowfield part way up the face, they woke up in the middle of the night to a weather front moving in. Descending in the dark from a site where falling rock and ice from above could be funneled on top of them during a storm, they got off the mountain just as first light touched the summit. Moments later a rock avalanche obliterated their tracks. They never returned to the climb.

All of these outdoor adventure stories about Doug depict a man who chose to climb or kayak with partners who were equally competent. How that translated to his flying with me, I wasn't sure. All of my flying had been without another pilot in the plane, except during flight instruction. What I knew about pilots flying with other pilots I had learned second hand from reading numerous accident reports in flying magazines.

Right after I first agreed to fly with Doug to South America in his plane, a dear friend of mine sent me a copy of *Unfriendly Skies,* a disturbing narrative of the complicated dynamics that often occur between two pilots in the cockpit. The author, a captain for a major airline using the pen name Captain X, describes a close call while flying a Boeing 727 into Saginaw, Michigan, after he turned the approach over to the copilot, who professed to have extensive experience in both the type of plane and the approach to the particular airport. Not until they nearly slid off the end of the runway did the captain realize that a lack of honest communication mixed with bravado had led them to the brink of disaster.

Before I'd given this two-pilot idea much thought, Doug called to cancel. He had crash-landed his new Cessna 206 in a field in Idaho. The FAA determined the cause to be vapor lock, but his fuel tanks were so close to empty as to be a possible contributing factor. Although the plane flipped upside down and was seriously damaged, no one was injured. Doug sent us a whimsical postcard he made of his aircraft, belly side up, with a casual description of how it was no big deal. As our plans to fly south were put on hold indefinitely, I was both disappointed and relieved.

"Everything happens for the best," my father always said. In this case, he was right. As it turned out, Galen and I could not have gone on the trip anyway. His proposal to do a book about Tibet had been accepted by His Holiness, the Dalai Lama, and we needed to return to Dharamsala, India, to finalize details on the co-authored project.

A year later, in the spring of 1990, we went to another one of Doug's chile pepper dinner parties in the huge garden of his San Francisco home. Following the breakup of their marriage, Doug's battle with Susie over control of Esprit had risen to such a crescendo that it became the subject of major features in the *Wall Street Journal* and the weekly news magazines. Soon after we arrived at his party, Doug singled us out and expressed his desire to get out of town and away from the mess. Déjà vu.

"Let's do that trip to South America," he said with firm resolve.

"Sure," I replied, feeling comfortable that plans made after glasses of French champagne are usually forgotten in the morning. I wasn't going to hold my breath.

"I'll give you a call," Doug added, "and we'll do it soon."

The idea of flying to Chile with Doug was both sweet and sour. On the sweet side, traveling with someone so smart, rich, and famous was intriguing. His strong character absolutely fascinated me. His total immersion in environmental issues and desire to change the way people think about the planet was evident, even at his outdoor party. A small, pesticide-free vegetable garden now graced what once had been a swimming pool in his backyard, and his guest list was sprinkled with a who's who of international environmental thinkers and activists. If we did do the flight, Doug's concern for the earth would add purpose to our trip as we photographed remote rainforests and pristine mountain landscapes.

The fact that Doug's plane was the same model as mine, only newer, would make flying his plane more straightforward. And my concern about airplanes being confiscated in foreign countries would not be my worry. Doug had enough money to easily replace his airplane. But best of all, he'd flown his plane to South America several times before; he was experienced. That alone was worth its weight in gold.

The fact that Doug was a multimillionaire could cut several ways. How do the very rich travel? His personal taste could be far beyond our pocketbook. I was afraid that when we checked into a hotel, I'd be looking up how to say, "What is your nightly rate for a broom closet?" in my Spanish dictionary. I certainly didn't feel comfortable enough around Doug to bring up such sensitive subjects.

Also on the not-so-sweet side, Doug sounded too adventurous, too risk-taking for my comfort zone. How would I handle being pushed beyond my capabilities in the cockpit? Would I cope or would I melt down? Would I be able to maintain my own sense of self, or would I do something stupid?

The last thing I wanted to do was fly south on wings of fear. Even though I clearly knew that I wasn't as brave as Doug or Galen and never wanted to take the kinds of risks they consider part of the game when they go climbing, another side of me felt the urge to bust some boundaries to learn how to better trust myself and my own instincts in risky situations.

I'd already taken a first step in this direction by marrying Galen and learning to live with his risk-taking and the idea that my life would be deeply affected if he never returned from some far corner of the earth.

During the first years of our marriage, it was impossible for me not to be consumed by worry while Galen was climbing. Hard work and staying busy kept my thoughts from blackening. When I was too tired to work, I would watch movies until I fell asleep. If I woke up in the middle of the night, I'd watch more movies. In 1983, a month after Galen had left to attempt a new route on Mount Everest, Joyce Roskelley, the wife of a climbing partner of Galen's, called to see how I was doing while Galen and her husband were gone.

"I'm organizing papers and putting things in order," I said.

She replied with a caring tone that indicated she knew what I was going through. "Oh, you're in the closet-cleaning stage. I always do that early on when John goes away. One time I went so far as to buy a new house."

I realized that if I were going to stay married to a climber, I would have to accept the risk, because if Galen doesn't get to spend time in the mountains, he is miserable. He's addicted to challenging himself by total immersion in the natural world, pitting his skill against vertical rocks like El Capitan in Yosemite, or the ice-covered Trango Towers in Pakistan. Climbing runs through his blood. To stop him would be the slow torturous death of his soul.

In the fall of 1981, I joined Galen on a lecture tour through England and Scotland. After each of his evening lectures, we caroused in the local pubs with many of Britain's most famous climbers, including Peter Boardman, Chris Bonington, Joe Brown, Dennis Gray, Alex MacIntyre, Alan Rouse, Doug Scott, Joe Tasker, and Don Whillans. Four years later, six of the climbers we'd partied with lay dead on high mountains around the world.

Galen is always quoting from climbing journals brimming with death-defying, first-person accounts, as well as tales of tragedy. In fact, most of the climbers I've been around seem to enjoy discussing intricate details of both current and historic expeditions. The more heroic or tragic, the more analyzed it becomes, and the more important its role in climbing history. I've never met a group more wild and unruly, yet somehow measured. Just beneath the surface runs a self-awareness of a political sense of their place in history. The contrast of their successes against so much tragedy makes their climbing seem ever more amazing.

Not long after Galen and I got together, I sent autographed copies of his books to my parents. As Dad began to read *The Vertical World of Yosemite,* he called to say that he had been the one who had dispatched a helicopter to rescue Galen off of the face of Half Dome in 1968. He had good reason to remember: it was the first big-wall rescue in the history of American climbing. After he had retired from the navy, he had worked for the State of California Disaster Office. As he recalled, "I got a call that two men were stuck on a rock face in a freak snowstorm. They had been there for quite some time, so I called the governor's office and got permission to use the National Guard helicopter. I wondered what those damn fools were doing up there in November."

When I complained to my mother about my husband's climbing, she asked, "Have you ever read his book *In the Throne Room of the Mountain Gods?*"

"No." I'd thumbed through the pictures but never read the text.

"You really should," Mom said in her wise-mother-knows-what's-coming voice. "You'll begin to understand what's driving him." The book was a gut-wrenching story of a failed expedition to climb K2, the second highest peak in the world. It gave clear insight to the motives that compel men and women to risk their lives again and again.

But it wasn't until I understood the title of Al Alvarez's book, *Feeding the Rat,* which profiles an obsessed British climber named Mo Anthoine, that I really understood what drives my husband. Like other devoted climbers, he is plagued by a hungry rat gnawing inside his gut, pushing him beyond normal human limits to endure exhausting, uncomfortable, and often dangerous challenges. When his rat has had a good meal, Galen comes away feeling terrific.

Now, nine years after my first exposure to this fierce species, I was about to fly off with not just one but two of the most voracious specimens of the climbing rat recorded in the current literature: Galen Rowell and Doug Tompkins.

As I considered being in the cockpit with two certified wild men, I began to wonder where the term *cockpit* originated. A pit for cocks? My thoughts began to drift off into the obscene. Oh my! All this time I've been flying in a *pit for cocks* without having one of my own. Does Galen's count as mine? My God, I'm having penis envy!

To learn more about the word, I dashed to the dictionary and first looked up the word cock. There were several definitions: an adult male chicken; a rooster; a leader or chief; a faucet by which the flow of a liquid or gas can be regulated; Vulgar: the penis."

I then thumbed to *pit*: "a natural or artificial hole or cavity in the ground; a concealed hole used as a trap; Hell; a miserable or depressing place or situation."

Now I was onto something. I thumbed back to look up *cockpit*: "the space in a fuselage of an airplane containing seats for the pilot, copilot, and sometimes passengers; an area for cock fights; a place where many battles have been fought."

These definitions were important to me. They held the key to the past and possibly the future. To be with Doug in the cockpit could be stepping into a battleground of hidden traps with an adult male chicken. My challenges were clear.

After my wild musings peaked, the reality of what Doug was offering me stood out: flying his airplane, traveling in countries close to my heart, and the opportunity to speak a language that I loved as much as my own—Spanish. If this trip materialized, nothing would stop me from going.

A few days after the party, Doug called us with a surprise twist: "Hey Barbara, I got an idea. Why don't you take *your* airplane to Chile, too?"

Seconds passed. This would mean a serious change of plans, but it would certainly address my fear about being in the cockpit with Doug. I would be at the controls of my own plane, in charge of my destiny. A brilliant idea!

"Sure. I can do that."

Galen cut me off. "Let's talk about this before you decide."

"We don't need to do that. It sounds great," I said quickly. "I'd love to fly my plane. Just tell me what I need to do before we go."

"I'll go over everything with you later and make out a list," Doug said. "We've got months to work out the details. You are instrument-rated, aren't you?"

"Yes, but I'm not current." I'd received my instrument license four years earlier, but I was no longer current because I hadn't flown enough IFR hours recently. In fact, I'd rarely used my instrument license in actual cloud conditions. The majority of my instrument flight time was in simulated instrument conditions, under a hood with an instructor at my side.

"You'll need to get current. I've been stuck in Panama for days waiting for good weather. That will be the one place you'll definitely need it. But the runway has a good ILS."

That sounded doable. The fact that Panama had an ILS (instrument landing system) was a relief. An ILS is a sophisticated system that guides instrument-equipped airplanes vertically and laterally to a precise landing. In the event of bad weather, it provides the most accurate and desirable method of navigating into an unfamiliar airport. My previous instrument flights had often ended with shooting the ILS for Runway 27 Right at Oakland.

After Doug hung up, Galen came over to my desk. "What the hell are you doing?" he asked. "You don't want to do that!"

"Why not?"

"You'll get left behind."

That thought had yet to cross my mind. Ever since I was a little kid, the idea of being left behind panicked me. Now my mind flooded with mental images of a blackening sky, horrendous thunderheads mixed with low clouds, heavy rain, and lightning bolts firing off in every direction. Then, like Moses parting the Red Sea, Doug probes the black clouds and disappears toward Colombia. Amelia Chickenheart stays in Panama, stranded and paralyzed with fear, unable to fly farther south, or return home.

Galen brought me back to hard reality. "Doug often flies eight or more hours in a day. You never want to fly more than about four hours. Don't be crazy!"

Galen was right that I didn't *like* flying more than four hours, but I *had* flown as many as eight hours a day en route to Alaska. I suspected that dollars and cents had much to do with his initial response to Doug's suggestion.

Galen's unspoken point was well taken. I had not considered how much this trip would cost. But since I had already told Doug yes, I wasn't about to back down on my word. We would work it out.

In the days that followed, my excitement about the upcoming flight became mixed with dread. As the plan changed from me being Doug's copilot to being pilot-in-command of my own plane, new worries began to surface. At the top were fears about my ability to fly like Doug and live up to his expectations. I was not alone when it came to a desire to please Doug. He seemed to have that effect on people. As another friend in common, Dick Dorworth, said, "At some level you immediately want Doug's approval. You know that he is a solid, honorable, and very real individual who lives essentially by sound values."

Dick was right. From the moment I met Doug, I, too, wanted his approval, his stamp that I was worth his association. The burden was on me to prove myself a worthy flight partner. Flying to South America was like playing hardball with the big boys in Yankee Stadium.

Being accepted as one of the boys had always appealed to me. Growing up as a navy brat, surrounded by sailors who doubled as babysitters, had made me more of a tomboy than most of the other girls I met in school. Navy men set off to sea while the women stayed home or worked in offices. I never had any doubt in my mind that men had much more fun at work than women were having at home. When my little brother got to mow the lawn or rake leaves while I was asked to fold clothes and do the dishes, I became determined to do things that the guys got to do. And as I gazed at photographs of Peru and Bolivia in *National Geographic,* explorers like Hiram Bingham were like gods in my eyes. They went places that I never dreamed would be possible for me. Photographs of Andean women dressed in flouncy skirts, wearing black hats, and walking beneath icy mountains became permanently etched in my mind.

Here, finally, I was the one doing a truly cool and adventurous thing. In one sense, I was in search of the power and the glory of success, like every other adventurer. But in another sense, it was not so much the accomplishment itself that was important to me. In the back of my mind, in a place I wasn't ready to share with anyone now—or perhaps ever—my flight would be so much more. My search was for the inner power and inner glory of succeeding at living life to its fullest—something that had been eluding me.

I needed to stop looking to other people for answers. I needed to bring my hopes and fears into balance in more ways in my life than just flying. Whenever I'd managed to do so in some lesser way in the past, hope won out and dangers fell away— but not before I gave them plenty of consideration. I grew up hearing President Franklin Roosevelt's famous words, "The only thing we have to fear is fear itself," but I no longer believed them. For me, it's a Spanish saying that rings closer to the truth: *Fear is the beginning of wisdom.*

DITCHING DURANGO

V

Crossing international borders in a private plane is intimidating, complicated, and highly regulated. Every country has special forms and procedures. A screwup could cost me my plane. In most cases, advance permissions are necessary. I'd heard horror stories of planes being confiscated for minor technicalities.

Approaching the infamous Mexican border from the air kept me on the edge of my seat. It was clear from a distance where the United States ended and Mexico began. Paved streets turned into dirt and family homes gave way to shacks. Orderly farmland suddenly looked less green and unkempt. Poverty was clearly obvious, even from a thousand feet above the ground. After so much television coverage of illegal immigration, I expected to see flocks of people running across the border into the United States, but I didn't spot a soul on the move.

"Mexicali Tower, Five Lima Yankee is crossing the border," I announced with bounce to my words. I was finally doing it!

"November Five Lima Yankee make a right downwind for Runway Two Eight."

After I answered the tower, I let out a silent "yes!" and shot my fist toward the headliner of the plane. The first border was behind me.

Doug turned from base leg onto final approach in front of me. Before touching down on Mexican soil, I made a quick mental note of where my black Cordura notebook was that contained all my required paperwork: aircraft registration, airworthiness certificate, radio station license, aircraft operating limitations, weight and balance information, pilot's license, current medical certificate, radio-telephone operator's permit, passport, and proof of Mexican flight insurance. Even though I had double-checked my documents, I felt the need to do it once again.

Just before we settled onto the runway, the stall warning bleeped, indicating that I was making a textbook-perfect, full-stall landing.

South of the border, I walk across the tarmac
back to my plane with Doug and Peter (left).

"Nice landing, honey," Galen said over the intercom.

I felt a warm glow wash over me, partially from pride and partially from the hot arid air.

I taxied off the wide runway and parked behind Doug's plane in line for fuel in front of a small shed near the base of the tower. No one came out to meet us, so we headed to the white stucco building next to the fuel pumps. Two men who were leaning against the wall outside motioned us toward the open door to immigration. There were three metal desks sitting in a row, empty. As soon as we stepped in the room, a polite gentleman came forward and directed us to his desk to the far left.

"Buenos días," he enunciated, so slowly it sounded as if he were mimicking us, even though we hadn't spoken yet.

"Buenos días," the five of us replied in unison.

He passed out immigration forms for us to fill out. Galen, Robert, Peter, and I already had procured our visas for transiting Mexico from the Mexican Consulate in San Francisco. At Doug's suggestion, we had gotten them in advance, yet Doug had forgotten to get his own. When he didn't produce his, the official said, "Señor Tompkins. You must go into town for your transit visa, but unfortunately it is lunch time and the offices are closed until two PM."

"Is there no other way but to go to town?" Doug asked. "The last time I was here, the visas were available from you!"

Doug was bluffing. He told me that I needed to have my visa in hand *before* entering Mexico. I was afraid things might get nasty very fast so I busied myself by walking over to the snack bar to see what was for sale. Among the meager choices were bottles of Day-Glo red and green sodas plus sandwiches filled with weird-looking chopped pink stuff. When I walked back to check on the visa situation, Doug was already on his way to the flight planning office with transit visa in hand, smiling like a brash little kid.

We couldn't file our flight plan until we knew where we were going, but Doug wanted to decide as we went along. We laid maps out on the lobby floor and reviewed possible airports along the coast. Doug wanted to see Durango, but because of making an unscheduled landing at Palm Springs, it was getting late and our choices were narrowing. We thought we could reach Durango before the airport closed, so we filled out our required flight plan, returned to the office where we started, and picked up a green slip of paper with our permission to have our aircraft in Mexico.

"This is an important document that we will be required to show at every airport in Mexico," Doug emphasized, reminding me of how my dad talked to me about serious things when I was a teenager.

We checked the weather map, which showed high pressure dominating our route of flight with clear weather, except for high clouds between Mexicali and Durango. We were in good shape to head down the coast of Mexico with the warm waters of the Sea of Cortés off our right wing tip.

As both planes were being fueled with 100 low-lead, Galen and Robert

transferred some gear to Doug's plane. They chose equipment that we wouldn't need until reaching Chile: three 165-foot climbing ropes, plus two oversize duffel bags filled with climbing hardware and freeze-dried food. I felt very relieved to see the excess gear go. With the lightened load, N735LY stood proud with its tail high above the ground.

As I jumped in my plane, I noticed something different. The nose strut was no longer fully extended, making it easier to steer during my taxi for departure. By eliminating some weight, my plane now looked and handled the way I was used to. My butterflies were gone.

For no reason in particular, Doug suggested that I take off first. I called Mexicali Tower and said I was ready to go. With no other traffic coming or going, I was cleared for an immediate departure and was rapidly airborne over the dusty outskirts of town. The higher performance of my much lighter airplane on take-

Orderly fields on the U.S. side of the border (left);
unkempt fields on the Mexican side of the border (above).

off was noteworthy. I lifted off much sooner and climbed like an angel headed home. The difference was dramatic. Doug lifted off behind me. Minutes later Mexicali Tower called and requested that we report reaching 10 nautical miles to the south. We made our required position report and the tower cleared us to leave their frequency.

Green farmlands beneath us gradually turned to arid desert as we headed for the northeastern shore of the Sea of Cortés. For over two hours we continued flying without speaking with anyone other than ourselves on the radio. We seemed to have entered a wild world beyond human habitation and official control.

Soon we began to realize that the short winter days and the loss of an hour by flying southeast into another time zone would bring sunset much earlier than we had expected. As we neared the town of Hermosillo, official sunset was at 4:30 in the afternoon. We were about to be required to fly on instruments, since flying at night is not allowed in Mexico under visual conditions, as it is in the United States.

I overheard Doug call Mazatlán Flight Center on the radio and request an instrument clearance to Durango. He waited for a while before anyone replied. Finally, the distant Flight Center answered: "November Niner One One Delta Juliett. Mazatlán Center, over," the controller said in such a heavy Spanish accent that I could barely understand him.

"One Delta Juliett, go ahead," Doug said.

"What time do you estimate arriving Durango?"

"Stand by."

"Roger," the controller replied, slurring the vowels in this simple word to the point that it was unrecognizable except in the context of the exchange.

Headwinds had slowed us down. After some calculations, Doug reported back that we estimated reaching Durango at 8:15 in the evening, 30 minutes later than we had originally planned.

"Sir, you will be arriving after dark," the controller said.

"Is that a problem? Aren't there lights on the runway?" Doug asked with a slight snicker in his voice. Since our flight plan to Durango had been approved when we filed it in Mexicali, Doug seemed both amused and confused by such an obvious statement.

"It will be late and the tower controller wants to go home," the controller warned. "You will need to pay a late landing fee."

"What is the extra fee for landing at Durango?" Doug asked.

"Stand by," the controller replied before disappearing from the air for several minutes.

Meanwhile, the sun was nearing the horizon and the wildly painted sky beautifully contrasted with the tortured landscape of desert peaks. Soon the controller advised Doug that it would cost $80 dollars U.S. to land at Durango 15 minutes past the normal closing time of eight o'clock.

"Is that eighty dollars for both planes?" Doug asked.

"Stand by," the controller said.

Doug and I check out flight maps on the lobby floor of the Mexicali terminal (left); flying over the outskirts of Mexicali just after takeoff (above).

Doug called me on the second frequency and asked how I felt about paying $40 to land at Durango. I said it was okay with me. I was tired and rethinking our flight plan wasn't my first choice.

More minutes passed before the controller called again to say, "It is eighty dollars for each plane, sir."

Doug and I talked on the radio and agreed that the price was very steep. I said that I was willing to pay it if Doug was, but he refused to pay that much to land, even though he could easily afford the extra cost. We decided on Mazatlán, a 24-hour airport, as our alternative. Doug switched back to the controller and announced our change in flight plan.

Doug's spirit of adventure was contagious. Now I was catching his fever with a twist of my own. Even though I had been in the air as many hours as I had ever flown in one day, I wanted to see exactly how far I could go. But something more powerful was driving me as fatigue settled deep into my bones and the last rays of light were casting long shadows on the twisted land below. As we flew ever farther into this foreign land, the captivating scenery outside the airplane was at least matched by a vision on the inside that began to capture my imagination in an even more mesmerizing fashion: I was rapidly exploring an uncharted inner landscape, in which I couldn't see beyond the next horizon.

There were so many things I didn't know about myself. How would my body and mind react to repeated days of more pilot hours than I'd ever flown before? How would I handle going through customs and immigration in countries farther south, where our American media said corruption and terrorism were rampant or governments were about to topple? What would I experience as a foreign female in these places? Would it work out flying tandem with Doug all the way to Chile? And would I feel relief or sheer terror flying over the Andes alone?

I wanted to do this flight as much as anything I'd ever tried to do in my life. My quiet reflections gave way to the silent laughter of emotional release. It seemed much less intimidating now, so almost normal that it had all worked out this way. As I watched the sunset off my wing over the coast of Mexico, I giggled to think how Doug had set the hook when he first invited me to be his copilot, reeled me in to that idea, and then released me to swim on my own. I ended up being pilot-in-command of my own aircraft on a flight to Patagonia after all.

Flying beside the Sea of Cortés (right).

Going Solo

VI

When I think about flying, my only regret is not learning to do it sooner. I admire women like Amelia Earhart, who had the passion, the vision, and the opportunity to begin young. She said, "I want to do it because I want to do it!" In her last letter to her husband, she wrote, "Women must try to do things as men have tried. When they fail their failure must be a challenge to others."

Though today I love everything about piloting an airplane, even when it gets downright frightening, I didn't learn to fly until I was in my thirties. While I now believe that there is nothing better than lifting off a runway and sailing high above the land, it's entirely contrary to my upbringing. My parents gave me plenty of reasons to avoid flying whenever possible, beginning with the story of how my mother's first husband was killed near Pearl Harbor when the wing of the military airplane he was flying low over the ocean struck a large wave.

My first flight, when I was only four, was very long and noisy. I have only vague memories of the thirteen hours my family spent over the Pacific Ocean in a Navy Mars seaplane before splashing down in San Francisco Bay after we moved from Honolulu in 1952.

During World War II, my father had served as a navy blimp pilot in the lighter-than-air division and as a navigator in the heavier-than-air fleet. After he was transferred to the Kingsville Naval Air Station in Texas, he recovered twenty-two pilots' bodies in two years as the aircraft crash claims officer assigned the grim duty of inspecting navy accident sites. He lost all interest in flying after he found an arm attached to a gloved hand on a morning long ago. Pulling off the glove, he saw a ringed finger. When he removed the ring and read the inscription inside, he realized that the hand belonged to one of his best friends. After that, we never flew anywhere again as a family.

Twenty years passed before I next saw the inside of an airplane. I went to Europe in 1972 to attend summer school at the University of Geneva. Months before departing, I began having fearful visions that the plane would crash. On the long overnight flight to Switzerland, I stayed wide-awake while everyone else slept, so I could watch for other airplanes. For the three months I lived abroad, I dreaded the

Flying my plane around Alaska's Mount McKinley in 1986 (left).

return flight home. To make things worse, there were two major airline accidents shortly before I was scheduled to leave. I'd heard the theory that these types of accidents come in threes, so I became even more concerned. When, just the day before departure, a third jet crashed, I felt a conflicted sense of relief.

A few years later, a boyfriend rented a single-engine plane and took me on several flights. I found that I enjoyed being in a small plane much more than being a passenger in a commercial jet. I especially liked the intimate view from up front, as well as watching my friend control the plane. But I didn't like hearing the changing sounds in the engine and concluded, then and there, that the only way I would ever be comfortable spending time in such a craft would be as the pilot, who would understand what the different sounds meant and be in control of them. However, the thought of becoming a pilot wasn't yet in my dreams.

Many more years passed without me having any desire to fly, until I went to New Zealand on assignment for my PR job at The North Face. I chartered three ski-equipped Cessnas to get six models and a photographer onto the Tasman Glacier to create images of our backpacks and parkas in use in an exotic setting. The pilot of my plane turned out to be the captain of regional Mount Cook Airlines, and our mountain guide, Gavin Wills, was a legendary bush pilot in his own right.

After the shoot was finished, Gavin prodded my pilot into surprising me with a stunning, low-level flight through the wild glacial gorges of New Zealand's Southern Alps. I was exhilarated. That kind of flying, with intimate views of exotic landscapes rushing past my window, struck a chord in me. The visual experience was so much more powerful than any movies or still photographs I'd seen taken from the air.

I was mesmerized by everything about flying, from the smell of the fuel to the sound of an engine starting up. I was especially in awe of my pilot. He seemed so in-charge, so competent, so strong. I felt attracted to him. Watching someone fly a plane that well was very sexy. My feelings toward him reminded me of a girlfriend's story about marrying an artist and later divorcing him before it dawned on her that her attraction to him had been that she wanted to be an artist herself.

From that day forward, I couldn't take my eyes off any little plane that flew overhead. It never occurred to me that the skill of piloting a plane could ever be within my realm because I didn't see myself as brave enough or technical enough to master something so risky and challenging. However, I did have the lurking tomboy side to my personality that I'd buried, for the most part, since adolescence. Skiing had been one of my few outlets for that sporty exuberance deep inside me.

Even though I was traveling more than ever with Galen, there was something about flying that reawakened my restless spirit in a way that left me feeling deeply unsatisfied with the way my life was unfolding.

"Find your own passion and follow it," Galen constantly chanted to audiences at his lectures and radio appearances. "Don't follow mine."

That was great advice for everyone out there, but what about for me? By the third year of our marriage, my life felt out of my control, and I went to a therapist at a girlfriend's suggestion. At the end of the first session, I was given a homework assignment: list as many things as possible that would "really turn me on." He said not to think about what these things would cost. It could be something as simple as taking a shower or as challenging as going back to college. "Just write it down," the therapist told me, "no matter how much time it would take to achieve. Just write down whatever comes to mind."

I went out the door smugly thinking, "Oh, this will be easy," but when I sat down to write out my list, nothing came to me at first. Each idea that popped into my mind seemed to come from someplace rehearsed since childhood. Oh, I thought, I should say that it would turn me on to be a veterinarian—that will impress Dr. Goldstein. That's what I used to tell my teachers in grade school, and they all loved that idea.

I should put down that it would turn me on to . . .

There was nothing. I sat there and stared at the blank piece of lined paper for thirty minutes. I could not believe that there wasn't even *one* thing in this life that would turn me on. How could that be? I was always so busy doing so many things. Wasn't there one thing that I loved to do? What about writing the Great American Novel? Didn't everyone want to do that?

What continued to seep out of my brain seemed to come from other people's voices: my husband was saying I wanted to be a photographer; my friends were saying don't be a photographer, that's too competitive with your husband; my dog was

My desire to fly came after I chartered these ski-equipped Cessnas to fly models onto glaciers in the Southern Alps of New Zealand (above).

telling me that I wanted to take him on a walk. I couldn't hear anything coming from Barbara.

I had always done things that my family, friends, and lovers liked to do because that's what allowed me to spend quality time with them. I wasn't willing to risk failure by revealing to myself or anyone else goals that I might never be able to achieve.

After sitting very still and staring at the lined paper until I couldn't stand it a moment longer, I had to put something down. All those lines begged, "fill me in." Then my mind began to wander. How can they put lines on paper like that? Those blank lines make failure so apparent. I dropped my head and tried to turn my eyes inside to see if I could see myself. What would I love to do no matter how much it cost? No matter how much time it took to do? Go to Peru and Bolivia? Yes, that was it! . . . to travel in South America, where women wear richly colored textiles, and children run in the Andes with fuzzy llamas. And Spanish! I love the Spanish language. I would love to be fluent, to be bilingual.

Now I was on a roll. I remembered how life sparkled in New Zealand as I flew in the backseat of that small plane around Mount Cook over glaciers and alongside wild peaks. We landed on the Tasman Glacier, got out, walked around in the snow, and I never wanted to go home. I was in love with life. Flying was like going to heaven while you're still alive—soaring with the eagles on metal wings.

Now I was ready to write down my short list, but a week passed before I was sure that what I had written down had actually come from me:

1. Learn to fly
2. Speak Spanish fluently
3. Explore South America
4. Write a book

Once these goals were down on paper, I had a sense of direction. I decided to begin right at the top, so one day I looked up at Galen and announced, "I want to take flying lessons!"

"Don't be crazy! That sounds dangerous!" he exclaimed.

I couldn't believe these words were coming from the man who made his living dangling off vertical rock walls with a camera in one hand. Who was he kidding?

"How can you talk about danger? You've said you've lost over a hundred friends in climbing accidents. You have no room to talk! I'm going to take an introductory flight lesson tomorrow. Besides, we could use flying in our business."

What a great idea! I was a genius.

"Okay. Check it out, but please don't decide before talking to me."

Could I really learn to fly? I'd never considered it before. I'd thought flying was for men, not women. But then there was Amelia Earhart; she was a woman. I got out the Yellow Pages and started looking up flight schools. I found one in Concord, California, 40 minutes away from home, and just $40 for a 20-minute introductory flight.

The next day I went to Buchanan Field. My instructor, Sue Clark, was a woman about my age whose self-confidence was comforting. Once she let me steer the plane, I was hooked. For the first time in my life, I had a little taste of what pursuing my own passion felt like. I signed up to begin flying lessons the next month, just after my return from a prescheduled trip to the Karakoram Himalaya in Pakistan with Galen.

As I drove to Concord for my first lesson, anticipation welled up inside me to a degree that I hadn't felt since I was a teenager about to go out on a first date. I felt wildly adventurous and petrified at the same time. The combination of emotions made the 40-minute drive whiz by.

When I checked in at the counter of the flight school, I was upset to discover that the instructor assigned to me, Peter Gaylord, was only nineteen years old. The idea of riding in a car with a teenage boy was scary enough; the thought of taking flight lessons from one was beyond even my wildest imagination. But Peter was a neat and proper young man who looked and smelled squeaky clean. He conducted himself in a very mature and formal manner. I soon found out that unlike myself at nineteen, he knew exactly what he wanted to do in life. He was building hours and ratings in order to become a jet pilot for a major airline.

The first day we spent 30 or so minutes talking about what we were going to do in the air. I hung on every word as if it my life depended on it. I believed it might, as Peter held a toy plane in his hands and explained what makes a real plane fly, but I still couldn't wait for him to stop talking so we could take off into the sky.

When Peter was done going over basic theory of flight, he led me out of the terminal past a row of airplanes and stopped in front of a Piper Cherokee he called 75 X-ray. As he did a preflight inspection, he named its various parts. In no time at all, I was sitting in the pilot's seat with the nose of the plane pointed down the centerline of Runway 01. My left hand gripped the control yoke while my right hand wrapped around the throttle knob for takeoff. Peter verbally guided me through each procedure as we sped down the runway. When he told me to pull back gently on the yoke, we lifted off the ground.

That this tiny two-seater box of metal managed to rise into the air at all felt unbelievable. Once we broke ground, it seemed as if I were floating on a magic carpet. The lightness and height made me tingle in somewhat the same way I feel aroused before making love. When I took over the controls, I felt as if I were at the center of my universe instead of orbiting someone else's. I felt certain then, and still believe now, that piloting a small aircraft is about as good as it gets.

The wonder of that first day—my hands on the control yoke guiding my craft into the sky—hasn't diminished. Since then, I've been in the cockpit of many jets during takeoff where I sense the difference between a pilot, a copilot, and a flight engineer sharing appointed tasks behind a panorama of highly automated instrumentation, versus what it feels like to be singularly in control of a small plane. When I practice touch-and-go landings, pushing the throttle nearly to the firewall between the landing and the takeoff phase, I feel as if I'm driving an Indy car with the added sensation of surging upward off the ground. The rev of the engine during takeoff pulses through my body. My heart races with anticipation, not only of being suspended high above the ground, but also in wonderment that I will remain so.

On that first flight lesson, Peter took back the controls and demonstrated climbs, turns, and descents. Then he asked me to do the same. He introduced me to the airport traffic pattern area by having me fly an imaginary rectangle over Suisun Bay. Each leg of the rectangle had a name: upwind, crosswind, downwind, and base, before turning into a final approach for landing. As we returned to the airport, he took over again for landing and explained each phase. He touched the plane down so smoothly that I barely knew we were on the ground.

When we taxied back to the terminal, I was sad the lesson was over. I signed up to fly again the next day, and the next. I couldn't wait to get back to the airport. Every time I drove there, I listened to instructional tapes and thought only about flying. Out of the corner of my eye, I watched for small planes in the sky and wanted to be in each one I spotted.

On my third lesson I did my first landing. The fourth day I practiced more takeoffs and landings that must have made my plane look more like a fish flopping on a pier than an aircraft touching down on a runway. On my fifth day, Peter introduced me to emergency landings by pulling the throttle to idle and taking me through a series of steps I would be asked to repeat at some point during every flight until I could prove they were second nature for me. The next lesson included stalls. By week's end, I was totally consumed. I had spent several hours a day in ground school studying flight theory, FAA regulations, weather, and much more. What kept me engaged was my time in the air and my dreams of how flying would fit into my life. I was surprised at how slow everything felt with the yoke in my hands, as the plane rolled down the runway and lifted off the ground.

Two weeks later, Peter said it was time for me to fly solo. I could barely sleep. For the next three days the winds were too strong by midmorning, when I was scheduled to take off, so he finally asked me to meet him much earlier the next time.

On March 22, 1984, I finally soloed. When I first arrived at the field, Peter joined me on a few legs around the pattern before getting out at the base of the tower. He wished me well, and I happily closed the door behind him, restarted the engine, and slowly taxied to the runway with anticipation. The tower cleared me for takeoff. I carefully centered the plane on the runway, hesitated for just a moment to collect myself, peeked at the empty copilot's seat to be sure that Peter was really gone, and pushed the throttle in all the way. My tiny plane sailed off the ground noticeably quicker without Peter's weight. As I slowed the plane on the downwind leg, I imagined him giving orders each step of the way. Once I turned onto the final approach, I felt that I knew exactly what to do. The feeling was so solid, so tangible, and so apparent that all I needed now was confirmation from the outside world, which I would receive as Peter and the tower controllers watched me smoothly place the tires on the ground. I continued around the pattern two more times, grinning ear to ear.

Soloing was the biggest thrill. I entered a whole new level of instruction where I alone was in control of an aircraft. After many more solo flights interspersed with hours of ground school, I passed the test for my pilot's license, just seven weeks after my first lesson.

A few months after I got my license, Galen and I bought the perfect plane for landing at high-altitude airports—a turbocharged 1979 Cessna 206 Stationair. It was Galen's idea to buy this particular model after spending a lot of air time in Alaska on climbing expeditions and photographing for his book, *Alaska: Images of the Country*. When he explained why bush pilots liked the 206, it answered my need for safety. Knowing Galen's passion for high terrain, I'd be flying in the mountains. I wanted a plane with a turbocharger that would give me the same power flying into thin air as at sea level. A turbocharged 206 is rated to fly up to 27,000 feet.

Since we made our living taking photographs, the visibility provided by a Cessna's high wings, located above the windows, was a major plus. We ruled out low-winged Bonanzas, Mooneys, and Pipers. Four versus six passengers was a moot consideration since we didn't have children, but we did want to carry our golden retriever, Khumbu, plus camping gear, camera equipment, mountain bikes, and friends.

A turbocharged Cessna 206 with 310 horsepower was a perfect choice, but I couldn't even rent one for a test flight because of my low flight time. To rent such a high-performance aircraft requires at least 750 hours as pilot-in-command. Since I had fewer than 100 hours, our only option was to purchase one and have me get a high-performance rating that would enable me to arrange for my own insurance.

An aircraft salesman at my local FBO (fixed base operator), Navajo Aviation, found a 1979 turbocharged 206 with a low total time of just over 700 hours. We negotiated a great price of $41,500, but Galen said I had to decide between buying a plane and buying a house. We could afford one, but not both. I chose the plane.

On August 31, 1984, our third wedding anniversary, I wrote a check for the 206 out of our savings. I wondered if the seller thought that we were drug smugglers, purchasing a type of aircraft prized for hauling drugs in and out of small of airstrips to be flown by a very low-time pilot.

Since my new plane was FAA-rated as a high-performance aircraft, I could not legally fly it without further training and an official sign-off in my logbook. After Navajo Aviation had the plane delivered to Buchanan Field and their mechanic gave it a once-over, they set me up to be trained and checked out by Bob Dye, a flight instructor with considerable experience in high-performance airplanes. By coincidence, Galen knew him from their race-car days when they both used the same machinist to build custom engines. Galen remembered Bob as being very quick-minded and precise, just the kind of instructor I wanted to have.

The first thing Bob had me do was to study the owner's manual and familiarize myself with the plane inside and out. On my second lesson, he quizzed me:

"What kind of engine does it have, Barbara?"

"A Teledyne Continental TSIO-M turbocharged, direct-drive, air-cooled, horizontally-opposed, fuel-injected, 6-cylinder with 520 cubic inches of displacement," I answered in one breath.

Bob beamed.

"What's its horsepower?"

"It is rated up to 310 for 5 minutes during takeoff and 285 after that," I replied, adding, "with 36.5 inches of manifold pressure initially and 35 inches continuous."

Bob smiled. He really liked my plane as well as hearing me accurately recite its engine specifications. He was as eager as I was to take off into the sky and begin my training. The 206's control panel, in comparison to that of any plane I'd flown before, looked truly ominous. There were so many more gauges and things to pay attention to, beginning with the three-bladed, constant-speed propeller and the turbocharger. I spent lots of time just sitting in the cockpit and studying the manual.

Bob taught me everything I was required to know, and then some, about handling the engine on taxi, takeoff, climb-out, cruise, descent, and landing. He knew Galen and suspected that I might be pushed into difficult situations, so he decided to tailor an unusual training program to keep me safe, promising that he wouldn't certify me until he was convinced that I could handle my plane like a pro. Given that I had only been flying for a few months, we clearly had our work cut out for us.

On our first training flight, we headed out over the level channels and marshes of the San Joaquin River Delta near Concord. Bob had me fly at 1,000 feet and follow the tight hairpin twists and bends of the river, insisting that I not bust out of any of the turns, some of which required at least a 45-degree bank. Then he had me try it closer to the ground. Only when I could do it at 100 feet would I be signed off. I loved the challenge and worked on it between other important exercises during each lesson.

"Barbara, take a heading directly toward those hills over there," Bob once instructed me. "I want to show you what it looks like when you're flying too low and won't clear the terrain. Set it up to fly at 90 knots."

I turned the plane where he was pointing. Soon, Bob took the controls to demonstrate. "Watch the horizon beyond the ridge and tell me if you're seeing more or less as we get closer."

"I see more," I replied.

"That means you're going to clear the terrain. Now watch again."

Bob turned the plane around and dropped lower. We were headed directly at the ridge, but this time the view on the other side became less and less until I was only staring at brown dirt. We weren't going to make it over. At the last minute, however, Bob pulled up steeply to clear the ridge. The dramatic difference became permanently etched in my mind. I tried the exercise myself several times with Bob beside me before we moved on to the next important lesson about obstacles: how to avoid high-tension wires.

After 9 intense air-hours of short-field landings, stalls, steep turns, low-level flight, no-flap landings, and, of course, flying the river without busting out of hairpin turns, Bob signed me off to fly the plane on my own.

Within the month after we purchased the 206, I did my first flight out of state. Galen was to teach a photographic workshop near the end of September in Telluride, Colorado, at the height of the fall colors. At that time, Telluride didn't have a suitable airstrip, so I planned to land at Montrose and drive the last two hours. To plan the flight, I laid out the CG-18 and CG-19 WACs (world aeronautical charts) on the dining room table and studied them for hours. Compared to the local flights I'd done, going to Colorado seemed like flying to the moon.

The richly colored map shifted from light green around the Bay Area and across the Central Valley to a rusty hue over most of Nevada, Utah, and Colorado. The colors correspond to terrain altitudes: light green starts at sea level and shifts to a slightly darker green at 1,000 feet. Above 2,000 feet, the color becomes beige, then shifts toward browner shades of sienna, first at 3,000 feet, and at 2,000-foot increments of altitude thereafter, concluding with a ruddy chocolate color for terrain above 12,000 feet. I could instantly see that my upcoming flight would take me over dozens of mountain ranges in California, Nevada, and Utah that exceed 10,000 feet.

As an inexperienced pilot, the idea of flying over high terrain far away from home made me especially nervous until I remembered a conversation I had with Steve Werner, the publisher and editor of *Outdoor Photographer* magazine, who had flown his Cessna into Concord from Los Angeles for an afternoon meeting with Galen. He also published a magazine called *Plane and Pilot,* and when he mentioned that he was about to fly his family to Wyoming for a vacation, I was quite impressed. Flying across several state borders seemed so formidable, yet when I asked him about it, he said, "It's just from one runway to another," in a matter-of-fact way that I came to know as his personal style.

Such a simple concept—one runway to another—made flying out of state seem so much less overwhelming. Taking Steve's simple wisdom literally, I divided my first long flight into three shorter flights: Concord to Tonopah, Tonopah to Moab, Moab to Montrose. Galen tried to talk me out of making so many landings and slowing us down, but I liked the idea of topping the fuel tanks off frequently and taking breaks.

We departed Concord early in the morning, but in full daylight, and climbed ever higher over the sharply defined shapes of farms in the Central Valley until they began to soften into a blue haze as we reached the rolling Sierra foothills. At 9,000 feet, I slipped on my oxygen mask, well before the required 12,000-foot level, knowing that breathing thin air can affect judgment in subtle ways.

High over Yosemite I cruised at 11,500 feet before climbing even higher to cross Tioga Pass at the crest of the High Sierra. As I expected, the great granite monolith of Half Dome dominated the head of Yosemite Valley, but instead of presenting its familiar postcard façade, it kept changing its shape into new configurations as we flew past. When Galen pointed out the sharp spire of Cathedral Peak to our right and almost directly below us, a peak that we had climbed during our first summer together, I was far more captivated by the lush green flatness of Tuolumne Meadows just ahead. We had driven through this huge subalpine meadow many times, but it had such a different personality when I could see all of it at once from above.

Through my windshield, the entire skyline was dotted with jagged granite spires, a bird's eye view in rapid motion that was too stunning to appreciate fully. I began to unconsciously raise the nose of my plane higher, causing it to climb, and before I knew it I was flying at 15,000 feet, far above Tioga Pass at 9,941 feet, which sits in a deep gap between Mount Conness at 12,446 feet and Mount Dana at 13,057 feet.

After several circles, we continued on over the alkaline waters of Mono Lake and across the California border into the high desert of Nevada. We stopped for fuel at Tonopah and set off again over dry lakebeds that stretched into the vast emptiness of a land that had held inland seas during the Ice Ages. From above, we could see the patterns of higher ancient shorelines, all but invisible to the untrained eye from the ground. Not long after lifting off, I spotted cumulus clouds building in the distance. The weather briefer at Oakland Flight Service Station had reported clear skies for my entire route of flight until the afternoon, at which time Colorado was predicted to have widely scattered thunderstorms. Staring into the distant sky, I couldn't venture a guess as to how far away the billowing clouds were. When I radioed Flight Watch on 122.0 for an update, they informed me that clouds were beginning to build all along my route of flight, but with bases currently far above my flight level of 13,500 feet.

By the time I crossed into Colorado and flew abeam Grand Junction, the bases of the clouds had lowered so much that they forced me down to 1,000 feet AGL (above ground level) in order to stay beneath them. Instead of the isolated white, puffy tufts I had first seen over Nevada, I was flying toward a solid mass of roiling charcoal as I neared Montrose. Realizing that I did not know how to evaluate the weather conditions around me, I considered landing at Grand Junction instead of heading up the valley to Montrose, even though it would complicate our plans. But Galen prodded me to continue on toward Montrose saying, "Bush pilots do this all the time."

The concept of deteriorating weather in the middle of a flight was something I knew more as theory than from practical, firsthand experience. During the seven weeks it took me to get my pilot's license, I'd avoided all clouds and had never even flown close to one. Now, the black sky was exploding with heavy rain showers as I neared Montrose airport. I dropped down to 800 feet AGL to keep the road in sight and follow it to the airport. I wanted to be on the ground then and there, but there was no escape. My naïveté and inexperience were bringing me almost to the verge of panic. Galen tried to comfort me by saying, "If you need to, you can land on the road," as I plodded on slowly, flying close to the ground so as not to lose sight of the highway.

I made it into Montrose without incident, but the fear I'd felt flying into rain showers and poor visibility would stay with me as a strong and upsetting memory. After this flight, it was clear to me why flying into bad weather was the number one cause of fatal accidents in general aviation. I was left with a gnawing feeling that the scenario that I'd just been through was going to repeat itself until I learned to evaluate weather forecasts through actual flight experience. Hopefully, I'd survive the steep learning curve that has cost so many private pilots their lives.

Not long after both my feet were securely on the ground, my fear of what I had flown through was subsumed by pride that I had successfully completed my first long-distance flight over wild mountains and deserts.

A few months later, on New Year's Day, Galen and I flew to Mammoth in the High Sierra, where I landed at 7,000 feet surrounded by snow. We put on our cross-country skis beside the plane to glide out to a nearby hot spring that comes up beneath a river. By sunset we were back home in the Bay Area, having flown what would have been two grueling, six-hour drives over the mountains in winter in just over an hour each way.

During the first year I owned the 206, I made many other long-distance flights to the Grand Tetons, Aspen, the Eastern Sierra, the Grand Canyon, Monument Valley, and up and down the Oregon Coast to photograph for a *National Geographic Traveler* story. During the second year, I flew north of the Arctic Circle and all around the wild peaks surrounding Mount McKinley in Alaska. I would find any excuse to take my friends out to lunch at an airport café within an hour of home (pilots call it the $100 hamburger), fly Galen to his lecture venues, or to head to the Eastern Sierra to go climbing or skiing. I was addicted to the aerial perspective.

Flying my very own Cessna 206
makes me feel so happy (right).

Sea of Cortés to Mazatlán

VII

As we flew the inland coast parallel to the Sea of Cortés, the controller gave Doug instructions to fly on instruments to the coastal town of Mazatlán, 430 miles to the southeast. By the time Mazatlán Control called me, the sun had slipped behind multiple bands of clouds on the horizon, and the sky was turning a vibrant crimson. Galen asked if he could open the passenger window and take a photograph of the breathtaking sunset. It was a reasonable request, but the timing couldn't have been worse. This particular controller spoke English with such a heavy Spanish accent that I could barely understand him with the window closed. Because he would be impossible to understand if it were open, I refused Galen's polite request.

"But Barbara, I really need to open it," Galen replied, beginning to sound frantic. "The sunset is gorgeous!"

"Please, Galen. Not now. Mazatlán Center is giving me instrument instructions."

"Oh my God!" Galen exclaimed, "This is the most beautiful sunset of the trip!"

Of course it was. It was our first and only sunset so far. When I looked over at Robert for support, he gave me a sheepish look and shrugged his shoulders. I knew he couldn't do anything to persuade Galen not to want to open the window, but I just needed to know that someone in the plane understood my point of view.

After telling Galen "no" for a third time, my next option would be simply to ignore him. A pilot-isolate switch that I had installed on the intercom allows me to separate my headphone and radio communications from my passengers. It was designed for just such an occasion, but before I could engage the switch and cut off Galen's microphone, he said, "Just tell me if the plane is going slow enough to open the window."

"No," I said firmly. It was a white lie. We were going 130 knots, and the owner's manual states that the window can be opened while the plane is going up to 140 knots.

On another visit to the Sea of Cortés
I photographed an incredibly red sunrise (left).

I flipped the switch to silence Galen's microphone and immediately heard the controller rattling instrument flight instructions to me: "Five Lima Yankee cleared to Mazatlán via Victor Four One, Cíudad Obregón, Victor Five Three, Culiacán, Victor Three Five, direct Mazatlán. Maintain niner thousand feet."

As I copied the instructions, I felt a tap on my shoulder. Galen had unfastened his seat belt and scooted up right behind me so that he could be heard through my headset: "If I can't open the window, then can you at least do a circle so I can shoot out my side?" He was referring to the 5-by-5-inch photographic port that we had just had installed in the pilot's side window positioned behind me to allow passengers in the second seats to take pictures without opening the entire side window. The port opens by dropping to the inside so it isn't very noisy. Unfortunately, my mechanic, Weldon, had not had time to complete the installation of a second photographic port on the right side window. Murphy's Law: the sun was setting on the side with the missing port.

After I finished writing the clearance on a notepad clipped to my lapboard, I read the instructions back to Mazatlán Control over Galen's muttering about his uncaring wife. When I was done, I flipped the pilot-isolate switch back on so that

As the sun set over the Sea of Cortés, Galen opened
the side window to make this photograph (above).

Galen could hear me say with fury, "Flying comes first, not photography!"

"Can I please open the window now?" Galen asked.

"Galen, how can you be so insensitive? Can't you understand how difficult this is?"

Robert sank down in his seat to escape the nasty crossfire.

"Go ahead and open it," I fumed. "A little fresh air might do everyone a bit of good." Galen was unstoppable.

I lowered 10 degrees of flaps and slowed the plane as Galen hurriedly unlatched the right window and guided it up with his hand before releasing it. The howling wind held the Plexiglas window up high alongside the wing. As Galen leaned over Robert's shoulder and aimed his camera toward the dramatic sunset, my ears were blasted by an even louder noise. Galen's voice-activated microphone had entered the wind stream. Over the roar he yelled, "Can you please lift the wing?"

I turned the control wheel to the left, which raised the right aileron and lifted the right wing up and out of view. The plane wanted to turn to the left, so I stepped hard on the right rudder pedal until it touched the floor. As I held it there, N735LY slipped along straight on course in a cross-controlled configuration. It's a technique I do to keep the wing out of Galen's viewfinder, while at the same time flying the plane parallel to the landscape he is trying to capture on film. Holding the plane like this in level flight is a natural adaptation from doing crosswind landings, where a pilot needs to hold one wing down on the windward side in order to keep wind from getting underneath it and flipping it up, yet still keep the plane straight at the moment of touchdown.

While I held the plane in this awkward configuration, I asked Robert to locate a thick brown leather binder with gold embossing that said *Jeppesen Airway Manual*, so that I could find the en route map for Latin America. After I identified the aerial "highway" named Victor 41 that we were supposed to follow, I dialed the Hermosillo VOR into my number-one radio and asked Robert to dial the Culiacán VOR into my number-two radio. I watched him slowly spin the dial with the trepidation of a beginner, until the needle centered vertically on the 124-degree radial. Victor 41 was on the 136-degree radial, so we were east of our new course.

"If we are east of the course, then we turn west to intercept it," I said. Robert would never need to know this much about VORs unless he wanted to learn to fly. But the joy of learning for learning's sake was something we shared, so he listened intently.

"Before we can fly to the appropriate Victor airway, we need to know where we are in relation to it," I said gently. "Center the needle on the OBS with a 'from' flag." This flying jargon made sense to Robert because he had become familiar with the OBS (omnibearing selector) during our session on my computer flight simulator at home, where he learned to recognize the little marker on the instrument that shows when the needle centers on a heading. I can center the needle until it reads either "to" or "from," depending on whether I want to know what my heading is "to" the navaid, or whether I want to know where I am "from" it.

After daylight had slipped away and we were about to be surrounded by complete blackness, Galen closed the window and settled back into his seat. As I lowered the wing and the tension eased, Galen said, "Thank you. That was great!" Galen seemed to have forgiven me or forgotten about the heated exchange that we'd just experienced.

As we flew southeast toward Mazatlán, I watched the last vestiges of light fade far off in the distance and wondered if some of my friends were seeing the sunset, too. Then my thoughts snapped back to the encounter I'd just been through. I still felt angry with Galen for treating his photography as more important at a time when flying should have been the priority. How would the Mexican controller have dealt with an American female who had replied: "Mazatlán Control, please stand by until the sun has finished setting; we're taking photographs."

Although it was true that flying didn't directly earn us money, that wasn't the issue. Our safety was paramount, but something else was disturbing me, too—a deeper issue that was much harder to identify. It centered on respect.

I wondered if Galen would have done things the same way if he were in Doug's plane. If so, how would Doug have handled Galen? Or would Doug have been as bothered by it as I was? I could not imagine a similar exchange happening between two men.

I felt caught between being a pilot and being a wife. How could I be a competent pilot and take care of Galen at the same time? Was it even my job to take care of Galen? One side of me couldn't help but believe his happiness was my responsibility; yet another side of me resented the inequality of it all. Now my interior landscape was looking as murky as the horizon merging into the sky. I could no longer visibly differentiate solid and dangerous from safe and penetrable.

The needle on the OBS began to move until it snapped to attention pointing straight up and down, which indicated that N735LY had intercepted her invisible radio course toward Mazatlán. I went back to staring into a black void broken only by distant clusters of pueblo lights glimmering out of the darkness. My head felt like it was being squeezed by vice grips after hours of wearing David Clark head-phones. The discomfort kept me from being able to relax. To make matters worse, we still had almost 3 more hours of flying before we'd be on the ground.

Other than the sweet purr of the engine and an occasional radio transmission between Mazatlán Center or a jet somewhere high above us, all was quiet. The first day of our flight was too stressful a time to think clearly about the complexities of life, so I put my anger on hold and focused my awareness on the eerie blackness outside the plane.

Night flight over unlighted terrain sets up pilots for the same loss of visibility and orientation they experience when flying into a cloud. The difficulty level goes up by a factor of ten. Day flying is to instrument flying as driving to the market is to racing in the Indianapolis 500. Although you might have an accident driving to the market, the attention and focus it takes to get there are minimal compared to what it takes to keep a race-car from crashing.

My thoughts were interrupted by Doug's voice over the radio. "Do you see me behind you? Be sure to keep your speed up so I don't catch you."

Robert and I simultaneously glanced back over our shoulders. Doug's flashing strobe lights were easily visible in the clear air, but it was hard to judge just how far back he was. I had no intention of changing my power setting, so his warning seemed unnecessary. It didn't seem right that I should be watching out for Doug when he was behind me. It's normally the responsibility of the approaching aircraft.

We continued southeast into a totally dark sky in which mountains had become invisible black holes. It was impossible to tell what lay beneath or ahead of the plane without looking at a map. Everything merged into a singular blackness. The intrigu-ing desert landscape that I had watched unfold for hours had disappeared. The sole defining feature was a single light in the distance. Only the instrument readings in-dicated what direction and at what height we were flying, quite unlike a night flight over a metropolitan area, where brightly lit skyscrapers and streets provide clear visual reference.

When the horizon turns into a void, a confused condition called spatial disori-entation, or vertigo, can easily overcome a pilot. If vertigo sets in, it can cause a pilot to lose control of the aircraft. If a spin develops before a pilot regains control, an obituary may follow.

I know from first-hand experience how quickly things can start to go wrong. Less than a year after I got my pilot's license, I flew from the San Francisco Bay Area to the Grand Canyon with Khumbu. Galen had asked me to join him for a few days while he was on a road trip in Arizona. I got a late start and flew over the High Sierra and Death Valley just before sunset. By the time I arrived over Las Vegas, the desert sky was lit only by casino lights. Once I left the cityscape bound for the Grand Canyon, darkness enveloped me. Only the dim lights of my instrument panel remained to keep Khumbu and me company.

When I had previously established radio contact with Los Angeles Center to ask for radar flight following, they advised me that I had jet traffic at my twelve o'clock position inbound to McCarren Airport in Las Vegas. As I tried to spot the traffic, I dropped my pen and bent over to pick it up. That action induced a state of vertigo. Not until I saw that the readout on the artificial horizon gauge indicated that the plane was on its side did I realize the plane actually was that way. It had felt like I was still flying straight and level.

Giddiness descended over me as I tried to regain control of the airplane and looked outside for some sort of reference. Without any lights on the horizon, I had no idea if I was upside down or sideways. I was not yet trained or certified to fly on instruments alone, but part of my training to be a private pilot had taught me to ignore what my body was telling me in situations like this and to trust only the artificial horizon. So I stopped looking outside and glued my eyes to the gauges on the inside until I fully regained control of the aircraft. Afterward, I was in a state of confusion for several minutes.

While my head was still muddled, Los Angeles Center called a second time. I misunderstood their communication to mean that I should begin an immediate descent toward Grand Canyon Airport's green-and-white rotating beacon. It wasn't until after I had lost several thousand feet of altitude that I froze with fear and finally realized my error. I had begun descending into mountainous high-desert terrain many more miles away from the airport than I had believed myself to be. As soon as I sensed my mistake, I felt nauseated. Fear penetrated every cell of my body. Instantly, I climbed back up as fast as I could until I was able to get a fix on my position. The clear night air had fooled my eyes, making the beacon look far closer than it actually was.

From that day forward, I had a healthy respect for flying at night and knowing my exact position all the time. That was six years before this flight. Being more experienced now, I would never let that happen again. To up my odds, I equipped my aircraft two years later with DME (distance measuring equipment) and Loran (long range aid to navigation) instrumentation to give constant ground-based read-outs of the distance from the nearest airport or VOR. GPS (global positioning system) navigation had been developed for the military, but was not approved for civilian aircraft at the time I left on my flight to Patagonia.

As we neared Mazatlán, the lights of the city stood out like jewels on display. From the sky, however, the gleam of an expensive light fixture and a cheap light bulb are indistinguishable. Slums and shantytowns look much the same as rich neighborhoods. All of Mazatlán had a deceptively equal economic appearance.

Mazatlán Tower cleared me to land when I turned onto the final approach. As the plane descended through the 500-foot level, I could feel the air turn warm and humid. After a total of 10 hours and 30 minutes of flying, I touched down and peeled my legs off the pilot's seat. I felt simultaneously exhausted and ecstatic. Not bad for the first day, I told myself.

Robert and Galen stumbled over each other in the dark as they both tried to collect a change of clothes for the night through the same door. Meanwhile, I secured the airplane and organized my maps. I was too tired to rummage through the heap of luggage to look for anything other than my toothbrush. Once both planes were locked, we joined Doug and Peter. The five of us marched like tired soldiers, single file across the tarmac to the main terminal.

We hired a taxicab to take us to La Siesta Hotel, facing the ocean in the heart of the old tourist strip. Unlike a New York cabbie, our driver waited patiently outside the hotel until he was certain that we had arranged for accommodations. When Doug overheard my request for a room for three persons, he insisted that Robert share a room with him and Peter. After traveling all day cooped up in a tiny plane with my husband and my brother, I was more than ready for complete privacy. Tonight I did not want to discuss with Galen the events of the long day's flight from Oakland. I was tired and still very upset with him over a number of things.

We agreed to go straight to our rooms, quickly wash up, and return to the restaurant before it closed. As soon as I sat down in the dining booth, a wave of sleepiness overcame me. I couldn't keep my eyes open long enough to finish the guacamole and chips, so I excused myself without eating dinner. After saying good night, Doug had the last word: "Tomorrow we fly nearly to the Guatemalan border. Let's meet in the dining room at six for an early start."

Oh my God! Boot camp. I shuddered at the very thought of getting up early for the second day in a row. But I remembered Galen's words: "You'll get left behind." With that threat in mind, I was determined not to let it happen.

With newfound energy, I bounded up the stairs to my room and laid out the flight map for a review of the next day's route to Puerto Escondido. After a few minutes of study, my eyes began to blur. I collapsed into bed and lay watching the ceiling fan spin round and round, redistributing the warm air in our room into a gentle breeze. The fan's hum masked some of the noise coming from outside my room, but not enough to block bursts of laughter coming from two men drinking tequila in the courtyard patio.

I had flown over 1,300 miles in one day, a very long day indeed. Although I was not out to break any significant flying records, I had broken my personal highs for distance and time in the air in a single day. I reminded myself that my goals on this trip should have nothing whatsoever to do with speed or public acclaim. I didn't care if it took me two weeks or two months to arrive in Chile, nor did anyone else. Only my closest friends knew that I had left on this trip. What mattered to me most was the quality of each day's journey and its lessons. I measured my success in private, personal ways that I didn't share with anyone, not even Galen. Little things done well or done poorly were teachings for me to learn from and improve my skills.

My mastery of basic flight techniques, like always holding the plane perfectly on the centerline during takeoff, were as important to me as any overall goals of completing the flight. I scrutinized the tiniest details, from paying close attention to the wind direction and correct aileron use during a crosswind takeoff, to remembering to close the cowl flaps after leveling off. Other important factors were proper radio communication, proper leaning of the fuel mixture, and stage-cooling the turbocharged engine smoothly on descent with adequate time before entering the landing pattern (yet not too soon). A perfectionist at heart, I'd never forget this morning's takeoff. I lay there, replaying it over and over in my mind and analyzing my actions every step of the way. It was my goal to never repeat my errors.

I took the words *pilot-in-command* seriously. Flying an aircraft is not a joy ride, although I expect to feel joy at certain times along the way. But I also expect other feelings, too, from fear and frustration to pride and passion. This flight to South America could be as complicated as the gamut of human emotions can get. I was thankful to have Doug flying along with me in his own plane, so I could look to his point of view for insight and direction. But I couldn't escape the reality that I alone would be responsible for the lives of those aboard my aircraft.

Sierra Madre sunrise (right).

ACROSS THE YUCATÁN

VIII

At the break of dawn, I woke up with a start, worrying whether my airplane had been stolen. Our travel alarm had not yet sounded, but I hopped out of bed anyway, jumped in the shower, and quickly washed myself from shoulders to toes. Determined not to make the guys wait, I skipped washing my hair and instead piled it into a cap. Within ten minutes, I was out the door with Galen and racing for the dining room to grab a cup of *café con leche*. Doug was already sipping tea, looking quite Australian in a pair of dark shorts that came to just above the knee and a crisp, white, long-sleeved shirt. He ordered toast and a blended fruit shake, which appealed to me even though I don't normally eat an early breakfast. I ordered a similarly blended banana *licuado* made with milk (but no ice) plus some toast.

After breakfast, we gathered in front of the hotel and stood in the cobblestone street waiting for a taxi to cruise by. But only the occasional bicyclist or motorist passed for at least ten minutes. Early in the morning, lazy Mazatlán hardly looked like the hopping beach resort it was cracked up to be. I'd been to Mazatlán once before in the early seventies during my ski bum days with friends from Lake Tahoe. We took the sleeper train from the Mexican border, which became the party train as it picked up American college students from Arizona along the way. It was an era when the thing to do in the spring was to mix quaaludes and booze and stumble your way to Mazatlán, San Blas, or Puerto Vallarta to lie on the beach, drink piña coladas out of coconut shells, and bargain for silver jewelry and embroidered shirts while browning yourself under the intense Mexican sun.

Just when we were about to have the hotel telephone for a cab, one finally stopped. It was too small to carry five people, so Galen and I waited for a second one and trailed the others to the airport. I was happy to be apart from them so that I could use the opportunity to practice Spanish and engage the driver in a little catch-and-release conversation. I quickly learned that our driver, Miguel, was born in

I rounded the cliffs of Acapulco dropping into the sea (left).

Mazatlán and was the proud father of three children—two boys and a newborn baby girl. I told him that I had flown my airplane from the United States.

"Muy bien," Miguel said, raising his eyebrows suspiciously.

"En serio," I said trying to convince him that I was indeed serious. Miguel flashed me a big smile and moved his head up and down and sideways. Either he didn't believe me or he didn't care. Probably both were true.

As soon as we arrived at the airport, I ran to catch up with Doug, who had made a beeline to the flight plan office while Peter, Galen, and Robert went out to untie the planes. When I caught up with him, he sent me to track down a fuel truck and place an order to refuel both planes. I accepted my mission like a dutiful member of our team, although as I jogged back to the Plan de Vuelo office to file my own flight plan, I tried imagining myself sending *Doug* off to order fuel—without success.

When I entered the office, Doug gave me a cool reception. Something was obviously wrong. He was leaning against the counter, staring at the ground and looking very upset.

"What's going on?" I asked cautiously.

"We are calling the hotel to see if I left my green permission form there," Doug replied with a slight edge in his voice.

I couldn't believe it! Doug, who had told *me* to guard my permission form to have a foreign aircraft in Mexico with my life, had already lost his own. I had been so worried about the documents for my airplane, as well as my passport, that I slept with all of them under my pillow. With a major screwup like this, we could end up with phenomenal problems, not to mention a big loss of time. The cab ride back to the hotel would be a minimum of twenty-five minutes each way. My concern was offset by the thought that rich people seem to have a way of getting out of most situations, especially *smart* rich people. But what really pissed me off was that I had gotten up early and rushed out of the hotel for nothing.

As I showed my permission form to the man in charge behind the counter, Doug called me over to look at his map. He wanted us to take a scenic route inland over the mountains just for fun. It made no difference to me. I was along to see as much of the country as possible, and I was game to go anywhere he wanted to go. After he showed me his flight plan to fly over Aguascalientes, I copied his route of flight and filed my own, leaving our time of departure blank because the gentleman at the desk had politely offered to do it for me as soon as Doug's permission form arrived from the hotel and his paperwork was complete.

When I walked across the parking ramp to preflight the plane and get the cockpit organized, I noticed that the tarmac was inundated with small planes with flat tires or no tires at all. Many of the planes were also missing propellers. At first I thought that either the owners didn't fly much or they were going to extreme measures to prevent theft. Then it hit me that most of the planes had registration numbers from the United States. Was I parked amid a mothball fleet of confiscated or stolen aircraft?

Just when I started patting myself on the back for the precautions that I had taken to keep my plane out of the hands of thieves and crooked government officials, Doug walked up and asked, "What is this purple stuff all over your plane?" He looked perplexed as he studied the little brush strokes of wax sealant painted in tiny strips across every opening on the fuselage and wing.

"Oh that!" I said as my face began to turn red. "My mechanic put that on so that no one can stash drugs on my plane without breaking a visible seal."

Doug shook his head in amusement. My worrywarts were showing, but I didn't care. Better safe than sorry. An aircraft has many removable plates and panels where it would be easy for crooked officials to plant drugs. If someone were to do that to my plane, I'd discover the broken seal during my preflight. Nobody was going to confiscate N735LY.

Doug didn't have to tell me that I was being paranoid. His facial expression made it clear. After that kind of exchange, I wasn't about to tell him what else I had done to my plane to avoid theft. Because my mechanic told me that most Cessnas could be opened with any Cessna key, I had tumbler locks installed on my doors. For additional protection, I bought heat-reflecting window covers to stick on with Velcro and block all view into the cockpit when the plane is parked. Jay at Bay Avionics had mentioned that if thieves couldn't see my expensive radios, they wouldn't be tempted to break into my plane in the first place. My most costly measure was the purchase of a custom steel guard that slips through both the pilot and copilot's control yoke to cover the entire radio stack and all my instruments. A serious thief with special tools might cut it off, but a casual thief would be stopped from either stealing the plane or popping out my new King navigation and communication radios with a screwdriver.

After Doug went off to see about his permission form, I checked over Five Lima Yankee with a fine-tooth comb. She was happy: tires, nose strut, and engine were filled with air and oil to perfection. Best of all, she was still there. Then, for no particular reason, I began to wonder if it was appropriate for me to be calling Five Lima Yankee a "she." Ships are usually feminine, but what about airplanes? One Delta Juliett sounded so obviously like a lady. But I certainly couldn't say that about Five Lima Yankee. The only way I'd ever heard the word *Yankee* used was to denote people or soldiers, generally men, who are from the United States. But Yankee is said to have come from the Dutch Janke, a nickname for Jan, Dutch for John. So perhaps I should be flying a "he" instead of a "she." That makes sense to me: men fly female airplanes and women fly male airplanes. I like that, but the aviation world isn't quite ready for me to give Five Lima Yankee a sex change.

It was late morning before Doug had his permission form in hand, brought to the airport by a hotel employee who found it in his room. Doug paid the man well, and we were finally allowed to depart. After takeoff, we climbed eastward from sea level and left the resort town without having seen a beach up close. Boot camp did not include bikinis.

As we climbed away from the airfield, I tried to see the port just to the south, famous for its shrimp fishing fleet. Thick haze made viewing difficult. Once we leveled out at 9,500 feet, we continued inland over numerous deep and narrow tree-covered gorges toward the fast-rising mountainous terrain of the Sierra Madre Occidental. Staying on our heading, we crossed Río Acaponeta and Río San Pedro until we were about 50 miles from the sea, and I lost VOR reception because of the distance and intervening landforms.

I began dead reckoning eastward and climbed higher to cross high mountain ridges and avoid peaks that rose to nearly 10,000 feet. The opposite side of the mountain range opened up to lush, broad valleys worked by corn farmers. As I passed by the towns of Zacatecas and Aguascalientas, I thought about how the landscape, which had now turned deep sienna, had provided the raw materials for the Mexican colonial architecture I so admired. Even from the air I could see that both towns were now haphazard mixtures of old pastels and new garish colors. After we passed by the village of Jalpa and began following Highway 54 toward Guadalajara,

I flew inland over the volcanoes of the Sierra Madre Occidental (above) and past Guadalajara, barely visible through the haze (right).

I was disappointed to see a haze layer rapidly thicken until it resembled mashed potatoes over the sprawling city.

Below me, the second largest city in Mexico and home to 5 million people spread for miles in all directions but gave me no sense of scale. I knew the city center was famous for its colonial charm and old-world atmosphere, but seeing the entire city for the first time dulled by muddy air from high overhead gave me the impression of looking at a dirty Persian carpet.

I continued on course, flying behind and above Doug's plane, which was wandering all over the place. I suspected that Peter, who was learning to fly, was at the controls.

As we cruised above the eastern end of leaf-shaped Lake Chapala, the largest lake in Mexico, I was struck by how charming it looked from the air. I wrote myself a reminder note to come back someday and explore the fishing villages on the shores of this sparkling, forest-ringed lake.

One hundred miles south of Guadalajara, I began a descent to 3,000 feet over Presa de Infiernillo, a vast reservoir set into desert gorges that reminded me of Lake Powell. At the lower altitude, the air was much warmer. Because we were nearing our next stop, Zihuatanejo, we stayed low and snaked our way through a stark gorge, following train tracks until we reached a bay just north of town. I called the tower 20 miles out and reported that two aircraft were inbound to land at the airport.

"Report reaching ten miles out and say airport of departure," the controller replied.

Galen videotaped me as I set up for the approach to landing. The stall warning gave a slight whistle as I eased the control stick toward my chest and held it there until the wheels gently touched the runway. I've had my share of bumpy ones, but when a landing goes well, nothing gives me more pleasure.

The flight from Mazatlán had taken a little over 4 hours, including our long sightseeing detour over the mountains. Another 2 hours of flying remained before we would reach Puerto Escondido, our destination for the night. After taxiing to transient parking, we hailed down a fuel truck, which arrived at the same time as a group of armed soldiers, who simply came to watch. Doug casually got out his ice chest, and we all sat down in the grass right in front of the Zihuatanejo Air Terminal to lunch peacefully on fresh avocados and canned tuna fish until a commercial jet arrived. It parked in front of us and nearly blew us away in its wake as we gathered our things. After it shut down, I stood there studying the row of jovial departing passengers, dressed in tropical shirts and heading for the beach seemingly without a care in the world. I thought about how differently I felt arriving in my own plane compared to arriving by jet. Though I would not have time to lie on Ixtapa's crystalline beaches and splash in its turquoise waters, I treasured the intimate connection that I now felt with the land after piloting my own plane above it.

Seeing the entire coastline at close range, not just the few places with road access, gave me a sense of rugged beauty far beyond the Mexican beach vacations I'd been on before.

In order to arrive at our destination before dark, we quickly reorganized our gear and departed over the coastline, staying low at 500 feet AGL above endless, creamy-white beaches. As I flew parallel to the beaches, I was charmed at seeing rustic thatched huts nestled in tropical vegetation bordering the sand. Doug flew much lower, directly along the beach, which caught the attention of children and adults who came running out of their huts, waving their arms wildly.

I watched Doug's plane begin to catch its own shadow on the beach as he dropped ever lower. It looked like he was having fun. I dropped down to 150 feet AGL, but my strict, law-abiding style kept me flying over the ocean in order not to violate the FAA regulation of remaining at least 500 feet above or to the side of any person or man-made structure. I had feelings of envy watching Doug cruise the beach at 20 feet just off my left wing. I had never flown below 200 feet before, except to land at an airport or in training with an instructor.

From my perspective, it looked like Doug was touching his tires on the sand, and at one point I told Galen and Robert that he was going to land.

"No. He's just enjoying himself," Galen said as he opened the window port behind me to take a photograph of Doug.

"Can you go a little lower, too?" Galen asked. "I'd like to get a picture of the huts behind Doug's plane."

I pointed the nose down gently and descended another 50 feet and leveled out. Every foot lower made the palm trees whiz by quicker.

"Can you go even lower?" Galen asked.

Lower and Slower is the motto of photographers. They have no idea what they're asking.

One of my flight instructors used to say that altitude is money in the bank. If an engine fails, the higher you are, the more time you have to pick a safe spot and land. Pilots are trained to follow standard procedures if the engine quits. The very first thing we are taught to do is to place the airplane in a flight configuration that provides the best glide ratio for maximum distance before touching down. My owner's manual says if my plane weighs in at 3,600 pounds (200 pounds shy of its revised gross weight with its new tip tanks), its best glide airspeed is  at 75 knots, which will give a descent rate of 750 feet per minute. In a no-wind situation that computes to a forward distance of 1.25 miles for every minute. At an altitude of 7,500 feet AGL, a pilot would have 10 minutes in the air before landing 12 miles away, possibly adequate time and distance to find a road, field, or even an airstrip on which to land safely. But if the engine quits at an altitude of 75 feet AGL, I would have at best 6 seconds before hitting the ground. That's not enough time to say good-bye.

As I dropped another 25 feet at Galen's request, I asked him, "Can you take some video for me, too?" It was hard not to get excited about cruising so close to the sea.

Doug and I flew side by side for a few miles. My heart raced watching the beach flash by. The fear of hitting something sticking out of the ocean plagued me even though there was nothing there. I couldn't forget how my mother was widowed when her first husband cartwheeled into the ocean while flying his navy trainer along a beach in Hawaii.

I followed Doug flying low over beaches north of Acapulco (left), and watched the shadow of his plane take people by surprise (above).

After we'd had enough low-altitude excitement, we climbed higher and continued south over the ocean following close to the shoreline. The vegetation became more tropical mixed with rugged rocks, as if the Oregon coastline had been stuck in the middle of Hawaii. The beaches disappeared into a wall of steep cliffs that dropped into the sea as far ahead as we could see. Doug was ahead of me, and he suddenly began a sharp turn seemingly into the rock wall. Within seconds, he vanished around the corner into the mouth of Acapulco Bay. I followed him around the bay's spectacular perimeter dotted by white houses that clung like guano to the sea walls. As we circled the entire bay to take in the scenery, Galen had me ask Doug to bank right in front of us for a photograph.

Doug complied with a steep bank beside the cliffs, then called Acapulco Tower for permission to overfly the airport at 1,000 feet. As we flew above its runway, I watched, with tinges of homesickness, as an American airliner taxied for takeoff. Farther south, the sky filled with clouds and rain began to fall as the setting sun tinted the clouds with pink. Soon light rain turned to heavy showers. A towering cumulus cloud west of our position was illuminated inside out with lightning.

"Oh my God!" exclaimed Galen.

My heart nearly stopped. "What is it?" I yelled, fearing that a wing had dropped off or oil was spewing down the side of the plane.

"Look at that rainbow!"

On the left side of the plane was a rare, 360-degree double rainbow. Seeing a full true rainbow—not a halo or glory—was a spectacular sight that I had seen only once before. But I couldn't help feeling anxious to land before showers got worse as the thunderstorm moved our way. I was certain that Galen would want to photograph it.

The only other time I saw a complete double rainbow had been on a flight in the Canadian Rockies, returning home from Alaska. Galen went wild when he saw the rare sight, but I went ballistic and refused to circle for photographs because the weather was stormy. I insisted we would see another one again soon, but we never did. I had always regretted it, so I decided to circle this time.

After I passed by that Canadian rainbow, Galen read to me from a book by atmospheric physicist Craig Bohren about the rarity of seeing a true 360-degree rainbow: "To the best of my knowledge, one has never been photographed." Bohren went on to offer "a suggestion for anyone who would like a bit of fame and fortune: photograph a complete rainbow. You will need an airplane. . . . You will also have to persuade the pilot to fly in stormy weather. If you survive your flight you will have acquired something rare indeed."

I lifted the wing while Galen used a 16-millimeter fish-eye lens to capture the whole rainbow out of my window. As the light rain gave way to heavy showers, Galen clicked off as many shots as possible before I headed toward the runway. Meanwhile, Doug was flying over the town to buzz the beach and let his friends, Tim and Marci, know that we'd arrived.

After landing, Galen climbed out behind me with his tripod before I even had time to shut the engine down. The sky had turned the deepest vermilion red we had

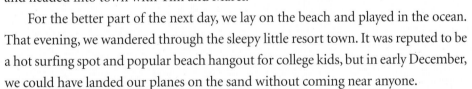

ever seen. Robert and I sat inside until the showers subsided and watched the splendid sunset. When we got out, Galen was still taking pictures as the wet tarmac reflected a sky so red that my plane appeared to be sitting in pool of blood.

"Tomorrow we'll have a rest day," Doug announced.

Rest day? I was just getting into flying. I didn't need to rest. But the idea of sleeping in did appeal to me. We tied the two planes down, closed our flight plan, and headed into town with Tim and Marci.

For the better part of the next day, we lay on the beach and played in the ocean. That evening, we wandered through the sleepy little resort town. It was reputed to be a hot surfing spot and popular beach hangout for college kids, but in early December, we could have landed our planes on the sand without coming near anyone.

The following morning, Doug had us up at five for breakfast. We said good-bye to Tim and Marci and caught a cab to the airport 45 minutes later. Unfortunately, we had to wait until seven for the Plan de Vuelo office to open for us to file our mandatory flight plans to Villahermosa, with Campeche as an alternate. A weather report was unavailable, so we would have to take a look from our airplanes and make our own call. If it didn't look good, we would return.

As we left the Pacific Ocean and headed inland, lightning from the remnants of the previous night's storm exploded inside towering cumulus just offshore. We

*I raised my wing so that Galen could use his
fish-eye lens to capture a rare 360-degree double
rainbow over Puerto Escondido (above).*

climbed up and over the mountains and crossed high above Oaxaca while only glimpses of the landscape pierced through the wispy layers of clouds. With nothing but clouds to photograph, Galen fell sound asleep in the backseat.

Doug was several miles ahead. I could still see the ground through wide spaces between clouds, but the weather ahead looked menacing, with clouds bunching up into solid overcast. Now I was getting worried about where Doug was leading me.

"What's the plan, Doug?" I asked over the radio.

"I'm calling Mexico Center on another frequency for weather," he replied.

"What frequency are you on?" I asked.

Doug gave me the Center frequency, and I dialed it in on the second radio to eavesdrop. Center reported the weather at Villahermosa as 400 feet broken. I quickly studied the approach plate for the airport and saw that Villahermosa was below minimums for making an instrument approach. The decision height for the missed approach was 520 feet. We would not be permitted to fly lower unless we could see the runway, and there were clouds at 400 feet. Weather was expected to improve, but for now, we were shut out from landing.

I called Doug again. "What are we going to do?"

"Follow me," he said.

I *was* following him. I just wanted to know *where* I was following him. Now I watched him closely, afraid of losing sight, which I had already learned was easy to do. Without another word, he began spiraling down through a hole in the overcast.

"Where is he going?" I asked no one in particular, somewhat stunned.

His spontaneous nature was not my style. Neither was his sparse communication. "What are you doing, Doug?" I asked.

"I'm going to look at something," he replied.

I flew over the hole where he had disappeared and turned the plane on its side to get a good look. This was beginning to get really interesting. Doug had twenty years of flying experience to my six, and he had flown to South and Central America several times before, but if he knew what he was doing he was the only one who did. We had agreed to a loose flight plan in order to explore interesting things along the way, and I had agreed that I was game for the adventure, as long as it was safe. But this seemed to be pushing the limit.

Robert, who had been studying the map, showed me that the terrain beneath us was near sea level and completely flat. I decided it looked safe to descend and began to reduce the manifold pressure and stage-cool the engine.

"Once you are under the clouds, Barbara, follow the railroad tracks to the southeast," Doug added.

I set up for a left 360-degree turn and circled tightly, losing 750 feet per minute as I continued down through the hole until I was just 250 feet above rain-soaked fields. Beneath the overcast I leveled out in an ominously dark and misty world. The visibility was poor—5 miles at best. The land was flooded from heavy rains. The terrain beneath me was so close that I climbed up toward the clouds until I skimmed their bases. Being near the clouds gave me the illusion of flying faster than I actually was.

Once I located the train tracks, I began following them, but I didn't see Doug. I blurted out over the radio, "Doug, where are you?" I knew he would think that I was a real pest, but I sure didn't like flying around without knowing where he was.

Peter answered on the radio, "Doug says to follow the tracks. Keep your eyes to the right and you'll see some spectacular Mayan ruins. Have your cameras ready. We'll be back. We are going to have a look at a narrow canyon and a waterfall shown on the map."

"I've got the tracks," I radioed.

I flew southeast along the railroad tracks at 100 knots. The land to the left was flat, wet, and partially cultivated. The land on the right was green, lush, and bumpy rainforest. Mounds of earth hidden beneath the forest canopy formed tightly clustered hills that made me wonder if they could be overgrown ruins yet to be discovered. The lower green hills were butted up against a backdrop of mountains that rose vertically into the black clouds. Squeezed from the right side and from above, I thought about a possible escape route if the terrain rose up in front of me, or the clouds lowered. I would make a hard left to the east. Then an apparition appeared off to my right. White temples stood out of the green forest. "I see the ruins!" I said. "Get ready to open the window."

I had never seen anything like it. Even in this dark light, the vegetation was emerald green and the ruins were ivory white. The splendid beauty of this jeweled and mystical landscape momentarily erased my fears, and I flew a circle as Robert opened the window on his side of the plane to shoot video. The cockpit filled with chilled, damp air, and my headphones roared with the wind passing over Robert's and Galen's microphones.

I lifted the right wing up and out of Galen's way for a few seconds so he could take a photograph, then dropped it, turned left, and circled back for another pass as soon as the ruins disappeared from view. When I called Doug and Peter to let them know where I was, Doug said that he was approaching the ruins from behind me. We both continued to fly counterclockwise circles, taking turns viewing the legendary Mayan ruins of Palenque.

After several circles by the ruins, the stress of flying low in an unfamiliar area peaked out, and I felt fatigued. Breaking out of the circling pattern, I flew to Palenque Airport a few miles away. To my relief, the runway was in perfect condition. As I touched down on the 105-foot-wide paved strip, a rusted DC-3 that had crashed long ago loomed out of the tall grass beside the runway. Doug soon came in behind me, and we secured our planes and hired a guard to watch them for the day.

A cab driver who had seen us flying near the ruins had already driven to the airport and was waiting for us. We asked him to take us somewhere nice to eat before touring Palenque's ancient city. He waited patiently as we lunched at an exotic outdoor restaurant with pools and palm trees. Afterward, the cab driver dropped us off beside a line of tour buses. We paid the entrance fee and hired a guide to take us through the mystical city of stone temples. After I climbed up the steep, hand-carved stone stairway to the top of the main temple, I surveyed the magical sight below and tried to imagine what it looked like at the height of the Mayan era. Was it as crowded then as it is today? Mexican families were exploring every nook and cranny. Foreign visitors were greatly in the minority.

We returned to the airport, paid the guard, and flew off over endless miles of flat jungle before landing at Campeche for fuel. From there we headed to Chichén Itzá to spend the night and see even more famous ruins. The monotonous, flat terrain appeared to go on forever, a sea of tropical jungle with almost no identifying features. Robert and I were constantly looking for roads and small villages to double-check our position on the map.

As we neared Chichén Itzá, a thunderstorm moved toward us, and I began dodging ever more frequent patches of heavy rain. The deteriorating weather made me decide to skip a scenic flight over the ruins. I was uncomfortable seeing an approaching thunderstorm that looked to be no more than 10 miles away when my flight training had taught me to stay at least 20 miles away from active electrical storms. Accompanying down drafts and winds that shear far out on the edge of such storms have proven fatal even to powerful jets, especially during takeoff and landing. I headed directly to the airport and hurried to get down on the half-paved strip before the heart of the storm hit.

"Doug, where are you?" I asked over the radio yet again as I reported my position in the airport pattern. Sounding like a broken record was preferable to becoming one if we were to collide in midair.

"I'm over the ruins," Doug replied, matter-of-factly. His calm amazed me. The combination of feeling anxious to get on the ground and a gusty 90-degree crosswind caused me to bounce my landing. It was my first rough landing of the trip, but I recovered it by holding the control stick to my chest and turning into the wind to prevent the plane from ground looping and to keep the propeller away from the gravel.

Minutes after Doug landed, the sky collapsed with a roar of thunder and curtains of heavy rain. A planeload of American tourists, hoping to return to Cancún after a day trip to the ruins, were standing outside a wooden shack that doubled as the terminal for charter aircraft. Their pilot was not about to take off until the storm had passed. We tied our planes down in the rain beside the unfenced strip surrounded by jungle.

Doug paid a night guard armed with a sawed-off shotgun to watch the planes until morning. The guard warned us not to return to our planes without first notifying him, because he might shoot first and ask questions later if he saw any unauthorized person near a plane.

We walked to the nearby Mayaland Hotel, an opulent structure built in 1930 with open verandas, surrounded by gardens and guest cottages with thatched roofs. By the time we checked in, it had become too dark outside to see the nearby ruins from our balcony. Rain pounded the tiled roof of the open-air lobby, while winds whipped the potted plants. Thunder roared throughout the building.

After Galen and I went to our room and opened the curtains, El Castillo, Chichén Itzá's most impressive pyramid, flashed into view several times a minute, illuminated by lightning strikes.

Thunder kept me awake most of the night. I lay there worrying that this is where I would get left behind. Doug had not seemed the least bit concerned about the storm as it approached. Perhaps he really would take off in such conditions. I wouldn't. Flying in bad weather terrifies me, and it didn't take a weatherman to know how bad it was out there.

In the morning the rain had moved on and given way to a thick fog that blanketed the ancient Mayan city. To kill time and wait for the sky to clear, we wandered through the ruins until the fog lifted. By the time we were ready to take off, the air was crystal clear, and it stayed that way as we headed toward the Caribbean coastline to see Tulúm. We circled low over the most picturesque ruins I'd ever seen. Brilliant turquoise waters lapped at the base of white limestone cliffs capped with a Mayan temple. We climbed up and flew on to Chetumal, our last stop before leaving Mexico.

After both aircraft were fueled, I tried to pay my bill with traveler's checks, but they were rejected and given back to me. I had to pay cash in U.S. dollars. We then filed international flight plans to Belize, hopped in our planes, and began taxiing to the runway. Just before takeoff, the controller called me, but not Doug: "Five Lima Yankee, return to the terminal."

As I neared the base of the tower, three soldiers armed with assault weapons surrounded the plane. "Qué pasa?" I asked, wondering if I was about to be taken into custody. The Mexican soldiers brandished their weapons and motioned for me to leave my plane. As I unbuckled my seat belt, my gaze alternated between the barrels of the AK-47s and the eyes of the most dominant soldier. Both were hard as steel. Three soldiers stepped forward, circled me, and led me into the same building where I had recently cleared immigration. A stern-looking gentleman seated behind a counter addressed me in Spanish: "You paid your bill with traveler's checks."

"No. My checks were returned to me, and then I paid in cash." I pulled out the signed-off traveler's checks to show him. He turned and talked to someone else, who then got up and left the room. Five minutes later, a young man dressed in blue overalls arrived. I recognized him as the sleepy, young fellow who had fueled my airplane. He huddled with the person in charge, who in turn came back to me and said apologetically, "Lo siento. I thought you paid your bill with traveler's checks. You are free to go."

When I got back and told the guys what had happened, Galen had a good laugh and said, "So much for that American Express ad: 'Never leave home without them.'"

The Mayan ruins of Palenque (right).

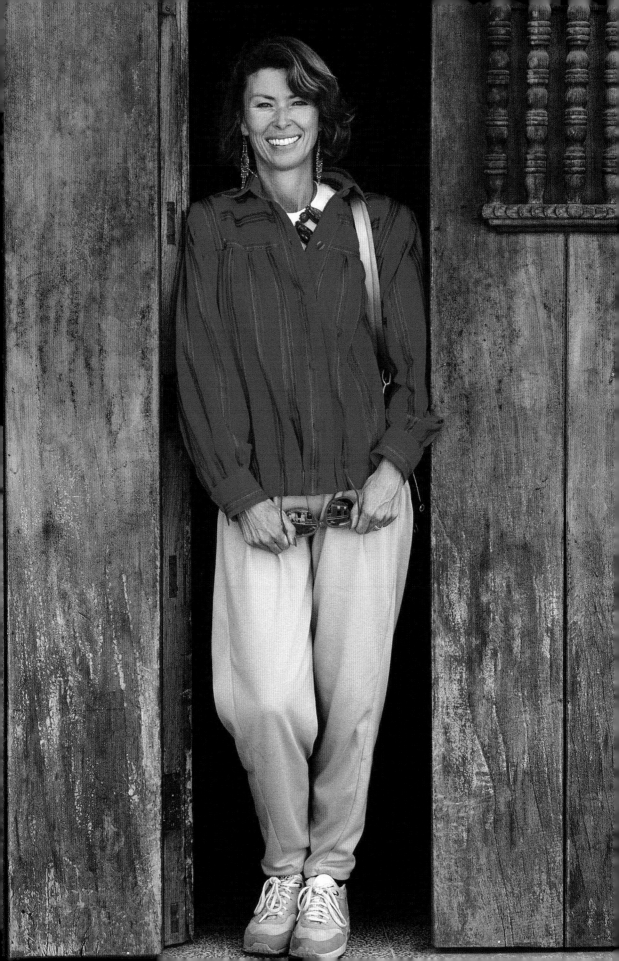

BELIZE TO GUATEMALA

IX

*S*econds after my tires left the ground, I turned right and climbed away from the Chetumal Airport. The Mexican controller instructed us to contact Belize Approach on 121.0, bid us a friendly good-bye, and wished us a safe flight. Three miles out over Chetumal Bay, I made my second border crossing and entered Belize.

Though we arrived at Phillip Goldson International Airport near Belize City just after lunch, it was late afternoon before we finally cleared all legal paperwork to be in Belize, the former British colony once called British Honduras. It is the only country in Latin America where English is the official language. Several of our friends had trekked through the country's famous rainforests, but our travel would be limited to the immediate vicinity of airports. Doug was not in favor of spending the night in Belize City, infamous for its petty crime, so we returned to our planes after clearing customs and flew northeast over the ocean for 30 minutes to the tiny town of San Pedro on Ambergris Caye.

When I first checked the map, the island appeared to be part of the Yucatán Peninsula, belonging to Mexico, but a closer look showed a canal separating the two countries. According to our guidebook, the canal had been dug long ago by Mayan Indians. The island itself has become a popular tourist destination because it parallels the Belize Barrier Reef, the longest of its kind in the Western Hemisphere. Unfortunately for us, the turquoise waters surrounding the narrow spit were dulled because we were arriving beneath overcast skies.

On my downwind leg into the short and narrow 2,579-foot strip, I reported my position in the blind to alert any pilot who was monitoring the airport frequency for San Pedro Airport. As I flew 800 feet above the ground and parallel to the runway, I could see bicyclists and dogs scurrying along the 33-foot-wide strip of loose crushed coral.

I wiped my damp hands on my sweatshirt and glanced at the windsock, which confirmed the report we'd been given: 15 knots, gusting 20, blowing at an angle of

At Spanish school in Antigua, Guatemala, in 1989 (left).

113

90 degrees to the runway. Just as Doug was about to land, everyone, including the dogs, cleared the runway. Either from past experience, sheer luck, or Darwinian selection, they made it off the landing strip just in the nick of time.

Because San Pedro had no tower to control the flow of airport traffic, I continued to call out my position over the radio as I turned onto the base leg of the traffic pattern and again as I turned onto final approach. I hoped that any other aircraft in the area would be listening and know where I was. As I was descending toward the ground holding the aileron all the way into the wind to keep the wing down and maintain a straight course against a strong crosswind, I heard four airplanes report on final approach, one right after the other. The sun was about to set and within minutes the unlit runway would be officially closed. Just before my tires touched down, a male pilot reported on short final and added, "I have Five Lima Yankee in sight." Seconds later, he yelled, "Get off the runway *quick!*" He was about to touch down in a faster, twin-engine plane.

"Barbara, come over where I am!" Doug called in an effort to help get me out of a tight spot.

I looked to see where Doug was and glimpsed his spinning propeller almost hidden in the tall grass off the right side of the landing strip, which lacked a parallel taxiway. Everything seemed to be happening in a strange combination of slow motion and nano seconds. I quickly considered my options as I struggled to hold my aircraft steady against a blustery crosswind and not allow the wind to get under the wing and flip us upside down. According to flight rules, I had the right-of-way, not the pilot who was in the air. He had the option of giving it full throttle and going around again. But I couldn't see behind me to know if he was indeed where he said he was. I did not dare count on his good judgment. My choices were limited to staying on the runway and chancing being hit by the airplane landing behind me or taxiing into the grass as soon as possible. In the midst of all this chaos, I never lost sight of the fact that I still hadn't finished my own landing.

As the other three pilots continued to give position reports right in line behind the pilot who had just called me, and without any more information about where he was, I decided to steer off into the grass before I had come to a full stop. Seconds later, the twin roared past me, taking up the full runway as it screeched to a halt. I had mixed feelings of pride that I'd successfully gotten off the runway in time and annoyance at the rude and reckless pilot landing behind me.

Doug and I waited into the twilight until the runway was clear of incoming traffic before daring to taxi to the far end of the field and park our planes in the grass. Finding nothing to which to tie my plane down, I pulled out my own metal stakes and nylon ropes that I had brought for just such a situation. Doug and I searched for the largest rocks we could find and asked the others to help us put them behind the tires to keep our planes from rolling in the strong winds. While a half-dozen children circled both planes, studying our every move, I set the parking brake. Instantly, several young boys tried to crawl inside to get a good look at my instrument panel. My fear of the situation getting out of control quickly passed as I recalled the times when curious children had circled my tent in Pakistan and Tibet, spending hours watching my every move from cleaning my camera to writing in my diary.

Having so many planes trying to land at once without a control tower was a free-for-all that I rated more dangerous than when I had once landed between jets at Denver during rush hour. Who would have guessed that I would encounter such heavy air traffic on a remote island in the Caribbean? The tiny San Pedro Airport was still buzzing with commercial passengers gathering suitcases as we started to walk into town.

Before we stepped off the field, a soft-spoken man who introduced himself as Daddy Paz appeared in a beat-up cab, collected us from the chaos, and drove us to a set of tiny beach bungalows. In a lilting Caribbean voice, he gave us running commentary during our brief minitour of an island under heavy construction to meet the demands of increasing tourism. As he let us off at the reception office, he said to call him at home at night if we needed anything more.

We quickly dropped our overnight bags in our thatched huts and regrouped to walk along the white sandy beach toward town. The man at the desk had suggested that we dine at the local hot spot, Elvis's Kitchen. We followed his advice and were pleased to find both a lively ambience and tasty food. After dinner, we continued wandering down the main street lined with colorful tourist shops. The local people were unusually warm and friendly. Background sounds carried by the humid night air of Latin Christmas music with a Caribbean-reggae beat were accompanied by the incongruous sounds of barking dogs and crowing roosters.

As we walked back to the hotel, I tried to contemplate the future of this little town. Although I liked the place a lot, it was apparent that its popularity had already begun to destroy its charm. It would soon become sterile, like everywhere else that travelers love to death.

Doug announced that we would leave San Pedro first thing in the morning, return to Belize City to clear immigration, and continue on to Costa Rica. After walking around town, I was sad that we were leaving this wonderful spot having had only a little taste of its rare treats. Before coming on this trip, I had been confounded by Galen's trying to turn this trip into his adventure. Now Doug's desires also seemed to be at odds with my own. If challenging my husband's wishes was difficult, the mere thought of suggesting a change in plans to Doug was even more intimidating. The net result of traveling with a second strong-willed man was beginning to feel like taking on a harem of husbands. The desire to please them first and put my needs last had seemed so ingrained in me that, up to now, I couldn't imagine it any other way. But it was finally dawning on me that I would continue to be trapped on someone else's express train through life unless I were willing to unravel the fabric of my soul and chance abandonment by weaving myself into a more confident and independent person. What I wanted was strictly for me. I was not thinking in terms of the bigger picture of women's liberation, and I certainly didn't want to be written off by men as just another angry and confrontational female with a self-esteem problem. I needed to figure out how to be assertive without losing my femininity, and I needed to figure it out soon.

An hour after we settled into our beach cottage for the night, winds began to howl and palm trees whipped as if they were mixing some frothy tropical concoction inside a giant blender. Heavy rain began pouring on the thatched roof and the sound of water hitting straw became so loud that it kept me awake most the night. I lay there quietly, trying not to wake Galen, but the more I wanted to fall asleep, the further away sleep would go.

At the first hint of daylight, I popped out of bed and went to the door of our room to check the sky. In the predawn light, it was impossible to tell solid gray cloud from clear blue. Try as I might, I couldn't convince myself that I was seeing any blue out there. All I knew for certain was that the rain had stopped for the moment. I crawled back in bed to cuddle with Galen. His powerful arms wrapped tightly around me. I felt torn between staying in bed with him to enjoy what in other times would be a romantic vacation spot and leaving to check on the airplane.

"What does it look like outside? Is it worth taking a photograph?" Galen asked.

"Not really," I said as I felt the first flutter of butterflies in my stomach. Galen got up and remarked that he couldn't see blue, either. He said it was one of those rare illusory situations that prove color is something assigned by our brains rather

*I photographed Fuego Volcano framed beneath
a colonial arch as I walked to Spanish school in
Antigua, Guatemala (above).*

117

than being a property of light or objects, as we assume. I tried to listen, but my mind was totally occupied with worry over whether Doug would take off into bad weather. Unable to stand the suspense any longer, I got out of bed and quickly packed what few things I had managed to get out of the plane the night before. Galen joined me as I headed out the door to walk to the airport. In the quiet of the early morning, the only sounds were those of palms gently swaying in a light breeze. No one was stirring in the shacks beside the sandy road.

The planes were soaking wet from the previous night's heavy downpour, but otherwise as we had left them. Robert showed up, and we quietly set about our individual tasks—Galen untied the plane, Robert wiped off the Plexiglas windshield, and I checked the oil. An equal division of labor had evolved quite naturally among the three of us. But no matter how hard we tried, we were never ready to go before Doug, who arrived later, but magically taxied into position for takeoff before I had even started my engine.

The sky was indeed gray and appeared to be darkening as we headed southwest over the ocean, back toward the shoreline of Belize's mainland. By the time we neared the international airport, Doug's plane was so far off course that I asked him where he was going. I wondered if he had changed his plans.

"Sorry," Peter replied. He was at the controls and Doug was in the copilot's seat acting as Peter's instructor. After watching Peter fly such an unusual approach into the airport, I guessed that he had never had previous instruction in flying proper airport patterns.

I was taught to fly as close to perfect airport patterns as possible. My instructor stressed the importance of making my turns precisely and always rolling out of my base leg onto the final approach leg with my plane lined up on the centerline. The airfield where I learned to fly had side-by-side parallel runways, so it was critical not to overshoot the turn from the base leg onto the final approach. Otherwise, I might hit an airplane on the opposite side rolling out on final for the parallel runway.

But if Peter Buckley had not learned proper pattern work before leaving on this trip, he wasn't going to learn it from Doug, who was not into form when it came to flying. Doug did things his own way, from casual radio communications to personalized airport patterns. His actions were difficult to predict, except for his frequent teasing about my precision and by-the-book radio communication style. He said I was a good pilot, just overly thorough. I thought he was a good pilot, just overly sloppy.

To keep from overtaking Doug's plane as I followed it toward the international airport at Belize City, I put down a second notch of flaps. I could see out of the corners of my eyes that the flaps were lowering simultaneously. The increased drag immediately slowed us down a few knots. To give myself more separation from Doug's plane, I continued my downwind leg beyond where I would normally have made a right turn onto the base leg. Even with 20 degrees of flaps, I was still continuing to catch Doug, so I lowered full flaps to drop my airspeed to 70 knots and began making S turns to put more distance between us. As I followed Doug's plane with my eyes, it looked as if it were motionless and just sort of dangling in space. For a few seconds, I stared at the strange vision sitting off the nose of my plane, trying to figure out what he was up to. Then it dawned on me that Doug was teaching Peter something new.

"Look at those guys," I said to Robert.

"What are they doing?"

"Doug must be teaching Peter slow flight. He's big on learning how to make low, slow passes over runways in the event you have to land on an unfamiliar dirt strip. This allows a pilot to get a good look at the runway before landing. Doug told me to work on the same thing before coming on this trip. But I wish he had warned me ahead of time, or at least offered to let me land first." Doug's STOL modification allowed his plane to fly very slowly without inducing a stall. Trying to fly a reasonable pattern behind him in slow flight was quite a challenge.

The tower cleared me to land as Doug's tires touched the ground. I watched in disbelief as his plane began slowly rolling down the centerline of the runway at a snail's pace.

"*Now* what is he teaching him?" I asked in exasperation. "The slow taxi?"

They were moving so slowly that it began to look like I would not be able to avoid catching up with them. That would force me to abandon my landing and go around the pattern again. I had heard a number of other airplanes report inbound to the airport, including a Boeing 747, and I did not want to lose my place in line to land. But I also didn't have the guts to order Doug to get off the runway quick, like the pilot had done to me at San Pedro.

Back at home, our controllers would already have ordered me to fly around the pattern again. Instead, Belizean controllers allowed me to continue flying slowly, just above the ground, down the first half of the 7,100-foot paved strip, while waiting for Doug's plane to taxi off. Even though they had given me permission to touch down, I didn't dare land while Doug's plane was still on the runway. It just wasn't safe. Instead, I hovered as slow as possible at a safe airspeed just above stall speed, feeling extremely frustrated and irritated.

I touched down when I was sure that Doug and Peter had safely reached the adjacent taxiway. I remained silent as I taxied to parking and pulled up alongside Delta Juliett. Glancing over at Doug and Peter, who appeared not to have a care in the world as they got out of their plane, I tried to look neutral. It wasn't easy, since my face had flushed hot as a fountain of fury welled up inside of me. I was ready to explode with anger, but who was I really angry at? What had they done to me?

Nothing, really. They were just doing what they wanted to without any regard for anyone else. Was that such a crime? Not crime enough to have triggered such strong emotions. The real issue was that they had done something that I would never dare to do: be completely self-centered. I was really angrier with myself for not being more like them. After pausing to think about it a little more, I should have simply passed them when they had flown so far off course. But something deeply ingrained in me kept me from doing that.

I'd spent a lifetime trying to please people, especially men, in hopes of winning their praise and affection. Because Doug rarely gave praise, I found myself trying even harder to get it from him. My desire to be seen as polite and feminine kept me walking on eggshells when I felt more like stomping and screaming. Could I ever be as powerful as he without coming off like a witch?

After Doug and I ordered fuel, we left the gang to watch over the unlocked planes while we headed over to the flight-operations and weather-briefing offices. We were told that no significant weather systems were in the area, but to expect multiple layers of clouds en route to Guatemala. After we filled out numerous forms, we set off like children on a treasure hunt to track down multiple officials scattered throughout the airport and have them stamp and sign our papers. The reward for successfully completing the mound of red tape was to pay a whopping $200 in landing fees. This was far more than I had expected. In the United States, there is no charge for landing, except at a few of the major airports like San Francisco International, where the fee was $24. Here in Belize, I wasn't sure if these fees paid for anything substantive, or if they went directly into someone's pocket.

By the time we were cleared for departure, the overcast had blackened. While everyone else headed off to do last-minute duties before starting out on a 6-hour flight, I sat inside my plane with my maps to study the instrument route that I was about to fly. Out of nowhere, a strange male voice asked, "Lady, how come you is sitting in the pilot seat?"

"I'm the pilot," I said, looking up to see who was speaking to me.

"No way," the stranger continued. From his uniform, he appeared to be a ground attendant for one of the airlines.

"Seriously, I am," I said, trying to hold back my nervous laughter. I appreciated the directness of his question, because I was so accustomed to people walking up to Galen, assuming that he must be the pilot and I his student. This was the first time that someone had come out in the open and said exactly what was on his mind.

"*He* have to help you," the man said, pointing to Robert, who was busy folding a map.

"No. He doesn't have to help me. He doesn't know how to fly," I added.

"Oh lady, you very brave lady," the man gasped with his mouth and dark eyes wide open.

He couldn't have been further from the truth. I felt anything but brave as I prepared for the upcoming instrument flight into clouds. What matters most in flying is good judgment. Making the correct decision to go or not to go is more important than "bravely" flying into situations where only the brave might come out alive.

In the field of general aviation no one tells a pilot whether she or he has permission to fly. That decision is entirely up to the pilot-in-command. Pilots are required to know everything about their upcoming flight, including forecast weather conditions, runway length, fuel availability, and aircraft performance for any given altitude and temperature. Unless the airport closes for some reason, pilots are allowed to depart, even if the tower controller thinks they are being stupid and may kill themselves. The controllers have control over the flow of traffic in and out of the airport, and that's it.

There is no system for a controller to assess the level of a pilot's skill or whether she has all the pertinent information to make a safe flight. For all a controller knows, I might be Chuck Yeager prancing around as a 5-foot 3-inch, 107-pound woman. Without X-ray vision, a controller can't know if my Cessna is equipped with the latest space-age instruments and de-icing equipment, or whether it has proper working equipment at all. Only the pilot knows for sure. Unless the pilot has an accident, no one knows the pilot's skill level. Only after a pilot crashes does everyone soon know about the history of the pilot, the plane, and the events leading up to the particular incident by reading the results of the investigation.

I was not going to be a story looking for an ending, like all those accounts I'd read in flying magazines where I knew what was going to happen at a point in the narrative well before the pilot did. My goal was to avoid all those kinds of sloppy little mistakes that can occasionally come together to drop a pilot out of the sky. Performing stunts to impress people was the last thing on my mind.

Just as we were ready to leave Belize, a British Harrier jet came roaring in over the runway and stopped right in front of us, hanging there in midair. I'd never seen anything like it. Airplanes that don't move are supposed to fall out of the sky, otherwise they must be helicopters. The Harrier hovered just 20 feet above the runway and slowly turned sideways to face us.

"Wow! Look at that!" I said as I hopped out of my plane to watch.

The jet stayed put and tipped its nose toward the ground, as if to bow and curtsy.

"I think they are putting on a show for the lady pilot," Galen said looking over at me proudly.

"Galen's right," Doug said, adding his two cents. Coming from him, it was more like a dollar.

We stood beside our planes holding our hands over our ears to protect them against the sound of the loud jet engine as the Harrier made complete circles, flying forward, backward, and vertically up and down. Even though the guys continued to say that they thought this wild show was a display of male machismo in honor of the lady pilot, I did not really believe that this performance might be happening for me. But then I remembered a similar incident on a flight from Oakland to Mendocino with a friend of ours. As a special treat, I flew over the Golden Gate Bridge and along the coast by the Point Reyes National Seashore. As I continued north, Oakland Center advised me that the MOA (military operations area) that I was flying through was "hot." They informed me that a jet trainer was buzzing around at 14,000 feet, but added that it would not be a factor as long as I remained at my present altitude of 1,000 feet. A few minutes later, Oakland Center called again and said, "Jet traffic now at your one o'clock position, at one thousand feet and less than one mile."

Just as I spotted the traffic, my friend exclaimed, "Look at that!" There, just a few hundred feet off my right wing tip, the cutest white jet I'd ever seen was paralleling me at 130 knots. Cute may seem like an odd choice of words for a machine capable of roaring through the sound barrier, but this one was traveling my speed and making all sorts of clever maneuvers. I assumed he knew that I was there too, but I rocked my wings to be sure. As soon as I finished signaling that I had him in sight, he mimicked me, did a barrel roll underneath me, and came up on my opposite side. When I smiled and waved, he rolled again back to the other side and remained there briefly before rapidly pulling away and climbing out of sight. Oakland Center called again to report: "Five Lima Yankee, traffic no longer a factor."

The jet trainer's close approach just after my voice had been on the radio had to be more than coincidence. Less than 6 percent of pilots in the United States are women, and less than 2 percent are women who are instrument rated. In Latin America, the percentages are much lower. With that in mind, it seemed far more possible that the military pilots flying the Harrier *were* performing for me. Male testosterone accounts for truly amazing things, and whether or not I had triggered the aerial display, I had to admit I was loving it.

Ten minutes later, the show ended. We resumed our familiar positions in the plane and taxied to the run-up area behind Doug, who of course was there first. I called Ground Control and said I was ready for my instrument flight instructions. He called back: "Five Lima Yankee is cleared to San José, Costa Rica. Climb via Romeo Six Three Zero, direct Rabinal, direct La Aurora, Uniform Golf Four Three Six, direct Liberia, Uniform Golf Four Four Zero direct El Coco. Climb maintain twelve thousand feet. Contact Departure Control on one two one decimal zero."

After I copied the clearance and read it back, I began setting up my navigation radios to follow the assigned route that we'd been given. As I dialed 215 degrees into my number-one radio, I caught a glimpse of Doug taxiing onto the runway. Before he started rolling, I asked him to report at what altitude he first encountered clouds. Just over a minute after departure, Doug disappeared from sight. He called to report going IMC—entering instrument meteorological conditions—at 1,500 feet and that he was still in the clouds as he climbed through 4,000 feet.

I can do that, too, I thought to myself before turning toward Robert to say: "I want you to back me up on this flight by double-checking everything I do. I'll be climbing on the two-one-five-degree radial, so the needle should stay centered. I need to be in a constant climb, and my vertical speed should indicate at least 750 feet per minute. Once I reach 12,000 feet, I'll be leveling out. It's straightforward, but I want you to act as a second pair of eyes."

Asking him to back me up was a precautionary request that made me feel more secure, given the limited number of hours that I had flown on instruments to date. Just before leaving on this trip, my logbook total for the amount of time that I had flown on instruments, wearing a hood to simulate clouds and block my view outside the plane, was 59 hours. Over a five-year period, that wasn't very many. But more surprising was my total time flying in actual clouds—a mere 8 hours. And those 8 hours were in bits and pieces, mostly flying in and out of my home airport. Very few of my hours were without an instructor in the airplane. No wonder my stomach was in knots.

While I anxiously waited for the tower to call me, I checked, double-checked, and cross-checked every instrument, map, and timer in the plane. I had checked so many times that I knew the position of every needle by heart. Even though I had done it before, I did it all over again, religiously. As the engine ran smoothly, I could feel all 310 horses in my bones. The plane rocked in place, ever so slightly, as they chomped at the bit, ready to sprint down the runway.

Ten long minutes later, Belize Tower finally called: "Five Lima Yankee cleared for takeoff."

I taxied onto Runway 25 and took a deep breath as I began my takeoff roll. Robert started the timer clipped to the headliner to his right, and I started the other timer clipped to my control yoke. As I rolled down the runway, I took a last glance down to reassure myself that the departure map and approach plate for Belize were in place. In the event of an emergency, I might need to return. I wanted all the paperwork close at hand.

As I left the ground, the VOR needle swung to life, and I turned on course, which was more like a veer as I watched my directional gyro pass from 250 to 245, 240, 235, 230, 225, 220 and finally to 215 degrees. In order to intercept the course, I flew past 215 to 210 and held it there until the VOR needle lined up, and then I gently brought it back to a heading of 215. Our route crossing over Central America from the Caribbean Ocean to the Pacific Ocean was southwest. As I flew, I announced, "I am climbing via the two-one-five degree radial."

Robert repeated, "Two one five is correct."

I continued, "Climbing through one thousand feet for twelve thousand on the two-one-five degree radial, heading two one five."

The sheer act of repeating my actions out loud helped me relax. I kept my eyes on the gauges on the inside panel so that I wouldn't be taken by surprise when we entered the clouds. When my altimeter read 1,500 feet, we went solidly into the clouds. Peripherally, I could see vapor swirling around us until we lost all sight of land and the world outside the window was completely white. My eyes quickly danced from one instrument to the next, scanning the aircraft's performance and direction of flight, as well as rate of climb.

Five minutes after takeoff, when it was obvious that everything was under my control, I felt the muscles throughout my body relax slightly. I knew exactly what I was doing, and I was doing it perfectly. At 5,000 feet we broke out into clear blue skies.

I cheered.

"Yahoo!" Robert added. He seemed as happy as I was. He understood the seriousness of it all and knew full well what the consequences would have been if I had not paid attention to my artificial horizon and accidentally held the plane level instead of raising the nose to climb, a slight difference on the gauge. Although our initial route of flight would take us inland over flat jungle, once we reached the interior of Guatemala, the jungle rose up into mountains. If I were to lose track of altitude and forget to climb, we could smack into the terrain. Boom! That would be it. But Robert and I were cut from the same cloth, and I knew that I could trust him to pay attention to my every move.

Earlier today, before I had flown into the clouds over Belize, I had indeed trusted Robert to take his job as backup navigator seriously. And he did. He has held enough dying people in his arms as an emergency medical technician to know that human beings are never infallible.

My brother is a gentle soul. It is a joy to watch him work as a ski patrolman at Squaw Valley. He glides down the steepest mountain, often carrying his ski poles in one hand and sign posts in the other, edging his skis through hard-packed snow like a knife through melted butter. But where his true nature is put to the test is in helping those who have been hurt. I've watched him lie down in the snow next to a scared child who has just taken a wild tumble and do a physical examination of the possibly broken leg without alarming the child. Not until Robert knows a person is okay and oriented enough to ski off safely on his or her own will he leave. Few, if any, ever know that the angel dressed in black with a white cross is the director of Ski Patrol.

Robert's medical emergency expertise comes from years of handling serious accidents on the ski slopes. One of the worst was that of a male skier who had taken a bad fall and slid rapidly down the snow slope, picking up speed along the way until he hit a tree. Robert was called to the scene and immediately began to administer emergency medical attention. The injured skier kept telling my brother that he couldn't breathe, yet he continually ripped the oxygen mask off of his face. Robert carefully moved him onto a special board designed to protect his back and had him transported down the mountain to the medical clinic on a Snowcat, all the while lying beside him. Robert put his face next to the man's chest, heard a gurgling sound, and began mouth-to-mouth resuscitation in a desperate attempt to save the man's life. Before they got to the bottom of the mountain, the skier had no signs of life. After that incident, Robert was distraught, but the doctors praised him for the outstanding care he had given after they found that the man had drowned in his own blood because a tree branch had pierced his heart. They said that he would have died even if the accident had happened on the doorstep of the best hospital in the world.

As a professional ski patrolman for over twenty years, Robert has seen a lot of grisly accidents. I have always felt that if anything bad were ever to happen to me, I would want him to be there. I would trust him with my life more than anyone in the world. That's one of the reasons it felt so right to invite him to join me on this flight, where his calm demeanor and competent backup could catch little problems before they got out of hand.

Seventy-five nautical miles west of Belize City, we crossed into Guatemala at an elevation of 12,000 feet, where I had previously leveled out. The clouds below the plane had now become widely scattered, and I could see three familiar volcanoes piercing the sky near Guatemala City. The sight of Fuego, Agua, and Acatenango brought back pleasant memories of the cobblestone streets and colonial-style buildings below them in the little, yet lively, town of Antigua, where I had spent four weeks attending Proyecto Lingüístico Francisco Marroquín, a Spanish-immersion school, two years earlier. I looked at these three glorious volcanoes every day from my bedroom while I was living with a local family as part of my course of instruction.

There below me was a town where every building, every cobblestone had a unique character, yet from up here in the air the streets were single pathways through town. I reflected on how all the individual cobblestones that I had laid down in my own life—graduating from college, studying the Spanish language, learning to take photographs, earning my pilot's license, getting my instrument rating, and running a business—were also a single pathway. I could see it more clearly now than before the trip, but where it would lead me, I did not know.

Cobblestone streets of Antigua, Guatemala (right).

126

The Galápagos Effect

X

For years I believed that I would have to wait for Galen to take me to South America. Since Galen seemed to have little interest in that part of the world, it would be a long time before I would see Bolivia, Peru, or Ecuador. Then one day it occurred to me that I could go on my own.

The Galápagos Islands were at the top of my wish list. I'd heard that the islands were little changed since Charles Darwin found animals and birds that were totally unafraid of human approach in the 1830s. I was captivated by the idea of sailing around the islands and speaking Spanish to native Ecuadorians in the same wild setting that had provoked Darwin to develop his theory of evolution. The islands had been preserved in his memory as a national park where  visitors must return to their sailboats for the night, experiencing the wildlife in much the same way as he had so long ago. Since we did not have photographs of the Galápagos, I could justify traveling there for business as well as personal experience.

When Galen blocked out the month of February 1988 to ski the John Muir Trail for *National Geographic,* it seemed a perfect time for me to head for the tropics. I decided not to ask permission.

"I'm going to the Galápagos Islands while you're gone in February," I said nonchalantly.

"Really? That's great!" Galen replied.

I was stunned. Wow! That was it? No questions? No argument? I could seriously go without him?

Galen sounded serious. He said that he wanted me to be able to follow my own passions. Before he had time to change his mind, I invited a girlfriend to travel

I first visited the Galápagos Islands (left) without Galen and took many close-ups of birds; my favorite shot is a more distant silhouette of boobies touching heads (above).

129

with me and called a travel agent to book a tour on a small sailboat, based in the Galápagos, called the *Nixe II*. Three days after my fortieth birthday, my girlfriend and I took a commercial flight to Ecuador, landed in Quito, and rented a car. We headed north into the highlands near the Colombian border for a side trip to Otavalo, famous for its lively outdoor market where hundreds of local people in wildly colored, traditional dress come down out of the hills to sell their wares. As we weaved our way over rolling green highlands dotted with farms, I fell in love with everything: the warmth of the people, their passion, their music, their food, and most of all their vivid use of color. My veins began to fill with vibrant red Latin blood.

I was so glad that I'd created the short list of potential life goals for the therapist. Next in line after "Learn to fly" were "Speak Spanish fluently" and "Explore South America."

By the time we caught our flight to the Galápagos Islands, 600 miles off the coast, the rest of the trip on the mainland had been so great that I couldn't imagine how the islands could top it. But they did. Due to a booking error, my girlfriend and I ended up being the only passengers on a sailboat that normally carries groups of six tourists. The Ecuadorian crew sailed in the night from one island to the next so that we could awake each morning to a new paradise teeming with wildlife. After breakfast we would board a small dinghy to visit beaches with marine iguanas, land iguanas, blue-footed boobies, frigate birds, albatrosses, seals, and sea lions that live in an island environment devoid of land predators and were wholly unafraid of our close approach.

The slower pace of life profoundly affected me. Life on the islands was so simple and pure that it was like being on a different planet. Even the giant tortoises fit right in with the casual pace of Latin living. I was so deeply affected that I did not want to go back to California. For the first time in my life, I had gone somewhere exotic that was my choice, and the experience surpassed even my highest expectations. Even mundane tasks such as locating hotels, finding routes, and changing money meant more to me when I was making the decisions without the help of a guide or husband. Now, more than ever, I was determined to see all of South America.

I began listening to more Latin music, honing my Spanish, and daydreaming about someday visiting the fabled rainforests, turquoise waters, and Andean summits of the southern continent.

Within a year or two, other feelings began incubating inside me. Besides feeling a growing discontent about primarily traveling to places that Galen wanted to visit, I was also beginning to resent flying to suit his whims. North American mountains were the love of Galen's life, not mine, and flying around them was nerve-racking. I didn't mind doing it now and then, but as a steady diet, it was getting hard to digest. Now I wanted to fly somewhere that enchanted *me*.

Despite these nagging thoughts, I believed that my life was headed in the right direction. I could see that flying was leading to positive changes in my social life. For the first time since we were married, people engaged me in conversations about something that I was passionate about instead of only asking me questions about my spouse. I felt a newfound sense of self and a special sense of pride in saying that I was a pilot.

Both men and women seemed genuinely more interested in what I had to say about things other than flying. It felt good having them ask for my opinions, rather than always turning first to Galen. But just being a pilot wasn't enough. Flying in and of itself did not hold the answers to my discontent any more than getting a medical license satisfies a passion for medicine. It's how you use your special skill that counts.

I didn't find the right direction until I went back to that list and no longer saw the three goals at the top as separate items. I could merge them into life experiences tailored especially for me. I would find ways to pursue flying, speak Spanish, and explore South America that would come together into adventures I couldn't yet imagine.

If I were going to continue traveling in Spanish-speaking countries, I would need to improve my Spanish. The year after my first Galápagos trip, I made flight reservations to go to Guatemala—at the same time Galen would be going to Bhutan for the World Wildlife Fund—after signing up for a month-long language immersion program in Antigua.

I loved the wild Latin colors of everything from textiles (left) to produce (above), which I photographed at a Sunday market in Otavalo, Ecuador.

Antigua felt like a second home to me. I spoke Spanish to everyone as I got to know the cobblestone streets and back alleys of this historic capital of the conquistadors, preserved without modern buildings, signs, or pavement by government decree. It had been founded in 1527 and soon abandoned because of earthquakes and volcanic eruptions. In the afternoons, I would study in open-air coffee shops that looked out on ancient buildings capped by mountains in the distance. As I looked over the rooftops at steaming volcanoes rising to over 13,000 feet on the outskirts of town, I felt as if I were in a lost world from a past century.

After a full month in Guatemala studying Spanish seven hours a day in private

classes, I came away with basic communication skills and set two goals for myself for the following year: to write my diary only in Spanish and to read only Spanish books and magazines when possible.

The first novel I chose was *Aeropuerto,* the Spanish translation of Alex Haley's bestseller, *Airport.* I labored for eleven months with dictionary in hand until I finished it. In the process, I learned a lot of aviation vocabulary. Concurrently, I read everything I could get my hands on that was published in Spanish and more within my reading level. The library of Spanish literature that I began collecting will take me a lifetime to read.

In Yosemite, Galen met a bold young climber from Venezuela named Kike Arnal, whom we hired to help us in our photography business. He made a private deal to converse with me only in Spanish, if I would correct his English when he was speaking with others. As plans for my flight to South America began to shape up, I talked a lot with him and confided many of my deepest worries, such as having my engine fail over the jungle or the sea. Just a few months before I was to leave, we were sitting in my car in the parking lot of a 7-Eleven near my office drinking a Big Gulp when I admitted that I feared that I might never return home. "People are saying I'm nuts to do this trip. I'm so scared."

The bold adventurer turned to me, looked me in the eye, and said, "This is for you. It's important, and you've got to do it! Don't let anyone stop you."

He paused and added, "It's true. You are taking a big risk. You might die."

I photographed a festival at Puerto Ayora in the Galápagos Islands (above) and boat life beneath a tropical sunset (right).

RETURN TO COSTA RICA

XI

As I listened to Doug speak to Cenamer Radio on 126.9, I felt deeply touched that he had asked me to join him on this adventure. I might have done this flight on my own someday, but it would have been a long time in the future. And I never would have done the instrument flight this morning without Doug paving the way. Instead, I would have waited for hours or days for better weather. The best part was how well I did on my own after Doug gave me the nudge. That gave me a great deal of satisfaction and took away much of the anger I had been feeling about being railroaded by the men on this trip.

Flying over Latin countries I had previously visited on the ground was so engaging that my conflicted emotions all but vanished as we flew southeast over Guatemala toward a corner of El Salvador that had been in a civil war over land ownership since 1980. I knew that tens of thousands had been killed by death squads and terrorist groups, but from the air, none of their strife was evident. Only volcanoes stood out from the checkerboard expanse of farms, emphasizing the fact that nothing in this world, not even a mountain, is immutable. Here in Central America, both the physical and human landscapes are subject to far more sudden changes than in the seemingly more stable world I had left behind in California.

As we continued on across Central America, we were required to make position reports at instrument intersections, which are like invisible highway interchanges, even though we had canceled our instrument flight plan. I spoke to a series of controllers, each one passing me along to the next. The process was just like flying cross-country in the United States. On this morning, each of the controllers spoke relatively clear English until I was transferred to a flight controller in Nicaragua, whose English was marginal. I tried speaking to him in Spanish, but he seemed to take it as an insult, which was absolutely not my intention. I wondered if his reaction was because he was required to know English and use it for international flight

I had seen and photographed the rainforests
of Costa Rica on other visits (left).

communication. I suspected that he was just too macho to speak to an American female pilot in Spanish, so I gave up.

As we flew the coastline of Nicaragua, the sight of white beaches set against green volcanoes draped in forest looked like a scene out of a storybook. Lago de Nicaragua, Central America's largest lake with over three hundred islands and the planet's only freshwater sharks, glistened in the background. After we had been in the air for 3 hours, I asked Galen to pass me the pee-bottle. Just as I unbuckled my seat belt, the Nicaraguan controller called me.

"November Seven Three Five Lima Yankee, Sandino Approach, over."

"Sandino Approach, this is Five Lima Yankee. Go ahead."

"Say destination Lima Yankee."

"El Coco, Costa Rica, sir."

"Five Lima Yankee stand by," the controller said before disappearing off the air for several minutes.

"I wonder what that was about?" I queried my passengers. This controller would have been informed of our flight plan and our destination, I was sure. Soon, Sandino Approach called back. "Five Lima Yankee, El Coco Airport at San José closed. Please say intentions."

Now I began to wonder if we were going to be coerced to land in Managua. I called Doug and asked, "What do we do now?"

Doug ignored me and proceeded to ask the Nicaraguan controller *why* the major airport in Costa Rica was closed. No sooner had the question slipped out of his mouth than I cursed myself for not having asked it on my own. What was my problem?

The controller called back with the answer: the airport was closing for repairs. As we flew over the Pacific Ocean, just off the coastline of Nicaragua, I worried that the controller might not be telling us the truth. Perhaps it was a veiled attempt to get us to land in his country and pay expensive landing fees. We had not requested the required advance permission to enter Nicaragua because it was politically unstable. In order to overfly both El Salvador and Nicaragua, I had Flint tip tanks installed, thereby increasing Five Lima Yankee's flying range by 2 hours. Depending on the winds aloft, I could go an additional 300 miles.

"Doug, what are our options?" I inquired over the second radio. We had already been in the air 4 hours and had enough fuel to make it to San José, Costa Rica, but not very far beyond that. Because landing anywhere other than at an official airport of entry is prohibited, our choices were extremely limited.

"There is a smaller airport in San José. Let me see whether it's an airport of entry and get back to you," Doug said.

In less than a minute he called with the name of the alternate airport, so I called the controller. "Sandino Approach, change our destination to Tobias Bolano International, sir."

"Roger, Five Lima Yankee," the controller replied. His weak and barely readable radio transmission gave me the impression that he was talking from inside a tuna can. As I looked over at the shoreline of Nicaragua, I imagined the controller was calling from the side of a volcano, playing a game of cards in between radio transmissions with foreign pilots. I wondered what he thought when he heard a female on the radio. After the comments the ground attendant in Belize had made to me, I could imagine the conversation between Señor Controller and his buddy at the airport: "Hey José, there is a señorita on the radio."

"Let's make her land and check her out."

My internal musings weren't a slam against Latin controllers. I love Latin people and their unabashed passion for life. My concerns centered around the inappropriate questions that men have asked me since I first started flying. One of my favorites came from a submarine captain in the United States Navy stationed in Honolulu. I was seated next to him and his wife on a commercial flight to Hawaii. His wife and I chatted openly while he read a book and ignored us. After she said her husband flew small planes, I mentioned that I had a turbocharged Cessna 206. He sprang to life, looked up, and asked, "What are you doing flying such a *serious* airplane?"

I gave him a straight answer about the need for power to fly in the mountains. After we parted, I reflected on his demeaning question. For the life of me, I could not imagine a man asking another man that question. I regretted not quickly replying, "What are you doing captaining such a *serious* submarine?"

Once I'd flown through the Southwest while Galen was on the East Coast working with *National Geographic*. When we talked on the phone one evening, he told me what happened when he mentioned to another photographer-adventurer we both knew that I was flying my plane around the Southwest. The other photographer replied, "That's great!" with perfect prep-school eye contact before they went out to have a few beers. After hearing every detail about the friend's forthcoming adventure, Galen said that he'd just talked to me in Santa Fe, New Mexico, and that I was worried about thunderstorms en route to Dallas, Texas.

"Don't you think Barbara should leave her worries to the pilots?" his friend asked.

"She *is* the pilot," Galen replied, realizing how often people don't take in information contrary to their narrow world views.

On another trip where I flew into remote dirt landing strips with a girlfriend who was also close to forty, I was asked if my father was paying my flight expenses. Later on, a man flying a less-powerful plane, who seemed shocked to have two women show up in a Turbo 206, had the audacity to question my sexual preference.

On a busy flight into Dallas, one controller ignored my call sign on initial contact and drawled, "Will the pilot with the *female* voice please stand by."

The red flags were up for me as I contemplated calling back the Nicaraguan controller, who had just told me that the main airport in San José, Costa Rica, was closed, to ask for a current weather report for that area. Earlier in the day, the forecast for Costa Rica had been good, but after 6 hours in the air, I did not want to fly on without a weather update. Off in the distance, I could see that clouds were thickening and the weather appeared to be quickly changing for the worse.

When I first requested weather information in slowly spoken English, he did not understand my question. Hoping he wouldn't take offense, I repeated it in clear Spanish. After a long pause, he answered back with a weather report in butchered English that I could not understand.

Doug came up with the brilliant idea of trying to call a commercial U.S. airliner flying overhead. Monitoring the center frequency, we soon heard United 888 check in. As soon as the transmission between the jet and the controller was complete, Doug called and said, "United Eight Eight Eight, this is November Niner One One Delta Juliett, over."

"November One Delta Juliett, United Eight Eight Eight, go ahead," replied a voice that sounded like John Wayne in the classic flight movie, *The High and the Mighty.*

Doug asked the airline pilot for a weather briefing and was politely told to stand by. After a few minutes, we received a complete report of scattered thunderstorms and rain showers.

We had canceled our instrument flight plan beneath clear skies somewhere over Guatemala. To switch back to instrument flight now would not be safe, flying through clouds in mountainous terrain with thunderstorms moving through, especially without weather radar on board to show us where the storm cells were.

Within the hour, we crossed the Costa Rican border and flew over Bahía Santa Elena, where Sandino Approach handed us off to Coco Control. Costa Rican controllers use sophisticated radio communications and radar facilities, and I was quite relieved to be speaking to a controller whose English was as good as any controller back home. But we were too low to show up on his radar screen because we had descended under the overcast to 1,000 feet. He advised us to remain clear of a military base located near the border, but we had already pierced the outer edge of it.

As we continued toward San José, the metropolitan capital of Costa Rica set smack in the middle of the tiny tropical country, we stayed low over farmlands and began skirting rain showers. At the first sight of a rainbow, I circled so that Galen could take a photograph and lost sight of Doug. With the weather deteriorating, I called Doug and asked what the conditions ahead were like.

"It's hard to tell. I'm being sucked up into a thunderhead," he replied.

"Seriously Doug, what does it look like ahead?"

"I am serious. We're in a cloud at twenty thousand feet and still climbing."

"Ha ha ha." I didn't need a neon sign to get the message. I had asked one too many questions.

Ever since we canceled our instrument flight plan, I'd been following Doug visually while Robert traced our position on the map. Robert's affinity for navigation had kept him occupied during the long flights and kept me abreast of our exact location. He frequently showed me where he thought we were on the map so that I could cross-check his accuracy. Next, I asked Robert to hand me the map so that I could get a very clear picture of the area in my mind before the flying got rougher and I wouldn't be able to look.

I was very familiar with how the terrain around San José looked from the ground. Just a year earlier, I had spent three weeks attending Spanish school there, so I was well aware that the city sits at 3,000 feet and is surrounded by high peaks and volcanoes. My look at the map determined that the terrain rose quickly in altitude between my present position and the airport. Visually, however, the land disappeared from sight as it climbed into black-and-white clouds hanging low in the sky. I felt like I was flying around the perimeter of a punch bowl rimmed with whip cream, looking for a safe way into the center without hitting the glass or getting stuck in the cream. According to the map, a river drained toward the Pacific Ocean through a crack in the punch bowl. Hopefully, the crack would be clear of clouds.

The map showed several rivers running in roughly the same direction on our route of flight. From the air I would not be able to tell one river from the other, except that the river I was looking for paralleled a main road. Just as I worked out my own plan, Doug called. "Barbara, when you get to a major river, follow it to the left. It's a tight squeeze, but it's workable."

"Thanks, Doug," I said, relieved to know he had found a way through the pass.

As I approached the river, the clouds had forced me down to 200 feet above the ground. "I may not be able to make this," I said to Robert and Galen, who unfastened his seat belt, leaned forward to look at the map, and proclaimed, "You're fine."

"Easy for you to say," I snapped.

I felt on edge, skimming just beneath the clouds. I did not like flying in low visibility and avoiding rain showers while being squeezed by hidden land where nothing was familiar, from names on the map to the river gorge below. It felt downright scary, and as I considered turning around, I wondered what would it take to scare Galen. Just then, a broad valley opened up in front of us, and I recognized San José spread out on the other side.

"See, I told you everything would be okay," Galen said.

"What a gorgeous sight!" I exclaimed, as the land dropped away beneath me, giving me room to breathe.

As we cleared the ridge, Coco Control picked us up on radar and vectored us toward the alternate airport, which was too small for commercial jets. Even with the controller's help, it was still difficult to pick out the 3,281-foot landing strip from the congested city. On my downwind leg for Runway 09, I contacted the tower and was cleared to land on the 60-foot-wide strip.

I was glad to be safely on the ground. After clearing customs and immigration quickly, we headed into town by cab to spend the night in a hotel near the main plaza, where street vendors were selling everything from hammocks to condoms.

Doug announced that we again needed to be up very early. Five out of six days of boot camp were beginning to wear me down. Flying all day long, day-in and day-out, was increasingly stressful. Without knowing it, I found myself in a race to get Doug and Galen to Chile so they could maximize their climbing and kayaking adventures. The feeling was all too familiar.

But Doug and Galen weren't the only ones abetting the race. Peter had left his wife, Mimi, at home with their three-month-old daughter and two toddlers. Mimi was not particularly pleased to have her husband flying to South America in a single-engine airplane with Doug. I shared her worry. Galen and I didn't have little children at home, but I could imagine how she must be feeling. I understood Peter's urgency to get home soon on the first available commercial flight from Santiago.

After we returned to our hotel, I tried to reach my Spanish teacher, Roberto, at Instituto Forester in Los Yoses. I was fond of Roberto and excited about letting him know that I had flown my own plane here. Doug teased me about feeling attached to my teacher, but admitted to having felt the same way about one of his instructors after he started studying Italian, a language about which he was equally passionate.

Perhaps it was childish to believe that Roberto would care that a student of his had returned to his country. But I had a special reason to care. Coming to Costa Rica to study Spanish had been an important benchmark: it was the first time in eight years of marriage that I had been the one traveling and Galen had actually stayed at home instead of being off somewhere on his own.

My horizons had gradually expanded from spending weeks in Spanish schools to exploring the whole of Latin America by air and ground. Now, as I lay awake early in the morning of our sixth day of flying with my stomach already upset, I thought about just what I had gotten myself into.

Santa Ana Volcano, El Salvador (above).

Into Troubled Lands

XII

*T*he weather forecast on our route to Medellín, Colombia, looked good, though cumulus clouds had already begun to form overhead. As I preflighted my plane, I felt well enough to continue on with Doug's plan to reach South American soil later in the day.

After takeoff we headed east toward the Caribbean Sea and were barely on our way when Doug advised me that he wanted to make a brief detour and fly very low over the Poch Hotel, where some friends of his were staying. He had a package he wanted to drop off.

Doug made several low passes over the hotel to get the attention of his friends while I patiently circled over the nearby town. Unauthorized airdrops are illegal in most countries, and this one certainly didn't seem to be worth risking our trip. When Doug had accomplished his task, we continued on course over banana plantations until we reached the shoreline and began flying side by side, dodging the increasing clouds.

Flying just offshore near the Panamanian border, Doug called and said, "Hey Barb! Listen up here. Since we didn't fill up the tip tanks, we can't make Medellín. I'm going to file an instrument flight plan to Panama City." The weather was rapidly deteriorating and clouds were building all around us.

Just as he finished speaking, his plane disappeared behind a cloud off my left wing tip. As I watched his plane appear again, I told him that I was worried about our proximity to each other. He replied, "I'll climb up two thousand to six thousand and you stay here at four."

I slowed several knots to put some distance between us and got my own instrument clearance immediately after listening to Doug receive his. Within minutes, the world outside the aircraft abruptly turned white and we went "solid." It happened so quickly that I had no time for concern. I felt as if a warm, white cocoon had enveloped us. Moments later, rain began to pound so hard that it sounded as if it was denting the fuselage.

Wild coast of Colombia (left).

"Barbara, didn't we need an airplane wash?" Doug teased.

"Very funny," I squeaked, as we bounced around blindly in the turbulence like a toy in the hands of a child.

Doug told me that shooting the ILS approach into Panama City would be a piece of cake. Soon after I began my descent toward the airport, I broke completely out of the clouds at 1,500 feet above the ground. A cluster of skyscrapers appeared from the gray murk on the horizon. I strained to see the Panama Canal, and was disappointed not to be able to view it from our flight path. On the plus side, I was greatly relieved to see the broad, 10,006-foot runway. With a sense of relief, I called Tocumen Tower and reported, "Five Lima Yankee has the airport in sight."

My plane felt like a bug on a highway as it touched down on the humungous runway. As I taxied off the empty runway and parked in front of the main terminal, something seemed very spooky. The rain had passed only moments before, and the tarmac was still wet with wide puddles of water, but there was not another airplane in sight. We had the entire international airport to ourselves.

As I was unbuckling my seat belt, a well-clad young man dressed in tan trousers and a colorfully striped shirt appeared beside my plane and said in perfect English, "Welcome to Panama."

"Where is everybody?" I asked.

"We are in the middle of a coup. No commercial flights are landing. Workers are demonstrating in the streets and a state of emergency has been declared," he answered in a melodic Panamanian lilt.

"We only want to stop for fuel. Will that be a problem?" I asked.

"No problem," he said. "I am here to help you, so please follow me inside."

Doug had told me about landing in Peru during a coup on a previous trip. I remembered him saying how he feared getting stuck for days or having his plane confiscated, so he simply took off without permission before anyone could stop him. Now, Doug didn't appear at all concerned as he walked with a slight shuffle alongside the towering young man who led us inside to the flight operations office. If Doug wasn't concerned, then I wasn't going to be, either.

Whether we were staying or leaving, we would still need to process a mountain of paperwork. But our young guide seemed to want to have it over with as quickly as we did. Perhaps he had been told to get us out of Panama immediately to avoid a potential international incident during the coup. Whatever his reasons, he took us under his wing, politely directing us to take seats before leaving to handle our paperwork personally.

Fifteen minutes later, he returned to say he had bad news. According to his records, I had landed in Panama without advance permission. The coup, he said, was not a problem, but being here without proper paperwork was. His friendly nature turned somber.

"I am certain that I requested permission to land in Panama several weeks ago," I insisted.

Quickly rummaging through my Cordura briefcase to find a copy of the telex I had sent to Panama several weeks earlier, I contemplated the ramifications if I could not prove that I had followed proper procedure. I could be in real trouble.

Luckily, I found my copy of the form and handed it over to him. He read it, and then left the room. Doug wandered off in search of a weather briefing. Galen and Robert followed behind to find a men's room, leaving me to wait in the empty office. Peter, meanwhile, stayed outside to guard both airplanes as they were being fueled.

The young man returned and said that he had located the telex that I had sent, but unfortunately it failed to include the most important piece of information: my aircraft registration number. In every other way my request for permission to land was in order: my name, number of passengers, type aircraft, and purpose of flight. When I checked his copy against mine, I realized he was right. N735LY was nowhere to be found. Both copies were missing my N number. How could I have done that? My knees went weak, and my face went hot. I had been so careful about each and every detail when I drafted the dozen or so telexes requesting permission to land or overfly and sent them to every country on my route of flight before leaving the United States. Had I done this to all of the permission requests? I was mortified.

I checked the remainder of my telexes requesting permission in other countries and was relieved to see that they all had my aircraft registration number on them. Only the one for Panama was missing my tail number. Though my mistake was unintentional, I was in an awkward situation. The authorities could take advantage of me if they wanted to. I didn't know what kind of power they had, but I suspected it ranged from charging me a gigantic fine to confiscating my airplane. To drive the point home that the error was innocent, I showed him the other forms.

"Is everything okay now?" I asked.

"Not to worry," the young man assured me. Troops from the United States had just been airlifted in. That gave me reason to hope the Panamanians would want to help me get me out of their troubled country as soon as possible while courting assistance from my country. I was still naive about the depth of conflicted emotions that Latin Americans feel about U.S. interference in their destinies.

I later pieced together more of what was actually happening in Panama on the day I landed, December 6, 1990. There hadn't really been a coup. President Guillermo Endara was using U.S. intervention to ensure that he would stay in power. He had come to power earlier in the year after the United States seized the previous dictator, General Mañuel Noriega. Regardless of the problems of the Noriega regime, the majority of Panamanians hated the United States for messing with their country's politics. After Endara became president, he felt the need to distance himself from the taint of the United States propping up his government, especially as it fell into economic and political shambles. But today's socialist street demonstrations and demand for a national work stoppage were such a threat to his continued rule that he risked calling in U.S. military support, using the ruse that a coup led by a recently escaped political prisoner was in progress.

My friends back home heard news stories about how our brave troops were protecting the Panama Canal, but the reasons behind our involvement in Panamanian politics were far more sinister. Noriega had been a CIA operative who was secretly promised by our government that all his heavy drug trafficking would be ignored if he supported the Contras in Nicaragua, who, in turn, were funded by even more secret U.S. arms sales to Iran. The direct connection between our political troubles in the Arab and Latin worlds was shocking. Only after Noriega stopped obeying the whims of our government did we seize him on drug trafficking and tax evasion charges. The word on the street in Panama was that the United States cared less about fighting the war against drugs than about fighting socialism in Nicaragua, which was bad for United States' big business there. Here in Panama, Endara remained in power after making a judgment call that bringing in U.S. troops to intervene would be less of a setback to his regime than letting the will of the people take over on the streets.

The young man who had been escorting us confirmed that we would not be required to clear customs or immigration, since we had only planned to land in Panama in transit for fuel. But what could have been an in-and-out situation took over three hours of red tape, plus $150 for landing fees and ground handling per plane, before we were finally free to leave.

After the long delay with the paperwork and a decision not to eat earlier when my stomach was upset, I felt tired and famished. I was granted permission to enter the main terminal to get a bite to eat before departure. When we went to get Peter, he said that he had been requested to pay $40 for a "narcotics inspection." The young man assigned to us said that Peter had been tricked, but unless he knew the name of who had done this, there was nothing he could do about it. Peter said that the man wore a uniform, seemed to be some sort of official, had dark hair, and was short and overweight, but he did not get his name or a receipt.

As we made our way toward the snack bar via the baggage department, Peter spotted the phony narcotics inspector, and we all chased after him. Peter publicly demanded his money back. At first, the guy pretended he didn't know what Peter was talking about, but after being pressed, claimed that Peter had given him money as a gift.

"That's ridiculous! Why would I give *you,* a perfect stranger, a gift?"

Peter's line of logic made sense to everyone. After the official who had illegally taken the money could not come up with a good answer to Peter's question, he returned the cash without further argument, but not without giving Peter a disgusted look. I was glad we weren't overnighting in Panama.

From the quiet hallways of the back offices where we had spent the last three hours, we entered a passenger terminal bustling with people waiting to get the first flight out of Panama. I found a fast-food vendor with sandwiches. Doug declined to eat, so the rest of us quickly gobbled our food and returned to our planes. It was already two in the afternoon and isolated thundershowers were now reported along our route of flight to Medellín.

Doug pressed us to move on. He had arranged for us to stay at the palatial estate of a friend who owned, among other businesses, the Colombian franchise for Esprit. Though I felt uneasy about spending the night in Medellín, based on what little I'd read in the news at home, Doug didn't seem the least bit concerned. He said his friend's home would be well guarded.

Medellín was the center of the Colombian drug cartel controlled by Pablo Escobar, the most powerful and violent drug lord in the world, who had been in a full-out war against his government for many years. Now the war had escalated to involve private citizens. Kidnappings and murders were daily occurrences. No one was spared, especially the wealthy, famous, or powerful. Journalists and judges alike were the cartel's targets. In retaliation, coworkers, friends, and relatives of Pablo's were butchered. But after Pablo ordered an Avianca airliner that included two American passengers on board blown out of the sky, he was declared a threat to the national security of the United States. The CIA and the U.S. Army joined in the manhunt. No one in Colombia was safe, especially if his or her disappearance could be used to send a message. Arriving with Doug, a multimillionaire, didn't seem like the wisest thing to do. I wasn't looking forward to spending even five minutes in Medellín.

We left Panama City on a visual flight plan, maintaining just 1,000 feet above the ocean along the marshy coastline. As the swamplands gradually rose into vertical cliffs covered with lush tropical rainforest, Galen's interest was aroused. He began composing photographs of the forest hanging just above the crashing surf, blanketing cliffs where black rock occasionally poked through. He offered to use the photographic port on my left side so that I wouldn't have to make a circle to put the terrain next to his window and lose sight of Doug.

By the time we crossed the border into Colombia, the clouds had forced us down to 500 feet over the water, and we lost radio communications with Panama. We were also too low to initiate communications with Colombian officials as we entered their country, a strict prerequisite for crossing their border. As we flew farther into Colombian airspace without any radio notification, I became concerned. A section in the Colombian flight rules states: "Patrol planes are prepared to destroy, in the air or on the ground, planes that try to evade controls." While we weren't evading controls, we weren't yet under anyone's control either.

I called Doug and queried him a second time about having crossed the border without verbal permission, casually mentioning that authorities could shoot on sight. He countered, "How is anyone going to see us? I can barely see you." I could vaguely make out his silhouette less than a mile ahead through increasingly heavy rain. Though I wondered how anyone could possibly identify us from shore as foreign airplanes, his answer was only slightly reassuring.

Speaking to flight officials soon became the least of my concerns. As we moved farther into Colombia, the clouds dropped lower, pushing us down to 300 feet above the ocean in rain showers. The weather was unlike anything I had ever flown in before. We were now doing what I had always considered to be unthinkable—scud-running in a storm just above the water. Without landforms directly in front of me, what was left was a visual horizon of water vaporizing into the sky. We were on the verge of flying into a whiteout.

I did not like being so close to the ocean, nor did I like seeing towering cumulus encircling above us through occasional holes in the lower clouds. Just as I was about to call Doug and question whether we should turn around, he called me. "If things get worse, our escape plan is to turn right and climb up into the clouds over the ocean. Once we reach a safe altitude, we'll be high enough to call for an instrument flight plan."

Escape plan? Whoa! Even Doug was feeling like we might get trapped. I was glad he had a plan, because I certainly didn't. I thought his idea sounded reasonable given our circumstances. Hopefully, it would keep us from smashing into terrain hidden by clouds, but it would not help us to stay out of embedded thunderstorms.

My sweaty hands were making the control yoke slippery, and I nervously wiped them on my shirt as I leaned forward to try to see the shoreline through the heavy rain. We were flying less than a mile offshore, surrounded in every direction by a gray nothingness that made it almost impossible to see land. I asked Robert to keep his eyes glued to Doug's plane, a tiny speck on the horizon in front of us, while I also followed its every move. To lose sight of Doug in these conditions was not an option.

After Doug's brusque answers to the questions I asked earlier as the weather was turning bad in Costa Rica, I did not want to bug him anymore and have him think poorly of me. If it had been up to me, I would still be sitting in Costa Rica, waiting for better weather. Right now, that seemed like a pretty nice place to be. I was beginning to regret this day's flight.

Following Doug was well within my current capabilities, but with our deteriorating situation and the looming possibility of needing to fly on instruments in truly bad weather, I could be pushed past my level of experience. What would I do then?

Galen sat quietly in the back, while Robert studied the map and kept abreast of our position. I talked to each of them in a nervous chatter to keep myself occupied. When I asked Galen to take a picture of the bad weather. He asked, "Why? It's all gray. There's nothing to photograph."

"I just want it for the record," I replied.

Doug straightened out the curvy shore as much as he could until we rounded a corner into a horseshoe-shaped bay. I spotted a dark mass on the water and flew over it before I figured out what it was. Beneath me, not much above treetop level, was a dark gray gun barrel aiming up from the deck of a military gunship. Surely we had been seen.

"I think the Colombians know where we are now," I said matter-of-factly over the radio to Doug, pretending to be calm. He didn't say a word. As he continued to lead the way along the rugged, virtually uninhabited coastline, I wondered how this day would end.

When the solid overcast opened up and turned to widely scattered cumulus, Doug immediately climbed to 8,000 feet and skirted the edges of more billowing white clouds that reached toward the heavens. I stayed directly behind him. Seeing Doug's tiny plane profiled against these towering giants made me feel insignificant.

Once we reached altitude, Doug finally made radio contact with a Colombian controller who gave him a weather report that included thunderstorms in all quadrants around Medellín.

"Even on instruments, Medellín is not an airport to fly into safely with a weather report like that," Doug warned. "It is surrounded by mountains. I think we should reroute to Cali."

Galen got out our guidebook to South America and read aloud: "Warning: Cali has recently become a center of both guerrilla and counter-insurgency activity, and drug and anti-drug operations. It is best not to arrive after dark." Galen said he didn't want to spend even one night in Colombia, since he was carrying thousands of dollars in camera gear. He argued to go on to Quito, two hours farther south. Soon it would be dark, and I knew that Galen didn't understand what he was suggesting: to continue on in unknown mountainous terrain embedded with thunderstorms after dark would be very risky. So far, we had narrowly escaped trouble. I was exhausted and not up to the idea of flying on. As it was, we would barely make Cali by sunset.

I touched down just as the setting sun painted the smog a milky red. I taxied to the west side of the terminal past broken-down airplanes and soot-covered buildings to where two armed soldiers greeted us. They gave only a cursory glance into both planes as Galen and Robert packed their personal gear for the night. Galen couldn't decide whether to leave some camera gear in the plane or carry all of it into

*I followed Doug over billowing clouds after we diverted
from landing at Medellín, Colombia (above).*

town. He asked me what he should do. "I don't know," I replied. Thinking about Galen's camera gear only frustrated me. I had an entire airplane to worry about.

In order to assess the situation, I struck up a conversation with one of the two young men. He assured me our planes would be safe and promised to watch them all night. I tipped him and left feeling a little more at ease.

Inside the main terminal, we simply flashed our passports and left. We hopped a cab into town without calling ahead to find a hotel. Once on the road, I took advantage of the opportunity to interrogate our driver in Spanish about his life, his family, and his green felt hat. He said it was typical of his village and that every village had a unique hat style.

On the way into town, a military roadblock stopped us. Armed soldiers forced us to get out of the car and searched our belongings. They asked me if I had a camouflage jacket. I thought it a strange question, but answered truthfully, "No." They immediately passed us through.

The first hotel we stopped at was smack in the middle of downtown. From the backseat of our cab, I perused boarded-up buildings plastered with ripped protest posters. I didn't want to get out of the taxi. Not even the militia standing on the corner with their automatic weapons comforted me. When Doug tried to pay the cab driver, he refused to take the money, insisting we pay him in pesos. He said that it would be impossible for him to convert U.S. dollars. At first, none of us believed him until the hotel refused to exchange our money, too. The banks were closed for the night, so we asked the hotel clerk if he would simply pay the cab for us and add it to our hotel bill. Nothing doing. Exhausted, everyone pleaded more aggressively with the clerk. Thirty minutes into a heated debate, he finally consented to change enough money to pay the cabbie and no more. We were experiencing a backlash from the cocaine cartels. I wanted out of Colombia.

Everyone else dashed to their rooms to get ready for dinner before the restaurants closed. I was too tired and nervous to enjoy a night out on the town, so I stayed back and took a leisurely hot shower, skipped dinner, and snacked on a chocolate bar that I'd stashed away for just such an occasion. As I lay down on the lumpy bed, I felt homesick. I closed my eyes and tried to imagine being in my own bed. A few minutes later, I decided I wanted to get up and dry my naturally curly hair so that I wouldn't look like Shirley Temple in the morning, but fatigue pinned me to the bed, and I dropped off to sleep.

Near midnight I woke up and discovered that Galen wasn't in the room. Had something happened? It was not like Galen to stay out so late, especially when we were getting up at the crack of dawn. I tried to go back to sleep but tossed and turned as I recalled a story that an American mountain climber had told me about having

been in South America with a climbing partner who left the hotel to buy a beer and simply never returned. No one ever found out what happened to him.

When Galen walked through the door, I blurted out, "I've been worried sick about you. Where have you been?"

He explained that Doug had taken them to a superb restaurant with very slow service. Even after Galen was safely back in my arms, I continued to lie awake for hours wondering whether I should have come on this trip. I hated spending so much time every morning pushing paper. We were losing the most valuable flying hours of the day filling out ridiculous forms. Being forced to fly later in the day, when tropical weather builds, was not safe. The only thing good to say about these morning rituals was that my desire to finish clearing customs, immigration, international police, narcotics control, health control, and the civil aviation department tended to erase my worries about the dangers of flying.

Cali proved especially difficult to leave. Without prior permission to land the evening before, it took us four hours to get the proper clearances to depart. Some of that time was spent typing out the serial numbers of every dollar bill used to pay our various expenses. Doug attempted to reach the family we were supposed to stay with in Medellín one last time. He even called his friend's sons without success. Only later did we learn that the entire family had gone into hiding because the father had been kidnapped by the drug cartel on the day we were to arrive.

At the Cali airport in Colombia, I greeted armed soldiers with
a smile (left); downtown streets were heavily guarded (above).

It was almost noon before we were in the air on a short 2-hour-and-20-minute leg to Quito, one of the highest major airports in the world at 9,223 feet. Our route of flight took us much higher, over exquisite hanging valleys and mountain lakes mixed with green fields nestled beneath the crest of the Andes. Soon after we crossed into Ecuador, I recognized Otavalo, the village with a famous market that I had visited twice from the ground. I couldn't quite believe it as we flew over places where I had been on earlier adventures.

The landing at Mariscal Sucre International Airport held my attention. The runway is nestled between a high volcano to the west, skyscrapers to the south, and a ring of lower volcanoes encircling the valley. As I taxied off Runway 35, I was startled to see my propeller blades stop as my engine quit in the thin air. When Doug landed behind me, he called the tower to say his engine had also quit. Both our engines instantly restarted after we adjusted the fuel mixture.

The flight base operator in Quito saluted and called me "Capitán." He made up for all our earlier hassles. He arranged for fuel and an oil change, and asked if there was anything more he could do for me. While I spoke to him about having my CD player repaired, Doug walked over to my plane and pushed on the tail. Then he walked back to his plane and did the same. My tail went to the ground much easier than Doug's did. I watched out of the corner of my eye as he asked Galen to do the same, saying, "See this? Your plane isn't loaded well. You have too much weight toward the tail."

Galen agreed and immediately began repacking the plane.

Their exchange seemed simple but represented something much more complex. Though Galen had already moved many things forward in California and switched with Robert to sit in the remaining cubbyhole on one side of the back seat, he had never repacked the back of the plane to move its center of gravity forward as much as possible. Even after we'd transferred some gear into Doug's plane in Mexico, we still had too much weight stashed too far back toward the tail of my plane. I had tried to move Galen's things myself, but he had stopped me and said, "Just leave it alone." We'd argued over this so many times that I had finally given up.

Now, I'd watched Doug say the same thing to him just once, and he immediately did it. I was happy with the result, but galled that Galen hadn't done it for me. I mused over how to get him to respond to me with the same respect he was showing Doug. I didn't have an answer, but I needed one for reasons of safety as well as for myself.

Highlands of Ecuador (right).

LOST HORIZON

XIII

The ninth morning of our journey dawned severe clear over Quito. We paid the flight base operator a flat fee that included coordinating all our necessary paperwork—a first-class service not available in other Latin countries so far. Within an hour, we were cleared to leave the country, and I received permission to taxi onto the runway behind Doug. I climbed out just high enough over the terrain to avoid using oxygen en route to Peru, where I wasn't sure I could renew my supply because the country was under siege by terrorists.

"Doug. Where are you?" I called when I realized that I had lost sight of him.

"I'm up here," he said in his normal droll manner.

"Up where?"

"Up here at 18,000 feet. I want to take a look at this volcano."

There were several volcanoes to choose from. Doug was referring to a giant snow cone called Cotopaxi. Its glaciers gleamed in the early morning sun.

"Why don't you come on up?" he added nonchalantly.

I put on my oxygen mask as I pulled the nose skyward and climbed to over 20,000 feet for a look into its crater. We played ring-around-a-rosy to get a photo of Doug's plane in front of the volcano. Below us, four brightly dressed climbers roped together were descending a great snowfield, looking like Mexican "worry dolls" sewn onto white cloth. The plane felt mushy, as if the wispy, thin air would no longer support our weight and we would drop out of the sky.

As we crossed the Peruvian border, my attitude indicator began to slowly droop to one side until it tumbled completely to that side. "Oh shit! This can't be real," I exclaimed.

"What's going on?" Galen asked.

"I've lost my attitude indicator," I said, pointing to the black-and-blue gauge directly in front of me, which loosely resembled sky above a horizon. It now sat

Llamas in the Peruvian highlands (left)

nearly upside down, falsely indicating I was making Top Gun maneuvers. "It's a vacuum-pump failure," I continued, pointing at another gauge on the far right of the cockpit in front of Robert, which read zero.

If there was anything good about this bad news, it was that my vacuum-pump failed while I was still VFR. If it had occurred after I was in the clouds, I might have trusted the broken attitude indicator and been led to do something very wrong. I continued to scan the rest of my instruments, looking for other failures. The sole purpose of a vacuum pump is to generate the necessary suction to operate certain instruments, but everything else seemed okay.

Though I remembered from my flight training that my DG (directional gyro) should be malfunctioning, too, it looked perfectly fine; we were heading south and the gauge showed a heading of south. I continued on with a gnawing feeling that something else was wrong. Then it occurred to me that without suction the directional gyro might be stuck on its heading, so I turned off course. The gauge continued to read south. Bingo! Both my artificial horizon and directional gyro had failed.

I had been trained to deal with this sort of an emergency, but I never expected it to happen to me. Training to fly "partial panel" had been a theoretical exercise until now. I had read about possible incorrect reactions, but I was still surprised to see myself respond just like the textbooks predicted. At first, I couldn't stop myself from staring at the failed instruments. I told myself to ignore them, but I could not stop myself from staring at them until I remembered what I was supposed to do: place anything I could find over the problem gauges. That would keep me from becoming confused or distracted by their false readings, which, in IFR conditions, could lead me to believe the plane was turning or banking when it wasn't. I folded two sheets of notepaper and stuffed them over the gauges until Galen located duct tape to hold them in place.

Instruments for attitude and direction aren't necessary in clear weather, when a pilot can follow landmarks on the ground and keep the wings level by reference to

*I watched the shadow of my plane trace the crater rim of Cotopaxi
Volcano as I circled above the peak at over 20,000 feet (above).*

the horizon, but they are crucial for instrument flight. The clear skies we had in the mountains of Ecuador were giving way to a thin layer of clouds along the coast of Peru. Though I was flying above it for now, I was starting to feel uncomfortable. I called Doug and reported my vacuum-pump failure, but he didn't seem the least bit fazed. I decided not to talk further to him about it.

Our next stop would be Talara, the nearest airport of entry in Peru. I was required to land here before proceeding on to Lima. Soon I would have to make a descent into the clouds by flying a nonprecision VOR approach on partial panel. By the report from the tower, I would come out beneath the clouds with plenty of time to see the runway.

Under normal circumstances, flying an "actual" approach into the clouds would have been exciting by itself for a neophyte instrument pilot like myself. But with a vacuum-pump failure, I would be forced to fly the approach without using my primary instruments—comparable to going from swimming in a pool to swimming at night in a shark-infested ocean.

Once in the clouds, I would guide my plane by a much-less-precise secondary set of instruments. As long as I kept on the proper magnetic course and altitude designated by my flight charts, I was assured of not coming close to any hills or tall structures in the area. On partial panel, neither turning nor remaining level would be so easy. Our lives would depend on an electric turn coordinator, a simple gauge located just beneath my airspeed indicator, which has a white silhouette of an airplane that rocks to either side. The little white plane hovers above a ball, which slides side to side. I was trusting our lives to an aviation version of a pinball game. Changes in heading would have to be made by timing my turns and rolling out level before cross-checking my heading on the magnetic compass, an even more sloppy gauge. Not a great situation. It would be easy to fly myself inadvertently into a spin or graveyard spiral.

Well before beginning my descent to the airport, I studied my approach chart and briefed Robert about the flight. The initial segment would start over the ocean and head back toward shore. I wanted him to double-check the compass as I entered the clouds.

When it came time to let down into white clouds, I felt as if we were sinking into quicksand and a claustrophobic feeling washed over me. I focused my complete concentration on the task at hand. My eyes darted between the altimeter, VSI, VOR, airspeed indicator, and turn coordinator. Even with so many instruments still functioning, it felt surreal not to have my attitude indicator. In the back of my mind I kept thinking that I could complete a barrel roll and not know it. My past dependency on that gauge was becoming abundantly obvious, as was my lack of extensive training for such an emergency.

With luck on my side, I quickly broke out of the clouds and spotted the runway glistening in the desert heat. I shouted, "Hooray!" with a deep sense of relief.

"Great job!" Robert replied. Galen patted the back of my shoulder as he congratulated me, too.

A hot wind of dry desert air blew into my face as I crawled out of the airplane

and walked across the scorching pavement to what looked like an abandoned outpost. We found our way to the office of the airport *jefe* (boss), who voiced a complaint that was difficult to understand over his cheap radio blaring Spanish love songs. He told me that there was a big fiesta going on near town. Because of us, he was still at work and missing a great party. Since we had been so rude as to arrive during his lunch hour, he declined to process our paperwork right away. He threw back the $20 tip we had given him and scowled. "Hace bromas?" (Are you kidding?) We offered more and he complied.

After we had cleared immigration, I inquired about getting my vacuum pump repaired. There was no one who could work on my airplane. Not today, not tomorrow, and maybe never, since the remote desert outpost had no mechanic. "What are we going to do?" I asked Doug.

"We'll go on to Lima," he said matter-of-factly.

Trying to be a good soldier, I followed Doug out to our planes without another word about how concerned I felt about my failed vacuum pump. As I taxied to the runway, I felt confused. How could I stop us from going on? If I stayed, what good would that do? How would I find a mechanic who would come to my aid in this dinky airport in the middle of a desert in Northern Peru? I didn't know anybody in Peru. It could take a week or more to figure out how to get a licensed mechanic flown into Talara with the proper parts and tools. The officials on the ground hadn't been

At Tolara airport in Peru, I posed between Robert and Galen for a self-timer photograph (above); my flight maps for much of the Andes had large white areas marked "Relief Data Incomplete" (right).

all that helpful; I couldn't imagine them going to any effort to get my plane repaired quickly.

Reluctantly, I followed Doug onto the runway and shoved in full power as soon as I saw his wheels leave the tarmac. I carefully traced Doug's every move. As he climbed upward, so did I. As we neared the cloud bases, I anticipated that he would level out, so I pointed the nose over and began level flight. I watched as Doug continued his climb and disappeared into the clouds.

"Oh my God! What is he doing?" I blurted out loud. Then I got on the radio: "Doug, where are you going? I was hoping we would stay under the overcast since I'm on partial panel."

"Barbara, the cloud layer isn't very thick. You'll be in the clouds for less than a minute," he said, making it sound easy.

I thought that to climb up though the clouds voluntarily on partial panel would be foolish. But that's a polite understatement. It would be downright stupid, and against FAA flight regulations back home. But we weren't in the United States and I wasn't about to leave Doug's side. When I was flying with Doug, I felt safer, as if he could help me if I got into serious trouble. I wasn't about to argue and have him say, "Okay, I'll see you in Lima."

Against my better judgment, I climbed back up through the overcast until I reached blue skies overhead. Doug was right: climbing through the clouds was easy. When I popped out, I looked around for his plane and spotted him climbing even higher. As I climbed up to join him at 8,000 feet, I felt a deep dread that something was very, very wrong. Nonetheless, I obediently followed him down the hidden Peruvian coast, navigating to the next VOR.

After we'd been in the air for awhile, Doug called to ask, "How's it going, Barbara?"

"I'm okay," I answered solemnly. Privately, even though I was comfortably flying above the clouds, my thoughts about what lay ahead kept me from enjoying the flight. I was on edge. The sound in my voice must have given away my apprehension. After a long pause, Doug added, "I hardly look at my DG, Barbara." His implication was unmistakable: What's the big deal? Just get on with flying. At this point, I had no other choice.

My aircraft was one of about 150,000 private planes without a backup or a warning alert for a vacuum pump failure. What I did not know at the time was that more than 2,000 of these planes had had vacuum-pump failures, resulting in 36 crashes and 82 deaths since the 1970s. When the Aircraft Owners and Pilots Association performed flight simulator tests on pilots trained to fly on partial panel in clouds without their vacuum-operated instruments, half of them crashed attempting to land.

Nevertheless, Doug was correct that I could navigate just fine once we were above the clouds. For the time being, the distant Cordillera Blanca range of the Andes demarked my horizon. The sawtooth row of the world's highest tropical peaks, reaching well over 22,000 feet, would have intrigued me much more, were it not for the paper taped over the failed instruments staring me in the face.

As I neared Lima hours later, the clouds thickened instead of dissipating, as I had hoped. The bases dropped down to less than a 1,000 feet and tops rose to 4,500 feet. If I maintained the advised descent rate of 500 feet per minute on the approach, I would be inside a veil of white for 7 to 8 minutes—an eternity on partial panel.

Doug's casual insistence not to worry was easy for him to say with his extensive instrument experience. Before this trip, most of my training had been with an instructor beside me, under clear skies, using a hood to block my outside view. The difference of knowing that I could rip the blinders off and see outside in the event of an emergency was roughly comparable to a sighted person wearing a blindfold instead of being clinically blind. An equally important factor was having a second, more experienced pilot beside me. Flying single-pilot IFR, even without a partial instrument failure, is so challenging that many bush pilots who fly my type aircraft for a living refuse to do it with passengers aboard.

The reality of my situation hit home when I overheard Center order Doug to descend and maintain 4,000 feet. "They'll give you a straight-in to the ILS," he said to me on a second air-to-air frequency. No sooner had he finished his sentence then he disappeared into the clouds. I was next.

After Center called me, I started down and leveled out at my assigned altitude. Embraced by solid white, I imagined that I was somehow safer with Doug on the instrument approach ahead of me. Emotionally, I was counting on him as a safety net. Physically, there was nothing he could do if I got into trouble.

Continuing on a 170-degree heading direct to the ILS, I was instructed in a thick

Spanish accent: "Five Lima Yankee, descend to two thousand and turn right three-sixty."

Everything felt more or less under control, and I was convinced that this would end up like all the other times I'd been scared and it had worked out okay, so I had not yet told the controller that I was flying on partial panel. But now he was waving me away from the field—my worst nightmare. Since Doug was ahead of me on the approach, the controller wanted to keep us separated, so I was being sent around to start my approach over. As I entered the turn, I asked Robert to call out compass headings, while I called out feet per minute of descent. When I reviewed what I was doing, it suddenly occurred to me that I might not have understood the controller's instructions. Did he say turn to a heading of 360 degrees, due north? Or did he ask me to make a 360-degree turn, and then continue heading almost due south to the runway? My mind went blank. Panic flamed through my entire body, and I felt out of breath as if I'd been punched in the stomach. Everything outside my body and inside my mind was white. Sheer terror paralyzed me into silence. I no longer had any idea where I was or where I needed to go. I felt completely disoriented as I watched the ILS needle swing to one side.

"Where in the hell am I?" I asked. Was I heading toward those hills I'd seen on the map? Was I about to hit something?

Doug's position in front of me had not worked as a safety net. Instead, it had seriously compromised my flight. Turning by reference to the little aircraft silhouette on the turn coordinator was of no use as it bounced around. The magnetic compass above my head had numbers, but they had lost their meaning. I was beginning to lose control.

"Fly the plane, Barbara," I said out loud. "Just fly the plane." My eyes scanned the turn coordinator. I wanted to look at a map, but I was afraid of inverting the plane if I looked away. With a non-pilot as navigator, what I needed was too hard to explain, so I called on the radio: "Lima Approach, this is Five Lima Yankee. Can I get a vector to the airport?" My voice cracked.

There was no answer, so I added, "I'm on partial panel."

"Five Lima Yankee cleared for ILS," replied the controller in broken English.

I no longer had any idea where that might be. Still in the clouds, I pleaded for the second time: "Can I get a vector to the field? I'm on partial panel."

"Five Lima Yankee report field in sight," came the reply. Not fluent in English, the controller was spewing out only memorized, cookie-cutter sentences. In my mental whiteout, it did not occur to me to switch to Spanish.

How ludicrous! "Report field in sight." What a joke! Everything outside my windows was white. I took a deep breath and tried to stay calm. If I didn't keep it together, we could be dead in a flash. I wanted to remain over the ocean to avoid contact with some unseen building or landform. A westerly heading would keep land on my tail, so I carefully turned until my compass read due west. When Robert began to get glimpses of ocean just below breaks in the clouds, I pushed the nose down until I spotted white caps 500 feet above the water. With forward visibility less than a mile beneath the clouds, I turned back toward shore.

"Robert, is the VOR on the field?"

"How would I know?" he asked innocently.

Oh Christ! How could he possibly know? I couldn't explain how to read it on the map now. Being squeezed between the water and the overcast was dangerously similar to flying inside a cloud. What was below looked the same as what was above as gray mists hugged the waters. I felt like a piece of sandwich meat stuck between layers of mayonnaise.

Simply controlling the plane in level flight was the most I could handle. For the moment, navigating was beyond me. I needed more clues to find the airport.

"How close does the runway appear to be in relationship to the shoreline?" I asked Robert, trying to pry a little more map information out of him.

"It looks pretty close, but I can't tell for sure."

"Hold the approach chart up over here," I said, directing him to put it in a spot where I wouldn't get disoriented while glancing at it. Sure enough, the VOR was on the field, which was so close to the coast that I should be able to see the runway once I crossed the shoreline. I centered the needle and headed directly for the airport.

As I neared land, my eyes searched desperately amid the low sprawl of brick-colored buildings and ramshackle houses for the airstrip set far from the center of the city. From my vantage point, the abject poverty of these endless barrios reminded me of the outskirts of Kathmandu. More than half of Lima's 7 million people are squatters subsisting in shantytowns without running water or electricity.

In the heavy fog combined with smog that blankets Lima eight months of the year, I was still unable to spot the airport. I castigated myself for having been so stupid as to have simply obeyed the controller instead of declaring an emergency and continuing straight on in to land. And then I spotted a long, open area through the gray murk.

"Robert! I have it! There's the airport!" Teeming with emotion, I called the tower and reported the field in sight. This time, they cleared me to land. As I touched my wheels to the pavement, I was more thankful to be alive than I could ever remember.

I took my time taxiing past rows and rows of dark helicopters and fighter jets belonging to the Peruvian military. Surrounded by tall fences and guard towers, the airfield had the aura of a prison compound. During my flight here, I was so busy with my own drama that I'd forgotten we were arriving in unsafe territory. For many years, Peru had been suffering from terrorist attacks by the Sendero Luminoso, known in English as the Shining Path. Though the entire country was in chaos because of widespread guerrilla activity, Lima authorities were the main target of bombings and killings, with the goal of overthrowing the government.

As soon as I tied down my plane, I went in search of a mechanic. I wasn't about to continue on with a bad vacuum pump and chance repeating what I'd just been through, no matter how much time it took. I was determined to get my plane repaired, even if I had to stay in Lima a week. This time, I would insist that Doug wait with me.

Everyone at the airport was helpful and outgoing. Two men gave me a ride in a golf cart to a small charter flight company on the other side of the airport, where they introduced me to the owner. He said that he had heard my desperate calls on the radio and was glad that I had made it down safely. Though his repair shop was only for his own fleet, he graciously agreed to sell me a vacuum pump he had in stock and sent me off with his trusted mechanic, Jaime.

I covered my failed instruments with paper (left)
before descending through the clouds into Lima
and getting repairs (above).

While Jaime worked on my plane, I stood alongside and practiced my Spanish on him. With adrenaline still pumping through my body from the flight, I rattled on a mile a minute about my adventure so far, and how I would never be pressured to depart partial panel again. Jaime proved to be an enthusiastic listener. By the time he finished installing the new vacuum pump, we were chatting like old friends. When he said he would like to work in the United States, I offered to help him get a visa. We both knew I was getting overly emotional. At the moment, I didn't care. I was ready to kiss the ground he stood on after he replaced my vacuum pump. I thanked him a million times, tipped him, and promised to write after I returned home. Then I headed off with the four guys in search of a cab.

We checked into the opulent but empty Country Club Hotel, located in the plush suburb of Miraflores. Here in the nicest, least touristy neighborhood we could find, the hotel's large garden and ballroom hinted at the lifestyle of the rich before the current political situation. Its restaurant was closed.

Doug asked our cab driver to wait for us while we changed into clothes to go out to dinner. During our ride to the Rosa Náutica, a seafood restaurant built on an old pier perched over Lima Bay, our driver told stories of thieves and terrorists who were known to stick guns to the heads of cab drivers and kidnap foreign passengers. Private guards stood at attention outside the restaurant, brandishing automatic weapons. I felt somewhat nervous until we stepped inside the five-star dining establishment, where charming, tuxedoed Peruvians took our order. The scene had the unreality of a movie set as everyone on the inside pretended they weren't living in that world just outside the doors, surrounded by poverty and crime.

The next morning, we returned very early to the airport and filed a flight plan for La Paz, Bolivia. After takeoff, we headed eastward over the Cordillera de Huanzo, along the high plateau of the Andes known as the Altiplano. Sections of the map said "RELIEF DATA UNRELIABLE. MAXIMUM ELEVATIONS IN PERU BELIEVED NOT TO EXCEED 23,000 FEET." The quadrants in my route of flight were marked 18,400 and 19,800 as maximum terrain altitudes. The lowest elevation was 12,500 feet.

In Lima, both Doug and I had been unable to refill our oxygen tanks, so as I climbed toward 16,000 feet Galen suggested I save it for later. I tried not using it, but began to feel slightly light-headed. In order not to run out completely, I compromised and began setting my timer to breathe oxygen for 5 minutes on and 8 minutes off. Robert and Galen opted not to use any at all.

I decided to crack a few jokes over the radio to make light of the situation. "Hey

Doug, Peter. This gorgeous terrain looks a lot like the Himalaya," I started. "Too bad Galen can't enjoy it."

"Why not?" Peter asked.

"You know how he is—he climbed high on Mount Everest without oxygen and this morning I couldn't get him to touch the stuff. Now he's passed out in the back seat," I deadpanned.

There was a long pause. Finally, Peter replied, "Really?" He sounded so seriously concerned that Robert, Galen, and I belly-laughed in unison. Perhaps the lack of oxygen was making us giddy after all.

Meanwhile, Peter was having his own set of problems. He didn't feel well after eating so much seafood and had terrible stomach cramps combined with foul gas and belching. He later told me that instead of receiving sympathy for being sick, Doug began cursing him for smelling up his airplane. He popped open the window so abruptly to air it out that the force ripped the hinges. "Can't you do something about this?" Doug pleaded. Irritation and poor critical thinking are early symptoms of altitude sickness.

As we hugged the Andes at 16,000 feet, rusty colors streaked the land. I could see snow-covered Andean peaks way off in the direction we were headed as we picked our way toward the Altiplano through low spots in the treeless, reddish mountains speckled with green vegetation. Robert kept extra-close tabs on our position on the map since we were too low to use radio navigational aids. I stayed close on Doug's tail so as not to lose him as I had earlier in the day when his plane blended in with splotchy patches of snow.

Just as we were leveling out over the vast Altiplano with Lake Titicaca glittering in the distance, Peter called again with an urgent request: "Barbara, call the tower at Juliaca and tell them we want to land. We want to rest."

"What are those guys doing?" I asked Galen and Robert. Our international flight plan was filed to La Paz, Bolivia, less than an hour away. We didn't have permission to land again in Peru, so I wondered what would cause Peter to make such a request. When I looked around to find the Juliaca airport, Doug's plane was already lined up for a straight-in approach off my nose. I had to circle to make room while I called the tower, "Juliaca Torre, es Noviembre Siete Tres Cinco Lima Yankee, cambio."

"Cinco Lima Yankee, adelante," the tower replied.

After calling the tower on behalf of Doug and myself, we were both cleared to land. Doug's plane bounced unusually hard onto the broad, paved runway perched at 12,546 feet. I was unaware at the time that Doug was not doing the flying. He was slumped over in his seat from oxygen deprivation. Peter was at the controls.

The speed of my landing in the thin air rocketed me onto the ground, but I touched down smoothly. This was the highest landing I'd made, but everything seemed fine until I spotted Doug standing next to his plane, vomiting. We hurried over just as he collapsed on the grass.

Meanwhile, Quechua Indian women had begun coming in from the surrounding fields. One of them opened a thermos of hot tea made from coca leaves, their cure for everything, including altitude sickness. While Doug sipped coca, locals  spread out alpaca sweaters, gloves, hats, and scarves on the tarmac beside both planes. We appeared to be tied down in the middle of a fly-in shopping mart.

Nobody felt good after flying at 16,000 feet for 4 hours, except Galen, who ran off into the fields to take photographs of Indian women dressed in colorful cotton skirts tending white alpacas. Robert swore I'd married an animal, and I agreed. The airport manager, however, sternly ordered Galen back to the airstrip. He didn't know quite what to do with a group of foreigners who did not have permission to be there, nor to take off again.

In his fourteen years of service, Héctor Sernaqué Yarlequé had never heard of a foreign private plane landing at Juliaca, and thus he was unfamiliar with entry or exit procedures for small aircraft. Other foreign pilots knew better than to drop out of the sky into an area with heavy Sendero Luminoso guerrilla activity, but we didn't know what kind of political conflicts awaited us on the ground.

Doug's sickness was brought on by a leak in his oxygen system, probably causing him to get less oxygen through the breathing tube than he would have from the straight rarefied air. After he had begun vomiting in his plane, Peter took control of their radio communications and landed the plane, though he, too, was feeling the lack of oxygen.

The airport had no repair facilities or oxygen to refill his tank. There was, however, a hospital clinic in town with a limited supply of medical oxygen. Héctor's wife took Doug to the small facility where the doctor on duty put him in bed to breathe pure oxygen. Then she joined us as we wandered around town and began snapping photographs and taking video of street scenes with Maoist graffiti on public buildings.

Noticing that she kept looking over her shoulder, I asked, "Is something wrong?" She admitted that she felt nervous for us because there were some very bad people here. It slowly dawned on us that we had seen no other tourists. Had we stopped in a war zone? Not quite, but we were in the heart of an area dominated by the Sendero Luminoso. When we returned to our multistory hotel well before dark, the lobby and dining room were eerily empty, with only a couple of Peruvians signed into the guest register.

Before dinner, the doctor released Doug and our group reunited in the hotel's large, empty dining room. Doug was feeling somewhat better after breathing pure oxygen for several hours, but all of us except Galen felt the effects of being at 12,500 feet, having flown to over 16,000 feet from sea level in the morning. When several different kinds of foods were brought to the table, nothing seemed appetizing, which is a classic symptom of mild altitude sickness.

I hoped we could leave as early as possible in the morning before one of us got really sick or Doug had a relapse. Just after dawn, we went to the airport and arrived in Héctor's office, thinking it would be a slam-dunk departure. He said we had no permission to leave. Even after he argued with the authorities in Lima on our behalf, trying to arrange permission for us to fly directly to Chile, bypassing Bolivia, the flight authorities insisted that we return to Lima first because we needed to leave the country from a designated international airport. Keeping Doug's failed oxygen system in mind, we requested a flight plan that would avoid routing us over more high mountains than necessary. He was still on the verge of serious altitude sickness and needed to get to a lower altitude as soon as possible.

When no approval was forthcoming, Héctor finally followed my suggestion and told the civil aviation authorities that we had a medical emergency. After a lot of argument, they granted us permission to fly on to Chile only if we followed an IFR

Peruvian tea made from coca leaves (left); Doug on oxygen in a medical clinic in Juliaca, Peru (above).

route at 22,000 feet. Doug finally agreed. He would do what he needed to do, once he was in the air.

I followed Doug on a left downwind departure until we were both out of sight of the airport. I continued to tail him as he veered off to find the lowest, most direct route over the Andes to the great Atacama Desert of Chile and the port-of-entry airport at Arica on the coast. Doug had asked me to make phantom position reports for both of us as we flew our own direction over the edge of Lake Titicaca, searching for the lowest road that leads over a pass into Chile.

"Barbara do you know where we are?" Doug radioed fifteen minutes later.

"Stand by," I said, assuming Doug had been keeping track of our position since I was following him. Besides, I was extremely busy calculating where we were supposed to be in order to respond to the frequent queries from the Peruvians about our position. My brother had put the map on his lap while he videoed farmlands and wooden fishing boats on the edge of the deep green lake and lost track of where we were. Galen had been busy shooting photographs. When Robert finally located us on the map, he turned it over to Galen to verify our position. Galen disagreed.

Quechua Indians rushed out to my plane at 12,500 feet on the Juliaca airstrip (above); passing over the edge of Lake Titicaca (right).

170

They started arguing. No one was thinking very clearly in the thin air at this high altitude.

"Doug, uh, we're, uh, a little confused. We're still looking," I confessed. "We may have passed the road." While everyone started debating our position over the radio, Doug and I headed west. We were low on fuel and we couldn't wait any longer to head toward the ocean. I scanned the instruments and continued using oxygen sporadically as I climbed up in order to clear the mountain range between here and the sea. Soon I was up to 16,000 feet in order to clear the lowest gap.

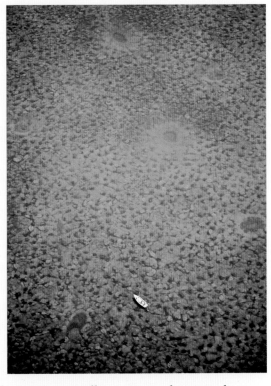

We wound our way between Andean peaks through treeless, moonlike terrain. We hadn't been able to buy fuel in Juliaca and were getting quite low as we skimmed the pass and flew unexpectedly close over a military installation. Minutes later, we we began to drop through a vast arid gorge, completely uninhabited and burnished by eons of intense sun without rain.

We were entering the Atacama Desert, the driest large expanse in the world. From a distance, the runway at Arica shimmered in the blowing sand like a piece of black opal. I felt thankful when the tower controller gave me a hearty welcome in English, but less so after we landed and health officials thoroughly searched our planes, confiscating all the salami, packaged nuts, and fresh foods we had brought for backcountry and emergency use. I had been unaware of the strict Chilean regulations on food imports. On the plus side, the Chileans expedited our entry formalities and charged us just $52 for a thirty-day flight pass that would allow us to fly anywhere in Chile without restrictions.

Back in the air again, we flew on toward Antofagasta, the only major town in the middle of the 1,250 miles of desert separating Arica from Santiago. Flying over the Atacama, I could hardly imagine how different the experience would be on the ground. Galen had a cousin who had been a mining engineer for an American copper company after World War I. In old age, he had regaled the family with tales of Northern Chile as a living hell of heat and sand, never mentioning natural beauty as he passed his hand through his hair and described how it turned gray overnight in his twenties, soon after he arrived.

The desert spread below us was anything but endless sands. Jagged peaks and spires of wildly colored rock separated dry valleys running toward the sea, where pink cliffs dropped the final 2,000 to 3,000 feet into breaking surf. The few settlements were at the base of these endless cliffs along the most rugged coastline I had ever seen.

Lining the opposite side of the long desert were Andean summits reaching to over 20,000 feet. From up here in the sky, the landscape was always intriguing as it unfolded ahead of us and on both sides. I wanted to come back someday when I had more time to explore parts of the region from the ground.

Antofagasta took us by surprise after the few dismal outposts we had already seen. In the middle of the desert we descended over a modern city of 200,000 people with public gardens, theaters, universities, a big sports stadium, broad streets, and inviting beaches flanking its major harbor. We spent the night in a tall hotel near the main plaza and departed early in the morning for Santiago.

The farther south we flew, the more interesting the great desert became. Occasional streambeds lined with green vegetation began to wend their way from the mountains to the sea. Ever so slowly, the barren rock and sands gave way to a blanket of dry scrub broken by green valleys with irrigated fields.

We were approaching the Central Valley of Chile, the lush heartland where two-thirds of the country's population lives. Much like California's Central Valley, it lies between snowy peaks and the sea, and has a Mediterranean climate. The whole country resembles a California stretched to three times its length and turned upside down with mountains half again as high as the Sierra. As I ended the five-hour flight on an inland path over vineyards and fruit orchards into little Tobalaba Airport on the outskirts of Santiago, I felt as if I were home again.

Flying beside Doug over the Atacama Desert (right).

Approaching Patagonia

XIV

*R*eaching Santiago after 65 hours of flying felt like the end of a journey, but it was only the beginning of our ground adventures. As planned, Peter hopped the first jet home to rejoin his family, while the rest of us stayed two nights with Doug's friends, Juan and Patti Abadi, who owned Esprit de Corps Chile. Their elegant, modern home in the hills would have fit in perfectly in Aspen or Santa Fe, while the European city below them was more attractive to my eye than any place of its size in the United States.

While our planes were having 50-hour servicing at the airport, Doug and Galen went off to arrange a 5-day raft trip down the Bio Bio River, 500 miles to the south. Doug chose the lowest bidder among a number of rafting companies that offered Bio Bio trips. Our guides would be Peruvians who had come to Chile because terrorism had brought tourism in their country to a standstill.

Galen and Doug also touched base with Rick Klein, the forest activist who was arranging a three-day trek into a stand of endangered alerce trees recently found to be over 3,000 years old. The redwoodlike giants were all but gone from accessible areas, cut for their decay-resistant timber. Ancient, huge, and endangered, the remaining trees were deep in the heart of the Southern Hemisphere's largest temperate rainforest. Rick founded a group called Ancient Forests International, based in California, after spending nine years as the only gringo park warden in Chile. He had contacted Galen before we'd left home about doing a trek to photograph the trees for *National Geographic,* saying our best chance to photograph virgin old-growth would be by doing a traverse of the rarely visited Alerce Andino National Park on the edge of Chilean Patagonia. We learned that no foreigners had ever crossed the park on foot, though trails were reported to exist the whole way.

As I circled a wild spire rising out of the clouds in Chilean Patagonia, Galen photographed me from Doug's plane (left).

Doug had instantly agreed to do the alerce trek before we left the States because of his strong interest in preserving the vast temperate forests of Southern Chile. Having just sold his interest in Esprit for over $100 million, he had a vision of buying huge private tracts of forested land to keep the trees out of the hands of Japanese timber interests.

He was clearly upset that world attention remained focused on saving South America's tropical rainforests, while the Japanese were systematically destroying the continent's last old-growth temperate rainforests. They were buying timber from private contractors and shipping it to Japan on two huge processing ships that  were constantly traveling back and forth across the Pacific from Puerto Montt. One of these carrier-size instruments of death was named "The Emerald Forest" in Japanese.

Rick planned to meet us in Puerto Montt a week from now. In the meantime, we hoped to explore into the heart of Patagonia by air. Our plans were somewhat open, with the only firm dates being the alerce trek starting on December 19 and the Bio Bio River trip on December 23. After spending Christmas week on the river, Robert would fly home, Galen would join Doug for climbs and adventures in the far south of Patagonia and Tierra del Fuego, and I would fly myself over the Andes to Buenos Aires, where a young pilot named Michael Craig would join me for the long journey up Brazil's wild coast and across the Amazon to Venezuela. I'd taken him on his first flight some years before, and now he was a commercial pilot who wanted the experience of flying a small plane in a foreign country. He planned to take a commercial flight home when we reached Caracas.

Doug intended to stay in Southern Chile for many months, adventuring as well as searching for forested lands to buy. Galen would join Doug for treks and climbs amidst the wildest peaks, then fly home commercial.

Meanwhile, Doug had arranged a climbing adventure for this week. An old friend of his and Galen's, Peter "Cado" Avenali, was bringing his teenage son,

Lake District of Southern Chile (above); Cerro Puntiagudo sticking out of the clouds (right).

Josh, down from Oregon for an adventurous Christmas vacation of rafting and climbing. We would fly Josh from Santiago to Coihaique, a small mountain town in Chilean Patagonia, and meet Cado driving a rented truck. After reconnoitering an unclimbed peak called Cerro Cathedral from the air, they planned to trek through the forest and make the first ascent in time to fly back to Puerto Montt for the alerce trek.

I wasn't too keen on the idea. I didn't want to thrash through rainforest or wait around in camp while they were climbing, nor did I want to be pressured to rush a flight to Puerto Montt on a bad weather day. The farther south we flew, the greater the odds of getting caught in a legendary Patagonian storm of the Roaring Forties and the Furious Fifties. I decided that Robert and I would fly south from Coihaique into the heart of Patagonia on our own time and meet the others back in Puerto Montt on the appointed day.

Early on the morning of December 13, we took off from Santiago for Coihaique, more than a 1,000 miles and 7 hours of flying to the south. Galen joined Doug and Josh, both to even out the loads and take air-to-air photographs of me flying through the Andes.

Level fields and vineyards soon gave way to forested hills cut by river valleys carrying melt water from the snows of the Andes to the sea. South of Temuco, we began dodging occasional clouds over an area of deep blue lakes and snow peaks that reminded me of Lake Tahoe. This was Southern Chile's fabled Lake District, which appeared far more spectacular than the Tahoe region from the air, with its twelve large lakes, fewer people, and snowy volcanoes spewing steam.

As we flew just west of the crest of the Andes, which forms the border with Argentina, the clouds below us came together into a continuous layer that blocked all view of the ground. Off in the distance, Argentina was totally clear, offering an emergency escape route if conditions were too poor to land in Coihaique.

The sky above was absolutely blue, while the cloud bank nearly at our level was white as a polar ice cap. Wild mountains began to poke through here and there as Doug called out their names on the radio—Tronador, Osorno, Puntiagudo. He'd climbed most all of them on previous trips. Then we entered a section of wildly sculpted summits that Doug didn't recognize. He believed that they were all un-named and unclimbed.

I was flying well above the highest summits, watching Doug skimming the clouds, and swooping low between the peaks so that Galen could get pictures, when Doug came on the radio with a request: "Barbara, can you go back again and fly slower and lower between that icy rock spire and the main summit? Galen wants a shot of you just as you come through."

"Okay guys," I replied, "I'll go lower and I'll put down one notch of flaps for one more pass." I took deep breaths as we circled once more around a knife-edged ridge of spires plastered with ice before venturing on over emerald glacial lakes and tree-cloaked ridges crowned with Himalaya-like snow mountains as the clouds gradually diminished. While Doug and Galen detoured to fly around Cerro Cathedral, I continued on and landed beneath clear skies in the paradise meadows of Coihaique, surrounded by peaks like the Tetons, rock walls like Yosemite, and wildflowers.

Cado came out to meet me well before Doug landed. When Doug arrived, he announced a new twist to our plans. He had circled so close to the top of Cerro Cathedral that Galen had spotted a rock cairn built on the summit. Since it had al-ready been climbed, they decided to attempt an alternate mountain rising out of the valley of the Río Milta, considerably farther north.

The next morning, Robert and I got a late start for Punta Arenas after helping Doug and Galen leave for their climb. Doug had one last word of advice for me: "If the winds get bad, call the tower when you arrive. Have them send out some men to hang on your wings." That sounded like loads of fun, and he wasn't kidding. The winds of Patagonia are infamous for building suddenly. Many planes that success-fully touch down end up ground looping out of control into an unplanned turn that sometimes results in a crash.

Skies were clear as we left Coihaique, but an hour to the south a line of lenticular clouds began lowering and the ride got rough. We were nearing the peaks of the Fitz Roy Range, sculpted by winds and ice into some of the wildest mountain forms on earth. I'd spent a month on the ground around these peaks when Galen climbed Fitz Roy in 1985, and I wanted to see the area up close from the air. But after another half hour in dicey winds, with my chest strap cinched down and visibility getting poor, I made a 180-degree turn back to Balmaceda. By the time I arrived an hour and a half later, a strong crosswind blowing 26 knots drifted me over the left edge of the runway as I came in for a landing. I turned the plane directly into the wind and flew across

the runway to the far right side before straightening out and touching down with full right aileron.

Very early the next day, we crossed the Argentine border to Bariloche, an exclusive ski resort I'd visited before on the way to Fitz Roy. It proved to be a big mistake. "Te están robándo de un montón de dinero!" Carlos, the flight officer exclaimed, reaffirming that both the customs and immigration agents were "robbing me of a bunch of money." Inflation and greed were peaking. They justified charging me $250 because I had arrived on Saturday. I sat in the airport cafeteria with my head in my hands. We had dropped into Argentina's biggest rat's nest, where rental cars went for $200 a day, plus mileage, and coffee was $3 for a tiny cup. Only the 30-day, $70 flight fee seemed like a bargain, until I asked Carlos, "Where can I fly?"

"Nowhere." He answered. "You must wait until I receive permission from Buenos Aires, or you can return to Chile." Carlos was as frustrated by his own system as I was. I opted to return to Chile on the first clear day, where I was to join Galen and Doug at Puerto Montt at the end of the week. That day happened to be the last possible one to meet Doug and Galen on time. Everything was so expensive that we stayed at a small inn high over the town, biding our time.

After landing back in Coihaique, I tied my plane to a fence (left); back in 1985, I photographed myself in front of Fitz Roy while Galen was climbing it (right); on my favorite day of the flight, I flew past peak after wildly sculpted peak just above a blanket of clouds (overleaf).

Meanwhile, the four guys lived through an epic on their chosen peak. It appeared close when seen from a point on the Carretera Austral, a new dirt highway opened the previous year, but what looked to be a three-hour walk through the forest to timberline turned out to be nearly three days of thrashing through primeval forest filled with chasms, waterfalls, bamboo, and leeches. In a fit of ecological passion, Doug had left the requisite machetes behind, and the men often had to crawl on their bellies with 60-pound packs through seemingly impenetrable stands of bamboo.

An *estancia* owner in the valley below told them the peak was locally named Cerro Barros Arana, and that to the best of his knowledge no one had even been to its base. Above timberline, the foursome climbed steepening snow slopes onto a glacier. After ascending an ice couloir in a whiteout and coming to a final rock headwall coated in ice, Cado and Josh decided to wait it out, while Doug led the hardest pitch up to the summit with zest. They made it down just in time for Doug and Galen to hop in the plane and meet me in Puerto Montt.

Once we were all there, Rick Klein was eager for us to begin our trek to the endangered alerce trees. We drove for hours on increasingly bad four-wheel-drive roads through freshly clear-cut sections of forest until we entered Alerce Andino National Park and set off on a narrow trail.

I thought that the first day and a half in light rain was going well, until two of the three guides said they wanted to turn back. We had already seen and photographed a fine grove of alerce trees, and both Galen and I questioned whether the rest of us should go on.

"Is the trail obvious from here on?" Galen asked.

Doug on the summit after the first ascent of Cerro Barros Arana (top); Doug leading ice-plastered rock on the final headwall (bottom).

"No problem, according to them," Rick said. "We cross a pass, descend to a lake, and walk a few miles to a road." After dividing up the gear that the guides had been carrying, we went on. Within the hour, we peaked over the crest and viewed a large lake several thousand feet below. I gasped at the unbelievably thick and forested steepness between here and the lake.

"Where can we get water?" someone asked.

"Down there," Rick said, pointing at the lake.

We started down a nearly vertical slope blanketed with vegetation that dropped off into sheer rock cliffs. "Hold on to the plants at their bases and lower yourself," Rick said as he swung out of sight like a monkey. At first I tried not to touch anything. Leeches were everywhere. I wrapped my feet in plastic sacks to keep the little bloodsuckers out of my shoes. When the terrain became too difficult to negotiate without using my hands, I finally gave up and started hugging the slimy slope.

Doug commented to Galen how impressed he was that I was handling our difficult situation so stoically. Little did he know that I was too upset at having been lured in to this "walk" by the two of them and too frightened to talk as I followed closely in my brother's footsteps. As we carefully worked our way through the thicket, we often ended up looking through holes beneath our feet onto nearly invisible cliff bands. Each time we came to one of these dangerous overhanging dead ends, Galen, Robert, and Doug would have different ideas about which way to go. When they fanned out in different directions looking for a way out, I would sit down to catch my breath and listen to them shouting and arguing with one another over whose route down was best.

The terrain was so tricky that we had taken several hours to go less than half a mile when darkness caught us far above the lake. We found a barely adequate campsite and quickly set up tents. While Doug built a fire, the others gathered damp wood. Running water was nowhere to be found, so Rick began tearing moss off granite slabs and squeezing black liquid into water bottles. I was thirsty, but unwilling to drink the brown ooze. Galen went off with a flashlight and came back with clear water from a tiny spring. With the mood in camp as dark as the night, I went to bed without eating dinner.

Starting off before dawn, we safely reached the lake after hours more of vertical bushwhacking. Just when the terrain looked easier, we came to the lake's far edge and stumbled through even more hours of treacherous jungle with mossy cliffs.

Not until afternoon did we spill out onto a jeep road where two battered vehicles picked us up as planned. No sooner had we begun to follow the dirt track paralleling the river than our driver accidentally ran his rear wheel off the road, leaving our vehicle dangling over a small cliff. I carefully climbed out of the teetering vehicle and stood back as several men fastened ropes to it and towed it to safety. Our travels on land were beginning to make the flying seem tame.

When we neared the outskirts of Puerto Montt, we begged our jeep driver to stop at a restaurant instead of taking us directly to the airport as planned. An hour later, I lifted off in skies so clear that it seemed I could see San Francisco. Small towns dotted the green countryside, graced with tall churches and storybook steeples. The perfect white cone of Volcán Osorno stood out like Mount Fuji, towering over rolling farmland spotted with cattle. The scenery beneath my wings was so peaceful and lush that for the first time I gave thought to living outside the United States and understood Doug's desire to move here. For the moment there was nowhere else on Earth I wanted to be.

Beyond the sparsely populated lowlands, Doug led me on a scenic tour over stunning lakes and wild rivers set into a thick blanket of temperate rainforest beneath the icy heights of the Andes. As we wended our way back north, the landscape was so fantastically gorgeous that I didn't want the flight to end. It made everything I'd been through so far seem worthwhile.

Nearing the town of Temuco, I watched Doug change course and swoop down for a low pass over some forested lands. Robert was in his plane and Galen was in mine. Instead of following Doug, I headed to the airport and radioed the tower

We descended mossy cliffs (above) to complete our traverse of Alerce Andino National Park after seeing a grove of the ancient trees (right).

for permission to land. Remembering that the Club Aereo de Temuco was in a log building near the approach end of the runway, I made a short-field landing just in time to turn off at the taxiway to the private flying club's entrance. Doug landed moments later, but didn't touch down in time to make the turnoff. By the time he taxied back, Galen and I had stepped inside the clubhouse to make arrangements for refueling and tying down our planes for the week we would be on the river. The walls were lined with photographs, dating back to the early forties, of the club's planes and pilots. A surprising number of the bush pilots who had flown all around Patagonia were women. One faded, signed portrait was of the first woman in Chile to become a licensed pilot. Nothing I had read in the United States had given me any hint of the long history of women's aviation in the wilds of Chile.

I hadn't given any special thought to my landing until my brother brought it up later. He told me Doug had been quite surprised not to see me as he taxied ever farther down the runway and more so to discover that I was already at the club, having landed short enough to make the first turnoff. Because I'd been trying to keep up with Doug all along, the fact that my landing surprised him made me feel elated. Flying day after day, I was reaching a new level of comfort and expertise that others were beginning to notice.

From Temuco, an hour's cab ride through pastoral fields brought us to Victoria, where our backbreaking schedule dictated that we meet our Peruvian river guides first thing in the morning.

Corcovado Volcano in Chilean Patagonia (right).

ON THE BIO BIO

XV

*O*n Christmas Eve we drove to the town of Lonquimay to begin the private river trip that Doug had booked a week earlier. There were to be six of us, so I bought badminton games and squirt guns to give to Galen, Robert, and Doug on Christmas morning and added a few stocking stuffers for Cado and his son, Josh, who had reconnected with us in Victoria.

I was not alone in feeling unhappy to see that three strangers from the United States had also been booked onto our trip. We had been told that our rafting trip was being arranged just for our private group in advance of the regular season. During brief introductions, we learned that two were producers for major movie studios in Hollywood and the other was a stockbroker from the East Coast. They were experienced river runners who had made a number of trips together during their vacations. After we helped our guides set up camp on the banks of the Bio Bio, Galen and I took a walk to discuss my reservations about going on the river.

"The risks aren't worth the thrill," I said, barely keeping my voice down.

"Doug says his ex-wife and kids did it when they were young," Galen reminded me, "so how bad could it be?" Then he added, "If you stay behind, you'll be all alone during Christmas week. Besides, we paid thousands of dollars in advance in Santiago. Cado and Josh are going. We'll have a great time."

Even though big whitewater intimidated me, the idea of traveling alone in a strange country during Christmas was depressing, so I decided to go along with the guys.

The first two days on the river were easy going. We floated long level stretches and encountered some big, relatively unchallenging rapids rated Class III with a few Class IVs. Doug paddled ahead of us in his kayak and waited by the shoreline to watch us shoot the harder rapids, which were exciting without seeming dangerous. In the evenings, we sat around a glowing fire and settled in to listen to Doug lecture our guests on the evils of producing the violent movies about which they had earlier bragged. At times, the nightly discussions became so heated that the fire seemed unnecessary. Both Robert and I moved our chairs away from the inner circle as the discussions boiled over. Though I privately agreed with Doug that it was a huge

Rafting the Bio Bio River (left).

waste of money to make movies about evil people, and that such films beget real violence in society, I didn't speak up. Doug's confrontational manner had a habit of silencing everyone, but he didn't seem to care. Meanwhile, Galen used the opportunity to photograph Doug waving his hands wildly in the air to emphasize his point of view.

On the third morning, the river guides told us to wear helmets. It was our first indication that the river was about to turn nasty. Up to now, we'd been laughing and lounging between rapids without a care in the world. Just before lunch, all that changed. With trepidation, I watched the guides scout Lava South, a Class V rapid named after Lava Falls, a crux section of the Colorado River back home. They paced back and forth on a cliff above the river's edge, nervously pointing to sections in the river. The sound of crashing water muffled their words, so I was unable to overhear them, but the excitement-filled air was unmistakable. The prospect of running this notorious rapid had everyone on edge.

Doug entered the river first. We watched him as he danced his way through boulders and eddied out into calmer water. The second raft, with the Hollywood producers, went next. Galen and I had already walked past the rapid to a vantage point, where I videoed them from high above the river. Galen had his camera set up on a tripod and was planning for us to walk around this rapid after we shot our pictures, but Chando, our boatman, convinced us to come back and raft it. When I asked him about the chances of flipping in this rapid, he said, "Barbara, don't worry about this one. It's the next one that's really bad."

Before climbing back into the raft, Chando instructed us to strip down to our bathing suits and rain jackets, "just in case." He did not want us wearing any extra clothing that could fill with water and weigh us down, or worse yet, catch on something. Obediently, I took off my pile jacket and long pants, fastened my helmet and life jacket, and sat in the back of the raft next to Galen.

As we approached the rapid, our raft spun backward and Chando lost control. He rapidly scrambled to get us turned around, but not until we hit a large boulder

As we entered Lava South (above), we flipped into a rock wall (top right) and I was thrown out (bottom right) with shattered teeth and jaw. (Photos by Doug with Galen's camera.)

in the middle of the river did we finally get faced down river. As we neared a jagged, overhanging rock wall on river left, I asked Galen if he would change places with me.

"Not now! Watch your hand!" he screamed. When I saw what he was yelling about, it was already too late.

My face hit the wall, and my mouth exploded. The freezing water stung momentarily; then I no longer felt the cold. Over and over, I clawed at the surface but kept colliding with the bottom of the flipped raft. The rapids dragged my body farther down river while I fought to get my feet downstream, but the water's force was too great. With my head leading the way, I repeatedly smashed into the jagged rock wall.

I remembered what Chando had emphatically said during our short briefing on river safety before we put in: "Get away from the raft. If you get tossed out, don't worry about swimming. Go down feet first. It's not so bad. Just be sure to go down properly until someone rescues you."

A whitewater river of this magnitude was beyond anything I'd seen before. The rules for safely swimming after a spill had sounded straightforward and easy on shore, but here in the river, nothing was easy. The river's flow funneled between jagged undercut cliff walls on river left and large boulders on river right. Against the fury of roiling waters, my strength was nil. Nonetheless, I continued to struggle, hoping to get my feet downstream, but the arrogant water tossed and twisted me like a rag doll going over Niagara Falls.

As my body traced each curve of the undercut wall, I occasionally pierced the surface, gasping for air. Water filled my mouth. I spit it out and tried again to breathe, only this time I swallowed foam. As the world crashed around me, I was no longer aware of anyone or anything other than myself. I lost track of my husband, my brother, and my friends. There was only the angry river and its black, bottomless void.

Confusing thoughts flashed through my head, until I heard a calm inner voice saying, "You must have the will to survive." The words came from a man I'd never met. I'd called him to inquire about taking a course based on his book, *Survival Sense for Pilots and Passengers*.

"Doesn't everyone have the will to survive?" I'd asked after a brief conversation.

Now, as his words came back to me, I wondered what I could possibly do differently than I had tried so far. His advice continued to haunt me as I took yet another blow to my head: "If you have an accident, the most important ingredient is having the will to survive."

I realized that my cheap helmet had slipped backward, exposing part of my head, and suddenly I understood what the man had meant. It was imperative that I do something—anything—to protect my head. I could not survive many more blows. With every ounce of my 107 pounds I fought the powerful water and raised my left arm to block my head just before I received the most violent blow of all, which left my arm feeling broken.

My need for air became urgent, but all I was finding was frothing water, cutting rock, and the rounded bottom of the raft. Then, miraculously, the water swept me away from the perilous wall for a few seconds. For a moment, I felt safe. But the river wasn't finished tormenting me. Ka-bam! I was sucked down into a deep, dark, twirling hole. I was certain my life was finally over and that I couldn't go without air a moment longer.

Contrary to some movie endings, my life did not flash before me. Instead, I felt sadly disappointed that I would not finish my trip. I wondered if my death would surprise my friends. It seemed peculiar that this was happening in a river and not in my airplane.

When the light of hope was nearly gone, the river churned me up once again. At the surface, I was certain I'd find air, but again there was only watery foam. Dying seemed so real, so obvious. The mystery of death was becoming clear. I could feel it approaching in combinations of little blows, one on top of the other.

When I least expected it, the hole finally spit me out, and I spotted my brother riding on top of the upside-down raft, grinning from ear to ear, completely unaware of what I had just been through.

"Robert! " I screamed.

He reached over, grabbed ahold of my life jacket, pulled me out of the water onto the raft, and held me tightly in his arms as the raft drifted across the river.

"I knocked my teeth out," I sobbed.

"No!" Robert yelled. His smile disappeared as we drifted to a stop in a calm eddy.

Chando stood in the back and hopped off to steer us to shore. He no longer wore his I-am-the-cool-guide-and-you-are-the-dumb-client look. As he surveyed the blood running down my chin, he seemed to understand my trauma because he, too, was dripping with blood. His face had two deep gashes, and when he saw me up close, his expression turned to concern. He swiftly picked me up in his dark, muscled arms and carried me to shore, gingerly setting me down on a rock. I shivered in the shade as I caught my breath. My left arm began to throb, so I unfastened a Velcro closure on my Gore-Tex rainshell and pushed the sleeve up to take a look. A hunk of bloody skin hung down below my elbow, exposing the bone. I nearly passed out, and the sight of the wound seemed to have the same effect on Chando. He spun away and began to retch. After he collected himself, he called over to Robert, "You take care of her. I'll get the medical kit."

Robert checked my arm. The look on his face said everything. The wound was ugly and in need of stitches, but I was in good hands. I relaxed into his care as he had me hold my arm up while he rummaged through the medical kit for a tourniquet. Once the bleeding was stopped, he went back to the kit to look for a sterile solution to clean it.

Above the roar of the river, someone screamed from the opposite shore. From a distance I could see several people milling on the beach and several more huddling over a body. I did not see my Galen anywhere. Then it hit me: there were six of us in the raft when we started out. Now we were only three. During my struggle with the river, I had lost all sense of everyone else. Where was Galen? Josh? Cado? My head began to spin.

I had sensed this river trip would end in disaster. Why hadn't I listened to myself? It was clear that Galen had doubts, too, because when I wanted to bet him that Chando would flip our raft in the first difficult rapid, Galen wouldn't take the bet. He thought so, too. We both agreed that the boatman in the second raft was more skilled. Neither of us had felt confident being in Chando's boat. Now I felt really stupid.

What made things worse was that neither of us gave a damn about this sport. We were only doing it to please Doug, who was passionate about kayaking. We were such fools. This wasn't Disneyland. There were no guarantees we would survive. I told myself that if I made it home alive, I'd go straight to a shrink.

Before we left our home in Berkeley, California, twenty-seven days earlier, I had accepted the possibility that I might die flying our single-engine plane. It is a risk that I accept whenever I fly. But I had never considered that the land adventures that Galen and Doug had planned would prove so dangerous.

My God! What about Galen? I began to feel queasy and thought I might vomit, but tried to hold it in so as not to spray my split lip or broken teeth with the contents of my stomach. My mind filled with things I wished I'd said to Galen.

"Is Galen okay?" I asked Robert.

He didn't know. Robert was too involved bandaging my arm to notice what was happening on the far side of the river. But I could tell that someone was stretched out on the ground with others huddled around. I was becoming frantic with worry.

"Is my mouth okay?" I asked.

"I don't know, Barbara," Robert replied. He sounded sad.

Gently patting the area beneath my nose, I felt something hard sticking out at an angle and pestered Robert to take a look, but he politely declined. He'd seen enough.

Chando took a second look at me and offered pain pills, but I couldn't chance having an allergic reaction on the river, given my previous history of drug sensitivity. Instead, I asked for a piece of gauze and soaked it in Novocain before sticking it in the open space between my teeth. This would have to do for the time being.

"Are they coming over here?" I quietly asked Chando.

"No. We have to go over there," he replied matter-of-factly. "The current is too strong, so we have to go to them."

He expected us to raft across the river. Was he serious? If this was a moment when I was supposed to be brave, I was failing miserably.

"Can't they come over here?" I queried again, watching in disbelief as he prepared to cross the river.

"What if I don't go?" I said to myself, looking around for an easy footpath out of here.

"How far is it to the nearest hospital?" I whimpered.

"We have several more hours of river rafting to get to a vehicle. Then it is another six or eight hours by four-wheel drive, depending on the condition of the roads. But first we have to get over to the others," Chando said, adding, "Robert, help me turn the raft right-side up."

After Chando helped me into the raft, my heart skipped a beat as we started for the other shore. He paddled wildly through the end of the rapid and reached the beach where Galen was lying, barely conscious. Galen regained consciousness minutes later, but still had water in his lungs.

The scene on the shoreline looked like a battlefield. The wounded were spread out on the beach with different crew tending to each of them. Galen was lying on his back, suffering from a concussion and a deep cut on his forehead that needed stitches. He'd been knocked unconscious the moment our raft hit the rock wall. Doug had spotted him floating motionless below the rapid and yelled at Josh to pull him to shore, which he managed to do despite having received cuts over his eye. Cado had injured his shoulder, but had no open wounds. My left arm felt broken and would be useless rafting in the Class V rapids ahead.

According to the whitewater enthusiasts, we were just now coming to the "good part" of the river.

Injured rafting party on the banks of
the Bio Bio River (above).

Escaping the Andes

XVI

A foul smell of blood and iodine wafted through the room as I struggled to open my eyes. My eyelids seemed glued shut from the inside, my mouth was parched, and it felt painful to swallow. As my tongue started its morning ritual of sliding over each tooth to check for cleanliness, I detected a bad taste. While I was trying to recall the last time I'd used a toothbrush, my tongue slipped over a sharp edge of a tooth and landed in a ragged hole. Hole? What hole? There was no hole yesterday. My tongue quickly explored the jagged porcelain and then went back to feeling the other teeth. The rest of my mouth seemed okay. The back teeth were still there.

My eyes shot open, but I still had no idea where I was or what had happened to me. My tongue probed around some more until it discovered a dangling tooth. I turned onto my side, and tried to curl up like a baby.

I remembered rafting the Bio Bio, but exactly what had happened escaped me until my tongue inadvertently touched an exposed nerve. Shock waves pulsed through my body, plunging my senses back into rushing cold water lined with jagged black rock.

Gradually, the events of the previous day began to come back to me. After I pieced together the accident, it took me quite a while to figure out that I was in a hotel in Victoria, far from the river, and I wouldn't have to get back in the raft again. I finally remembered five of us cramming into a small jeep and driving late into the night until we arrived at a medical clinic. There, ten hours after the accident, I waited an hour for the lone doctor, called at home, to come in and sew up my lower lip with twelve stitches and my arm with eighteen more.

After a cursory look at the more serious injuries inside my mouth, the doctor said that I needed to get to an oral surgeon immediately and that the nearest

Flying past ice-capped Osorno Volcano (left); flying over the vineyards south of Santiago reminded me of the Napa Valley back home (above).

specialist who could deal with injuries as extensive as mine was in Santiago, 500 miles away.

I sat up in bed and looked around the room at a scene that appeared to be straight out of *M*A*S*H*. Right next to me, Galen was sleeping soundly with half of his head bandaged over stitches. Josh was on his back on the floor, wearing a blood-soaked bandage above one eye. Robert was sleeping—the only one unscathed. Cado and Doug were nowhere to be seen. It came back to me how Cado had injured his shoulder but decided to stay back on the river with Doug and the other Americans, since there had only been one jeep available for our evacuation.

For the first time since the accident, I raced to the mirror and looked at my face. My lower lip was puffed out where the stitches formed a Y. I gently touched the area under my nose and stopped when I felt a small, sharp protrusion beneath the skin. Something seemed very wrong, but I was too scared to investigate further.

After the initial shock of seeing my face and body so torn, I ventured outside, crossed the hotel grounds, and headed to the restaurant just as the sun came over the horizon. In the sudden daylight and silence of the morning, I became aware of audible growls coming from my stomach. It had been a long time since I'd eaten.

When I reached the hotel dining room, I spotted a group of Americans dressed in trendy adventure-travel clothing. I hid in the bathroom to collect myself before approaching their breakfast table. "Is anyone here a doctor?" I queried.

"No, but we have a nurse from San Francisco. Would that be any help?" a woman replied.

As I walked off with the nurse to talk in private, she said they'd come to raft the Bio Bio. By the looks of me, it was all too obvious that I had already done so. After glancing at my mouth, she said there wasn't anything she could do and that I should find a very good dentist as soon as possible.

As I was thanking her for her advice, a deeply tanned man in well-worn clothes walked up with a look as if he knew me. "You must be with the Tompkins group," he surmised. After I briefly described the accident, he revealed, "Doug asked me to take your group down the river and I refused. He wanted to run it too early in the season and the water is unusually high this year."

My face turned red with embarrassment mixed with anger. As his group gathered around to listen, I carried on polite conversation, holding back my true feelings about my experience on the river. I wanted to get on with making an immediate decision about how best to get myself to an oral surgeon.

The sickening stench of blood that had awakened me was from the piece of gauze soaked in Novocain that I'd crammed into the hole between my teeth the night before. I had good reason to leave it in. The exposed nerve wasn't painful so long as I kept my mouth closed, but even the slightest rush of air from breathing through my mouth as I talked was enough to send me through the ceiling. I had not taken anything for pain in the field or since, partly because of a history of adverse reactions to codeine and related painkillers, but even more because I held onto the possibility of flying myself to help, which I wouldn't attempt with my mind dulled by painkillers. Now, flying injured to Santiago this morning seemed to be by far my best option.

After a breakfast during which I only sipped liquids through a straw, Galen, Robert, and I took a long cab ride back to the airport in Temuco, where I phoned Doug's friend Juan in Santiago and asked him to try to set up an appointment with the best oral surgeon in the city. He offered to meet us at the Tobalaba Airport.

As I lifted off in clear skies, Robert and Galen oohed and aahed at the glorious vision of snowy Andean peaks off in the distance. I limited myself to conversation required with controllers and quietly reflected on how much I preferred being in charge of my own destiny behind the controls of my plane to rafting dangerous waters passively, my life dependent on the skills of a boatman. If I were to continue with an adventurous life, I needed to figure out how to stay in control and avoid letting others make critical decisions for me. For better or for worse, I needed to take full responsibility for the outcome of my own actions and not acquiesce to other people, especially men who always want to be in charge. The male urge to "help" the "weaker" sex was constantly getting me into troubles I might not have encountered had I followed my own intuitions.

When I touched down in Santiago, I was relieved to see Juan standing by the runway, waiting to take me to an oral surgeon. He'd chosen one of Santiago's best, a dentist who had trained in the United States and had kept up with all the latest techniques.

As the oral surgeon removed jammed pieces of fractured maxilla bone from my jaw, I couldn't stop myself from screaming. My torn gums had already become infected from the contaminated river water, rendering useless his multiple attempts to numb them. He apologized profusely for causing such pain. I didn't blame him. Having never screamed in a doctor's office before, I felt as upset as he did about my reaction. He continued working to remove a loose tooth still dangling in my mouth, and I finally managed to calm myself. When he was finished, he took some time to show me photographs of dental implants and explained how I would need to heal for a long time before any surgeon could begin reconstructing my mouth. He encouraged me to fly home promptly to see a specialist.

While I was being fitted with temporary false teeth, all of us stayed at Juan and Patti's home. Doug called after having just finished kayaking the river, looking for Galen and sounding as nonchalant as ever. Much of Galen's outdoor gear was in Doug's airplane, but he was not coming back to Santiago anytime soon. He asked Galen to join him flying and trekking around southern Patagonia and Tierra

del Fuego, as they had planned to do before the accident.

Galen was still dazed by his concussion and needed a lot of my attention. I barely had the energy to take care of myself, let alone him. Though he was willing to go home with me on a commercial flight and return later for my plane after my mouth had healed, I knew I wouldn't sleep well worrying about N735LY and it would be months before my mouth healed enough for me to come back.

Robert immediately started making arrangements to catch a commercial flight home. Though he wanted to return before he lost his girl or his job, he was torn about leaving me to fly home alone. I assured him that I would be just fine without him, even though I would sorely miss his calm presence and great sense of humor. I reminded him that I didn't want to disappoint Michael Craig, whom I was meeting in Buenos Aires on the other side of the Andes in just three days to fly through Brazil to Venezuela.

Michael, the son of a climbing friend of Galen's, was a professional pilot working summers for a flying service in Colorado and Utah. He was counting on joining me on the leg from Argentina to Venezuela during his semester break from college and had already bought his air ticket.

Even though I didn't know him very well, I was a close friend of his family, and I knew that he was looking forward to flying with me in a foreign country.

Before crossing the Andes, I recuperated at the home of
Juan and Patti Abadi in the hills above Santiago (above).

But something deeper was driving me, something others probably wouldn't understand. This was the trip of a lifetime for me, and I wasn't about to give up now. I needed to continue on and finish the journey in my own plane, on my own terms. I thought it better to get my plane up the coast of Brazil while I was in the flow of flying day in and day out, than to return with Galen months later.

Since Michael was joining me, Galen opted to explore farther south with Doug for a week or two, then return home on a commercial jet with all his climbing and camera gear, thus leaving me a much lighter plane to fly over the Andes and the Amazon. I wasn't at all keen on the idea of Galen leaving me when I was injured, but I didn't tell him so. I wanted to appear strong and independent like one of the guys, but it was more than that. I was at least as adamant about following through on my own personal venture as Galen seemed to be about joining Doug on a climb in Patagonia.

After Galen and Robert departed for opposite ends of the continent and I had time to myself, I thought about how, since Galen and I first got together in 1981, he had always been in a relentless pursuit to achieve the goals he set his sights on. I had sought him out just after I returned from directing a North Face catalog shoot in New Zealand, Australia, and Fiji. I wanted to publish stories by well-known adventurers who regularly used our products. The marketing department suggested I call Galen Rowell, a local mountaineer who was indebted to us because we'd supplied him with gear for several expeditions. They bet me that he would never let me use his name in our catalog without a big endorsement fee. I took the bet as a personal challenge and called him.

"I'll take you to lunch," I offered, hoping I could disarm him in person and entice him to write about one of our backpacks as well as a parka. People at work said climbers would do anything for a free meal. Though Galen was leaving for Tibet in two weeks, he agreed.

On the way back to my office, he asked me out. I turned him down. My rejection seemed to surprise him and he roared off in his loud Chevy V8 station wagon acting very flustered, which made me believe that I'd made the right decision. The next day he was back like a boomerang with a charming write-up of the parka. I was impressed by his promptness. Also, he seemed to write very well for a climber.

Galen showed up at my office every day after that, accompanied by a showcase of friends, and continued to ask me out. He was unstoppable. I turned him down for five days in a row until he invited me to a lecture that he was giving at the Marin Civic

Center. I went with a friend and sat in the front row, listening intently to Galen talk about the backcountry of China. The slides he showed were magnificent, but what impressed me most were his brilliant insights and his sensitivity to foreign cultures. Finally I was hooked.

After the show, my girlfriend decided to go home, so I joined Galen at a San Francisco bar for a glass of wine. I'd never met anyone like him. He was bursting with raw energy. All my life, my high energy had made me feel like a misfit. From my parents to my boyfriends and roommates, everyone had been telling me repeatedly to slow down. For the first time in my life, here was a man saying, "Yes! I love your energy!" He could relate to my fast pace and hard drive.

We talked until the bar manager kicked us out around midnight and continued our conversation out in the parking lot in Galen's car. We learned that each of us had been married once before. I'd married my high school civics teacher at 18; 7 years later, I had divorced. Galen married at 22, had 2 children, and divorced 14 years later. I had been single for 7 years and he for 4 years.

Galen was a splendid combination of brains and athletic ability. He didn't smoke or seem to have any vices, other than climbing. He was attractive and seemed very loyal. I was not interested in dating just for fun. If I dated someone, I considered him for marriage; there was nothing in between for me.

Then and there, we decided to go together. We were not drunk, we hadn't even kissed, and it wasn't lust. It seemed like magic plus a lot of logic, pure and simple. Why not? We were energetic, athletic, and attracted to each other. He was a climber and I worked in the outdoor industry. He was eight years older than me, but I liked older men. And we both hated dating.

"Let's just go for it!" Galen said, leaning forward to kiss me.

It would be a wild thing to do, but I was feeling wild, so I accepted. It never occurred to me to ask him what he did for a living. When we got to his home, I picked up a book on the mantle with his name on the cover. Speechless, I quickly thumbed through the pages of text and breathtaking photographs. Beneath that book were four more large-format books with his name.

"You wrote and photographed these?"

Galen gave me a sheepish smile and a nod.

My God! What had I just done? I hardly knew this man! He was famous. I couldn't wait to call all my girlfriends in the morning.

Within two weeks, Galen embarked on a trip to Tibet just as it was opening up to the Western world. He was the guide for the first American trekking group permitted to visit the Tibetan side of Mount Everest, and he had an assignment to photograph the area for *National Geographic*. He promised to write often. With each beautiful love letter from Tokyo, Beijing, Shekar, Shigatse, and Chengdu I fell more deeply in love. The days between letters passed like months. After the third week, he'd been gone longer than we'd been together. The letters kept my heart warm and my hope alive, but then two weeks passed without a word. I prepared myself for the worst. When I left for New York on business and still hadn't heard from him, I asked a friend to check my mail. When a letter finally came postmarked weeks before, I insisted she read it to me over the phone.

> *Dear Barbara,*   *Chinghai, Tibet*
> *They are calling breakfast, but I'm staying for my last chance to get a letter out before going into the Anyemachen mountains. The last three days have been boring, bouncing bus rides through overgrazed mountains that once were a "zoological garden" for tens of thousands of rare Tibetan animals. We did see Tibetan gazelles, an antelope at close range, and a fox, and we hope to see much more in the mountains.*
>
> *Oh Barbara, I miss you even more, and my heart is 1,000 percent yours. My fantasies might get this letter censored, so they'll have to wait until we're together again. I've tried to phone from two cities, but with problems at this end. I'm going to try again on the way out and either talk to you and giggle and say I love you, or at least leave a message.*
>
> *Your life sounds exciting, and I can't wait to share more of the simple joys with you. Now these two months are getting long for me, and I know they must be even longer for you, even with your jaunts to Washington, Alaska, and the East Coast.*
>
> *I, too, have forgotten exactly what it was like holding you in my arms, but I remember the sheer pleasure and wonder, and what we had and can have is worth more than any mountain or all the money in the world. I am ready and oh so willing.*
>
> *All my love,*
> *Galen*

I moved in with Galen after his return. As soon as the gloss wore off, we fought like cats and dogs. He got fan mail from designing women; I got jealous. He loved junk food; I liked health food. He liked red meat; I liked fish. I showered frequently; he didn't. In many ways, we were polar opposites.

In many other ways we were very much alike. I'd been a high achiever all through school and students picked on me because they thought I kissed up to teachers. But that was never my intention. I simply related better to adults than to other kids my own age. School-age games were painful. In seventh grade, girls in my Tri-Hi-Y locked me out of a slumber party in midwinter because I'd arrived late. I had no way to reach my parents, so I slept curled up in a ball, shivering all night in their garden until first light. When the winter sun peeked into view, I ran three miles to my house.

Before Galen became interested in climbing rocks, he collected them. He became so fascinated by mineralogy that he could sight-identify all the major minerals by the age of twelve. Professors and adult collectors were constantly calling his home to take him out on field trips. Kids his own age thought he was a nerd and began to pick on him intensely by sixth grade. Galen felt the need to hide his interior mental world from then on.

As we exposed ourselves to each other, we realized that we had finally found someone with whom we felt comfortable sharing our most outrageous aspirations. Each of us bore an intensity and high energy that complemented the other's.

Late one August night in the middle of a heated discussion, Galen asked me to marry him. We'd been together physically all of ten weeks.

"When?"

"How about tomorrow," he said. "On our way to Jackson Hole."

We were planning to drive there to have Galen photograph backpacks for The North Face under my direction. When I told my boss about Galen's marriage proposal, he agreed to have The North Face pay for everything except the license, so long as we got good catalog photos. We stopped in Elko, Nevada, and got married in cowboy boots by a justice of the peace on August 31, 1981. That evening, we arrived at Lupine Meadows in the Grand Tetons, where we pitched a North Face dome tent on Guides' Hill as invited guests of Kim Schmitz, the climbing friend whom Galen had suggested as the best model. Smack in the middle of the living area for professional mountain guides, we had little privacy on our wedding night. I was not a happy camper.

Going out to a local restaurant with Galen's climbing buddies was hardly the romantic, candlelit dining experience that I'd hoped for on my wedding night. It was more akin to dining in a pool of flaming testosterone, trying to stay afloat on a stick of dynamite. The fuse grew shorter by the minute and ignited when my husband of ten hours asked, "Would it be okay if I climb the North Face of the Grand with Kim tomorrow? It's his only day off. We'll be back by noon." He was syrupy sweet, promising they would bring back the photos that we needed for the catalog in spectacular dawn light.

How could I say "no" in front of everybody? I felt like I had been set up.

Galen snuck out of the tent around 3:30 in the morning. He wanted to get the photos and climb the face before the ice melted and rocks began to fall. I woke up alone, wondering if this marriage would work. The message that Galen was not about to take care of me was loud and clear.

Well after dawn, I slipped into a T-shirt and pair of jeans and headed off to the bathhouse to cleanse myself of my newlyweddedness. As I latched the door, one of the mountain guides began pounding on it and yelling from outside.

"This shower is for guides only!" he bellowed, ordering me to leave. I grabbed my things and ran back to my tent, mortified. At that moment, I hated climbers.

I'd had no preconceived notion of what married life with Galen would be like. Though up until now he had spent every available minute entertaining me, the day we returned from our honeymoon, he started writing *Mountains of the Middle Kingdom,* which was due in six months. He wrote from early morning to late at night and was too busy to spend time with me when I came home after work. I began to wander around the house feeling lost. A week after we were married, I felt more alone than I had ever felt when I was single. I had grown accustomed to having my nights and weekends filled by the attention of men. The honeymoon was over.

Our first year was a hard one, but life was certainly exciting, and I became determined to make our marriage work. Now, nine years later and alone with my thoughts in the guest room of Juan and Patti's Santiago home, I contemplated whether we were really right for each other. My emotions were mixed. Before Galen left to join Doug, I had felt as much like pushing him away as having him hold me in his arms and tell me everything would be okay.

On New Year's Day, I began making final preparations to cross the Andes. Patti kindly drove me to the Tobalaba Airport and waited while I topped off all four fuel

tanks. Before I finished my chores, a young pilot from a local flying club spotted my N number from the United States and asked where I was flying. "Qué valiente! We never fly over the Andes without another pilot. Sometimes it's so turbulent, the controls can be ripped out of your hands," he exclaimed, after hearing that I would be flying alone.

"Really?" I answered. "Do you know anyone who'd like to fly with me tomorrow?"

"Lo siento," he replied. "Not on such short notice."

"Adiós," I smiled, self-consciously holding my hand over my swollen lip as he trotted off toward his plane.

When I returned to Juan and Patti's house, I went to my room and cried myself to sleep. In the afternoon, I studied again what route to fly. The peaks between Santiago and Argentina rise to over 20,000 feet immediately, so no flight path east looked easy, but choosing the least of the evils would take me almost directly over the spot where the rugby team had crashed and the survivors had eaten each other, as explicitly described in the bestseller, *Alive*.

I took Doug's advice and called his friend and old ski-racing buddy, Hernán Boher, a Chilean businessman who owned numerous aircraft. Even though he had

Directly behind Santiago, Andean peaks
rise to over 20,000 feet (above).

many pilots who flew for him, he was an accomplished pilot himself. Doug had described him as a bold and flamboyant risk-taker who had become a wealthy industrialist, but his attitude toward flying over the Andes was sobering.

"Check the difference in barometric pressure between Santiago and Mendoza," he told me. "Don't go if the spread is more than ten points. Normally we file IFR, but fly only in VFR conditions. Take Victor way UA305 direct to Ezeiza," he instructed.

He then turned me over to one of his Chilean commercial pilots who added, "As soon as you take off, climb at your best rate and tell the controller you're climbing to 21,000, as required. Turn your transponder off and make the crossing at 14,000 through the first low pass to the south. Mendoza Radio may order you to land there, as the first point of entry into Argentina, but by filing IFR you're legal to go on to Buenos Aires. Tell them they're 'breaking up.' Say 'can't understand,' and add 'flying as filed.' Then turn your radio off, too."

He explained that this was a common maneuver among the flying community in Chile. The controllers know exactly what is going on and keep calling the pilots for frequent altitude and position reports. The pilots stay busy throughout the flight inventing where their plane should really be.

I found this cowboy style of flight more amusing than enticing, yet after considering the best route of flight over the Andes, it made perfect sense to me. Santiago sits beneath a wall of mountains to the east. Some of the highest ones pierce the heavens at altitudes ranging from 17,000 to over 22,000 feet. Given the height and closeness of these monsters in relation to my departure airport, I would need to spend forever climbing to get over them. Querying local pilots about their home turf is always a good idea, and I was unable to come up with a better plan to cross the Andes in a single-engine plane.

Before hanging up, I asked Hernán if he would go with me. He answered, "Sorry, I don't have the time right now. I'm already going to Buenos Aires later in the week for a morning meeting, so I need to go by jet."

"Do you know anyone who could accompany me to Buenos Aires?"

Hernán thought of a friend's teenage son, who would appreciate catching a ride to his family's vacation spot in Argentina. He said he could arrange everything, so I instantly agreed.

The next day, the kid showed up at the airport with his mother and grandmother, who looked me over to see whether or not they could trust me to take care of him, which put an additional onus on me. I thought: I'm injured, I'm flying as a single pilot across the Andes, and now I have the additional responsibility of taking a young boy on a flight that would be a personal challenge for me even on one of my best days. I felt sick inside, and I wanted to warn his mom not to let him fly with me, but I couldn't bring myself to talk to a complete stranger about a fear so deep. And I still wanted the company.

After his family bid us good-bye, I flew a short hop over to the international airport, from where I would need to depart after filing an international flight plan. It was only 8 nautical miles or so, but it gave me enough of a view to get a good look at some nasty midlevel clouds already building toward the mountains. After the meteorological department confirmed that the weather over the Andes was indeed turning really bad, I didn't fly any farther. I just paid for the kid's long ride home for the night in an expensive taxi.

Before departure, I had not been able to locate more oxygen at either the national or international airport. I had just enough left in my tank to fly over 12,000 feet for brief periods of time, but not enough to make the much higher flight that the controllers would require. Now it was even more imperative that I fly as low as possible in case my remaining oxygen were to run out. So when we went back out the next day, I decided to try what I'd been told about faking my departure the South American way.

The plan began like clockwork. As I climbed past 12,000 feet, I put the cannula in my nose and turned the oxygen on. As I climbed higher, the boy didn't say a word, but looked as if he expected me to put him on oxygen, too. I felt guilty that I didn't want to share it with him, but I couldn't take the chance of running out. After running short on oxygen over Peru, I was well aware of my slowed thinking and reduced powers of concentration when I wasn't using it full time. It was more important that I stay clearheaded and keep us both alive than it was for me to take care of him for the moment. Besides, I wasn't required by law to provide him with oxygen until we reached 14,000 feet. Reminding myself of the FAA regulation gave me far more comfort than it would have given him had I quoted him the law.

On a clear morning with a tailwind of over 120 knots, the kid and I shot through the Andes into Argentina registering 240 knots on the gauge. For the moment, the views of snowy peaks and glaciers were too wildly savage to appreciate. Though there were no footprints in the air to mark who had been here before me, I felt certain that Saint-Exupéry must have flown this route in the thirties during his pioneering

flights to deliver the southern mail by air. His book, *Wind, Sand and Stars,* has a poignant description of being blown around by the winds of the southern Andes: "Hanging on with all the power in my engines, face to the coast, face to that wind where each gap in the teeth of the range sent forth a stream of air like a long reptile, I felt as if I were clinging to the tip of a monstrous whip."

Luckily for me, I was flying with the wind, not against it. After we crossed the mountains, I was thankful to find smooth air. I immediately descended over the flat, grassy pampas. The transition was so abrupt that I felt like Dorothy arriving back home in Kansas.

As we cruised over the vast, empty plains that stretched to the Atlantic, out of the blue came a radio call from a Chilean airliner: "Noviembre Siete Tres Cinco Lima Yankee. LanChile cambio."

"LanChile. Cinco Lima Yankee adelante."

The airline captain said he had a passenger on board who wanted to speak to me. "Hi Barbara. How's the flight going?" It was Hernán on his way to Buenos Aires.

"Everything is great. Thanks," I said, tickled at the surprise call.

As I was crossing the Andes, Doug and Galen spent
a stormy week beneath the Fitz Roy Range (above)
without doing any climbs.

"Let's meet for dinner," Hernán added, "I'll send a car to pick you up."

On the final descent to the airport, the plane bounced about slightly in turbulence. I thought nothing of it, but my young passenger turned green and vomited. He sat there with his head hung low, staring at his mess on the floor.

After landing and taxiing to the terminal, my airsick passenger bounced back to life and bid me adiós while I stayed behind and cleaned up the plane. When I entered the building, a young, well-dressed man greeted me and said "Barbara?"

"Yes."

"I am Mr. Hernán Boher's chauffeur. He sent me to take you to your hotel," he said, gently relieving me of my heavy flight bag. "Señor Boher would like to take you and your companion out to dinner this evening. He will come to the hotel at seven o'clock if that is okay with you."

The driver helped me through customs and then took me to a medical clinic to have my stitches taken out before taking me to the hotel. It cost more to have my stitches removed in five minutes in Argentina than it had for all the surgeon's time to put them in, in Chile.

Michael met me in the hotel, as planned. Seeing his fresh and familiar face filled me with joy. It had been days since I'd spoken English with anyone, so I reveled in my own language as I told Michael every detail about my trip so far and about the rafting accident. He listened eagerly, yet stoically, and when I was finished, he shared his own tale about a frighteningly wild taxi ride from the airport into town. I'd already forgotten how tame and regulated the highways were back home in the United States. Driving on any South American highway is challenging enough, but driving in Buenos Aires, where four-fifths of the population is of Italian descent, is like making a wrong turn into the middle of the Grand Prix course at Monza.

In the evening, Hernán took Michael and me to an elegant restaurant, where we all shared flying stories over dinner. When I learned that he had flown to the United States many times, I probed him for as much information as I could get.

"Barbara, what are you doing?" he asked me during dinner. "Do you want to die? If I were making the flight right now, I wouldn't fly through Brazil. I'd go back the way you came—up the western coast where it's drier. You're heading into Brazil at the height of the rainy season."

As I gained altitude above Santiago,
rows of icy peaks came into view (right).

Spitting Pennies

XVII

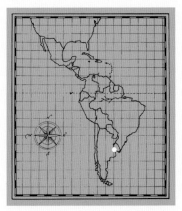

Though northern Argentina was in the middle of a good weather pattern, Michael and I got up before dawn to get an early jump on the day. After what Hernán had said about the weather, I felt uneasy about going through Brazil, which had been Doug's idea, and though Doug wasn't with me, I was still following his plan. Right now, I couldn't envision doing anything else. Rearranging flight permissions might be too big a hassle to deal with while trying to maintain the momentum to get my airplane home.

After a light breakfast at the hotel, we took a taxi to the airport and immediately filled out the required paperwork for making an international departure. As we chased down each of the separate official stamps for our flight plan and general declaration through dark and lonely corridors, I explained the crazy process to Michael. He had come here for the experience of flying in a foreign country, but before we were in the air on our first day, he was already finding the red tape somewhat irritating.

After takeoff, I navigated directly to a VOR named Capitán Corbeta C.A. Curbelo, a mouthful to say to flight controllers. The huge cosmopolitan city of Buenos Aires, with over 3 million inhabitants, ended abruptly on the banks of the Río de la Plata, the river that divides Argentina from Uruguay. Our direct route would take us 250 nautical miles over choppy water as we angled across its wide delta past the point where its muddy waters spill into the blue South Atlantic Ocean. As I looked down at the merging colors, I felt deeply relieved to have Michael sitting beside me in the copilot's seat. His enthusiasm for flying and his desire for adventure was just what I needed to keep me going after the accident on the Bio Bio. I felt distinctly more confident with another pilot onboard.

Michael is the son of Bob Craig, a well-known Colorado climber, skier, and educator. I first met Michael in 1983 on a trek to Tibet to visit the base camp at the

Flying my Cessna 206 on instruments just above the clouds (left).

north side of Mount Everest. He was a teenager going to see his father, who was the expedition leader of a team of Americans trying to reach the summit, without oxygen, via the unclimbed Tibetan side of the West Ridge. Galen was the climbing leader.

Michael was trekking with his mother and his older sister, Jennifer, who was my tent mate. She and I became good friends. When I visited her several years later on their family ranch in Aspen, I peeked into Michael's room and saw a huge poster of an aircraft cockpit on his wall. After Jennifer told me that he had never been in a small plane, I offered to take him flying around the Maroon Bells, a group of 14,000-foot peaks that rise above Aspen. He accepted and had such a great time that we went together to inquire about flight instruction for him.

Soon after I had taken Michael on that first flight in the early eighties, he became a professional charter pilot and now had far more airtime than I did. Initially, he towed glider pilots out of the Aspen airport before working for a charter service to fly tourists from Las Vegas to remote rivers for rafting. Within a few years, he had 2,000 hours; I had just over 700 hours by the time he joined me in Brazil. His quiet, easygoing style reminded me of a young Jimmy Stewart, and I was counting on him to support me on the flight through Brazil more than either of us knew.

Buenos Aires, Argentina (above).

When we crossed the border, a little over three hours after departing Ezeiza Airport in Argentina, the first Brazilian controller radioed me in perfect English, although he used Portuguese with most of the local pilots. Before leaving home, friends had told me not to worry about speaking Portuguese in Brazil. Everyone said that my Spanish would suffice. The two languages are similar, but from the radio dialogue I was now beginning to overhear between Brazilians, there were clearly major differences. Compared to the pure, soft vowels I was accustomed to hearing in Spanish, the complex chords of Portuguese sounded as different to me as Russian from English. I found it impossible to understand who was coming, who was going, or if someone was flying nearby. I didn't like being out of the communication loop.

Michael and I were intrigued by the beaches, lagoons, and lowlands passing beneath us. The landscape looked so much friendlier than the rugged Andes I'd just crossed. Being able to see a country that I'd only read about had me forgetting all my physical ailments after the rafting accident.

By the time we approached the sprawling city of Porto Alegre, I'd been flying 4 hours and 20 minutes, but it had been such an easy flight in such perfect weather that I didn't want to stop. Unfortunately, I had no choice about putting down at the first port of entry in Brazil. I was required to land at Porto Alegre and check in before going on.

As soon as I landed, a man in a van met me on the tarmac and began asking me questions that I couldn't understand. Eventually he made it clear that he wanted to know how long I was staying. "It depends on the weather," I answered in Spanish.

He didn't seem to know what I was saying, so he handed me a form to fill out that asked me for the date and time of my departure and for my next destination. Since I didn't know yet, I made it up.

We were directed to immigration, where I went first and was immediately passed on through. Then Michael stepped up to the officer's cubicle.

"May I see your general declaration?" the officer asked.

"My what?" Michael said, looking confused.

"Your general declaration," the officer repeated. "You are the pilot, no?"

"No sir. I am her copilot, sir," Michael answered softly.

"She is the pilot?"

"Yes sir," Michael said, as I walked up and handed over the form.

The befuddled look on the immigration officer's face melted as he let out a hearty laugh and addressed me, "Comandante!"

I smiled. The officer gave me a big toothy smile back. While I went upstairs to get a flight permit for Brazil, Michael stayed with our suitcases. No one in the flight operations office spoke English or Spanish, making it difficult to understand the incessant questioning that followed. Two men in their twenties demanded to know the tiniest details, such as what the C meant between Barbara and Rowell on my pilot's license. I explained that it was for Cushman, my maiden name, using my Spanish to say, "nombre de mi padre."

When they began studying my medical certificate, I thought I might be in real trouble as they started pointing to the expiration date. It appeared to them that it had expired. I knew it had not. I tried to keep my Spanish very simple as I explained a difficult concept. I had taken a Class B medical examination required for commercial pilots only to know if I would qualify to become a commercial pilot later. Since I was strictly a private pilot, not a commercial pilot, the expiration date did not pertain to me. Class B medicals expire in one year and default to a Class C, good for two years, for private pilots. Since I was not a commercial pilot, my medical certificate was current. That detail alone took about thirty minutes of questions and answers to get across.

Michael and I took a taxi to a cheap downtown hotel that had offered an unusual view out our window of shacks built by very poor people, blanketing the tops of high-rise buildings.

After quickly washing up, we went out to get a bite to eat. I felt frustrated not being able to recognize most of the items on the menu. I was hoping to eat chicken, but anything close to the Spanish word pollo was nowhere to be found. I did not have a Portuguese dictionary to tell me that chicken is called frango in Brazil. We both ended up eating something quite different from what we thought we'd ordered.

Early in the morning, I woke up with pain shooting from my elbow to my wrist in my injured left arm. The pain was most intense where the stitches had been removed the day before, and I was surprised that it still throbbed so much. I would have sworn it was broken, were it not for the X-rays that had been taken. Even so, I immediately sprang out of bed to check the sky. Slots of bright blue were barely visible between all the high buildings, and we headed out as soon as possible.

On our drive to the airport I scanned for any evidence of bad weather, but didn't see a cloud anywhere in sight. We appeared to be having a streak of good luck, with two days of back-to-back good weather along a coast known for its high rainfall.

Before we'd left the hotel, we'd quickly studied the map and made a tentative plan to fly all the way to Rio de Janeiro. The flight would take close to 6 hours. That was right at my limit, since with normal fuel consumption it would leave me just one extra hour in case I couldn't land at Rio.

At the flight operations desk we asked for a weather briefing, but it was virtually impossible to understand. Michael and I came away believing we would have good VFR weather conditions all the way to Rio. We hadn't heard anything to the contrary, but we both admitted to each other that we weren't really sure. On such a beautiful morning, good flying weather seemed a pretty safe bet.

Just before takeoff, I was informed that I owed a $125 landing fee that had to be paid in cash in U.S. dollars. Brazil is a huge country, nearly the size of the United States and the fifth biggest in the world. Its coastline alone is almost 5,000 miles long. To pay such a high fee every time I touched down on a runway was going to drain me of most of the cash I had left. This was not like Chile, where I was charged a small fee that allowed me to land anywhere for a month, or like Ecuador, where I was charged a high fee, but only had to land once. Since this trip had already cost me much more than I had budgeted for, I felt pressure to stretch each flight by filling the long-range tip tanks and going as far as possible.

Michael was itching to fly. Since my arm was hurting, I asked if he wanted to do the flight to Rio. He seemed pleased and immediately said yes. But I instantly felt uncomfortable. The idea of switching places with him in the cockpit made me uneasy, if not a little insecure. I'd never flown my own plane from the right seat, where everything would be reversed and the primary instruments would not be right in front of me. I'd never even ridden in the right seat of my own plane. If something happened and I needed to take back the controls to land or do a takeoff, I would need to control the throttle with my left hand, which I'd never done.

Michael said he was checked out to fly from the right seat and was perfectly comfortable doing so, since he'd often flown right seat as a commercial copilot. We agreed that I would stay in the pilot's seat and he would fly from the right-hand copilot's seat.

From the time we arrived at the airport, it took us over an hour to complete the required steps that I had now come to accept as the normal way of life for a foreign pilot who simply wants to fly in another country.

Finally, a man in a white van gave us a ride to the plane. No sooner had we settled into the cockpit than the man in the van returned. He parked in front of my plane, blocking our departure. At first I thought that I might have left something behind and he was just doing me a kind deed, so I got out to see what was up. Using a combination of body gestures and words he ordered me into his van and drove me to the terminal. I couldn't imagine what was wrong now. I obediently followed him up a set of stairs to a business office, where a woman behind a counter said I had stayed thirty minutes beyond the time I had written on the form when I'd first arrived from Argentina. She demanded an additional 50 cents in cash for parking. I didn't have change and neither did she. Since the fee was for parking, rather than landing or permits, Brazilian currency was okay. I went downstairs and broke a large bill to buy a soda and returned with the proper amount. After I paid, I started to head out the door, but my driver made me wait until the receptionist typed out a receipt in triplicate.

I had to laugh at the absurdity of it all. I wondered if, by the time I got back to the plane, I'd be marched back in again because I hadn't paid for another thirty minutes of parking. Rules like this, where the government had just spent far more in gas and employee time to chase me down than the 50 cents they collected from me, gave me some idea as to why the economy of Brazil was floundering. It seemed so ridiculous to take 30 minutes of several peoples' time to collect a measly 50 cents, but I'd seen the same kind of mentality at work in places like India and Nepal. The poorest countries seem to require the most paperwork.

When Michael took off down the runway flying from the right seat, he seemed immediately at ease with my aircraft. I was impressed. He didn't miss any procedure, from closing the cowl flaps upon reaching cruise altitude to adjusting the fuel.

Though it felt odd not being at the controls, I was happy to have the opportunity to gaze at length at the land as he flew us over rural farm country. I kept the map on my lap and marked down the time as we passed notable landmarks. After we reached the coastline, I found the blue water and white sandy beaches so enchanting that I scrawled "pretty here" in many places on my map, hoping to return someday with Galen to see them from the ground. They have a distinct Mediterranean look, like parts of the Riviera.

As we passed over the classic city of Florianópolis, a beach resort half on an island and half on the mainland, clouds began forming overhead. I made a radio call for an update on the weather en route to Rio. Neither of us could understand the controller's response. I called again. When the controller responded the second time with something that was still impossible to understand, Michael and I looked at each other and shrugged.

Michael continued flying along. The thin layer of clouds above us began to thicken gradually. With the shoreline relatively straight and easy to make out, I felt only slightly concerned as he was forced to fly offshore now and then to skirt the occasional rain shower.

As we continued north along the coast, Michael dropped down to look at a beach. He shared his fantasy with me about landing on one someday. That took me by surprise. It wasn't something I would have come up with on my own. I'd never daydreamed about landing on any surface other than a paved or gravel runway simply for the adventure of it. I knew that there were pilots who regularly landed on beaches in Baja and on tundra in Alaska, using special oversize tires, but the furthest my fantasies had taken me was to imagine landing on a country road in an emergency. Adding more risk to a flight than was already inherent wasn't something I would intentionally go out of my way to do.

Michael, however, had some experience landing clients on riverbanks as a charter pilot in Utah. His fantasy seemed to me to be a guy thing, so I just replied, "Oh yeah. That would be really cool."

As the rain showers became more frequent, I calmed myself by thinking about what Doug had told me while we were scud-running in Colombia: All you have to do if you get into trouble in bad weather on the coast is turn toward the ocean and climb up to an altitude high enough to orient yourself to the nearest VOR. Then you contact flight center, get on an instrument flight plan, and continue flying IFR to your destination. His comment had stuck with me. It sounded like a great backup plan in case of an emergency.

As we flew along the wild coast, just abeam the inland megacity of São Paulo, the rain showers worsened. I asked Michael if he thought we should climb up and file IFR. "Not yet. It still looks okay ahead," he said

The weather continued to deteriorate, and I began feeling more uncomfortable. I turned to Michael and asked again, "Don't you think we should go IFR now?"

"No, no. I can still see," he said confidently.

This made me feel slightly uncertain about what to do next. On the one hand, if Michael didn't think we should file an instrument flight plan, I would defer to his judgment, since he had many more hours flying on instruments than I had. On the other, I had a gut feeling that we should just bite the bullet, call a controller, and request an instrument clearance. But having already experienced a vacuum-pump failure on this trip that affected my primary instruments on the approach into Lima, my confidence in my aircraft and myself had become seriously eroded. I felt more intimidated about flying IFR now than before coming on this trip. Before I'd insist that we fly in the clouds, Michael would need to appear confident about going IFR.

When I checked the map, a mountainous region just south of Rio de Janeiro had me concerned. The last thing I wanted now was to have a flight controller vector us inland over high terrain and have the vacuum pump fail again, only this time over mountains. I was also concerned about the chance of thunderstorms later in the day over hot, hilly terrain, where the tropical air would be mechanically lifted by the land.

Though I hadn't admitted this to anyone, I believed that the only reason I'd survived landing at Lima was due to the fact that I was able to descend safely under the clouds out over the ocean until I saw the water. This prevented me from hitting any unseen obstacles, such as hills or radio towers. I thought our chances of making it to Rio would be better if we continued VFR and stayed along the coast over water.

As the weather worsened, Michael was forced to descend below 300 feet to stay clear of lowering clouds. Almost instantly, the scattered rain turned to heavy showers. I turned around and looked at the weather behind us, thinking perhaps we should do a 180-degree turn and get out of this miserable stuff, but the rain had closed in behind us. When I tried to see out the front, the rain was coming down in sheets so heavy that I could barely hear Michael talk, let alone see. Suddenly, our forward visibility was virtually gone. Michael instinctively moved very close to the land so we could keep visual contact with it, like keeping the Queen of Hearts in your hand during a game of hearts so that you don't get handed her by surprise later.

In quickly trying to decide a course of action, I noted our time, which placed us more than three-quarters of the way to Rio on a six-hour leg. Our only safe option would be to employ Doug's emergency plan and turn toward the ocean, climb up until we had radio contact, and go IFR, but when I looked at our directional gyro to see what compass heading to give Michael, something was very wrong.

The DG indicated we were flying south. That seemed impossible. We had been heading northwest. No sooner had I said, "Michael, something is wrong with our DG," than I knew what had happened. This time it wasn't a vacuum-pump failure. We had turned into a bay, and we really *were* going south. The straight beaches were gone, and all we could see were steep rock walls covered by dense Atlantic forest.

From our large-scale flight map I was aware of a few islands just offshore, towering as high as 4,000 feet, but I couldn't see any of them. A regional map would have shown me that Angra Bay has 365 islands, one for each day of the year, as the locals like to say. At 15 nautical miles to the inch, my map's wiggly rough lines failed to show the true nature of what were in fact a series of miniature Norwegian fjords cutting into steep terrain within Angra Bay. Only a few of the biggest ones, up to 5 miles long, were depicted on our map. Flying too low to pick up any VOR station left us no choice but to follow the coastline precisely.

Clouds continued to force us lower until Michael leveled out at 175 feet over the ocean to better see the shoreline, but that did little to help our forward visibility. Land kept appearing out of nowhere off our nose, and Michael was repeatedly forced to make steep turns to miss it. Minute by minute, it was getting harder to see anything.

Michael was barely keeping up with the zigzagging shoreline, so I suggested that he slow to 90 knots. Though I was impressed with his ability to maneuver the plane in these conditions, I wasn't certain he could continue without making a fatal mistake. This was no video game—both of our lives were in Michael's hands. Doing steep turns so low to the water and slow would be dangerous in good visibility, but in torrential rains, the danger was infinitely greater. Every time he was forced into a steep turn as a last-ditch effort to avoid hitting the mountainous shoreline, the plane came imminently close to stalling. We were too low to the ground to recover from a stall before hitting the ocean, but to fly any higher would put us solidly in the clouds where we'd lose all visual contact with the land. To fly any faster would mean we'd hit something for sure. Michael had no option other than to just gut it out and hope for the best.

At one point he warned, "I think we might be flying around an island."

"No. I'm absolutely certain we are not circling an island," I told him. I'd been watching the coast like a hawk. If there was one thing I did know, it was that we had never left the shoreline and were still following the mainland. Just to reassure myself, I glanced down at the ONC map sitting on my lap. I felt too panicky to look away for long, so I quickly looked up again just in time to see terrain coming up fast off the nose. We were headed straight at a green wall of trees.

"Michael, make a steep turn now!" I yelled. Forest filled our windshield.

Michael abruptly made a hard right turn just in time to avoid hitting the side of a mountain. Once we were parallel to the slope, he turned back to the left to avoid losing track of the shore. He was cutting S turns like an Olympic slalom skier. Even though he was obviously getting tired, it was apparent that he could not hand the controls over to me. It would be difficult for me get up to speed in time, and I didn't want to chance it. The best I could do was to keep looking in front of us and advise Michael of terrain he couldn't see, while he kept his focus just off our left wing tip to miss vertical cliffs covered in deep forest. We both kept looking for any reasonably level place to land: a beach, a parking lot, anything.

We finally got to the point where we were so close to hitting something at any moment that there was no way that I dared check the map again. Michael glanced out over the ocean and suggested the unthinkable: "We might need to ditch the plane."

"No way," I countered. I was clear about that. With about an hour of fuel left, we still had a chance in the air, even if we didn't know where we were, and it was a chance I wanted to take. Ditching the plane in the ocean would be the last thing we'd do, and then only if the engine quit and we had no other choice. Of course, it was my plane, so it was harder for me to conceive of losing it. But I wasn't thinking about the monetary loss. I couldn't handle the thought of being in deep water crashing against a rugged shoreline. It gave me flashbacks about hitting the wall in the Bio Bio. I wanted out of this alive without swimming.

"You're doing an excellent job, Michael," I said to try to calm him as well as myself. He was doing really well handling the plane, given how desperate things had become. "Just keep breathing," I added, after observing him hold his breath.

I made a call on our last radio frequency in hopes of talking with someone. When nobody answered I dialed in the emergency frequencies in both my radio and transponder.

"This is November Seven Three Five Lima Yankee, over," I said, stopping short of saying anything descriptive. I wasn't sure what more I should say. I didn't want to say something that would upset Michael more than he already was, and I didn't really expect anyone to help us. I just wanted my family to know where we were in case we didn't make it. No one replied. I tried several more times, but still no one answered. Finally, I decided to try the frequency that commercial airliners might be using. I heard a faint male voice. It sounded Brazilian. After trying to make contact with no response, I went ahead and declared an emergency anyway, just in case someone out there could hear me.

My mouth was so dry it felt like it was stuffed with cotton. I had lost track of how long we'd been flying and I had no idea where we were. I kept hoping to see a skyscraper or the famous statue of Christ for which Rio is known. I believed we were somewhere on the outskirts of Rio, but I wasn't sure. All I could see were sparsely inhabited, rocky cliffs and forest. I even wondered if we'd somehow passed beyond Rio without knowing it.

My heart pounded so hard that my chest began to ache. To follow every nook and cranny of this coast would run us out of fuel. We had crossed beyond hope to the other side, where the only uncertainty that now remained was the way in which we would crash.

I'd heard pilots talk about spitting pennies—when you're so afraid that you get the taste of copper in your mouth and you think you're going to die. It was clear that Michael thought he was going to die, and I thought so, too. All I knew to do was to stay calm and keep saying in as many ways as possible, "Michael, you're doing a good job. Keep flying the plane." His only job, for now and what might be forever, was to keep ahead of this wildly curving terrain. We seemed to be going very fast, even though, for a plane, we were going very, very slow. Time had lost its meaning. Nothing existed outside of Michael, me, and the storm, except for brief flashes about my family.

Suddenly, a miracle appeared. I screamed, "Michael! There's a runway right below us!"

*Storm south of Rio along the Atlantic
Coast of Brazil (above).*

WHERE'S ANGRA?

XVIII

*W*hen I first spotted the little airstrip nestled at the end of the bay, we were virtually on top of it. I was certain that we were too close to get set up for landing without circling first. But Michael didn't want to chance losing sight of the airfield. He had one shot at making the approach and landing. If he missed, we'd be back in the clouds that were obscuring the mountainous coastline; if that happened, then ditching the plane would have been a safer option than flying blind into rapidly rising terrain. In those moments, I prayed that he would get us down in one piece.

He instantly chopped the power, lowered full flaps, and began a steep left turn in an attempt to aim the plane down the runway's centerline. Each second mattered if Michael was going to touch down in time to get stopped before the end of what appeared to be a very short runway. The fact that we were already 800 feet lower than the normal altitude for entering an airport pattern—just 175 feet over the water—was now working in our favor.

I watched anxiously as we left the flat ocean and flew directly inland toward the towering mountains that we'd tried so hard to avoid. To my great relief, Michael touched down gracefully beyond the start of the runway and managed to stop before the end. Under enormous pressure, he had flown the plane onto the ground with professional certitude. I was glad that he was at the controls.

After the plane stopped, we sat there in the cockpit, speechless. As we looked at each other, Michael began slowly shaking his head back and forth while I started to tremble. My feelings of relief and disbelief were overpowering—a rush of conflicting emotions about how unbelievably lucky we were to be alive and how stupid we'd been to have gotten into this situation at all.

Michael finally broke the silence: "I'm so sorry."

"Don't be sorry, Michael. It's not your fault," I said to cut him off from further apology. He'd done a remarkable job keeping it together and remaining focused

*Had we missed the runway at Angra dos Reis, we would
have flown into these shipping cranes in the next bay (left).*

225

while we flew through hellish conditions. Now his eyes seemed to reflect a deep sadness mixed with astonishment. I understood how he must have been feeling, but I could only watch helplessly as he looked away and turned his head toward the floor, appearing more lost now than he had been in the air.

Though we were safely on the ground, we'd journeyed to a world beyond this one. We were both returning as changed individuals. We would need some time to understand how deeply changed we truly were.

I sensed that the whole misadventure was my fault because I had not trusted myself when the weather turned bad. I should have insisted that we climb up and go on instruments while we still had the ocean in sight, but instead I'd allowed Michael to continue into the rain showers without a viable alternative in case things got worse, as they did. What was wrong with me? Why did I fold so easily around certain people? Was it them? Was it me? Was it always when I was around men? What in the hell was it? I'd come so close in Lima, and then there was the Bio Bio. What was going on here? Though I'd asked myself these questions before, I'd never taken the time to pursue the answers. After coming so close to dying today, I needed to face them now. Continuing to ignore such deeply ingrained behaviors was bound to lead me into tragedy. But if personal examination of my innermost workings had intimidated me before, such deep self-evaluation now looked like a walk on the beach compared to the flight I had just survived.

I didn't know all the reasons I trusted other people more than myself, and perhaps I didn't need to know, especially if I was truly able to learn from my mistakes and change my ways. But I did need to arrive at some basic understanding of what made me tick to avoid falling victim to the same kind of situation over and over again. The bottom line was perfectly clear: it was high time to stop looking outside of myself for my answers.

Though it seemed that I let myself be unduly influenced by certain men's opinions, that wasn't always the case. Strong-willed older women often had a similar effect on me, intimidating me from following my best intuitions. Throughout my childhood, both my parents had barked, "Because I said so!" anytime I questioned them. "Children are to be seen and not heard!" was another way I was silenced into submission.

Looking to others for advice and answers had been my strategy to gain their approval. I grew up with a deep need to be liked by everyone as my navy family moved from place to place and I was constantly having to make new friends.

Carrying that over to aviation, I had been contorting myself in order to be liked—perhaps dead, but liked.

Even at this moment, I knew today's flight would forever change me. I would never forget the terror, and I would never forget my resolution to drop my old ways. The hole in my gums would always be a reminder in the event I should forget.

As Michael taxied off the runway, the rain cut loose even more. It was impossible to imagine it coming down any harder. I'd been in Asian monsoons and in Costa Rica during the rainy season, but I'd never seen it rain so heavily. When Michael shut down the engine, the expected silence never came. Instead, it sounded as if our wings were being strafed by machine-gun fire from above. The rat-tat-tatting was so loud that it made me wonder if the paint was being chipped off all the exposed surfaces. We weren't in any hurry to get out of the plane.

As we continued to sit in our cocoon, I spotted an old man dressed in tattered shorts emerging from the jungle onto the airstrip. He ran barefoot toward us, carrying a purple umbrella, talking a mile a minute as he neared the plane. I couldn't understand a word he was saying, but he clearly wasn't congratulating us on Michael's smooth landing.

I watched with curiosity as the man moved right up under the wing, put his face next to my window, and lectured us. He was speaking Portuguese, but he made himself perfectly clear: we were totally crazy to be flying in weather like this. He carried on about rocks and mountains, alluded to God, set the umbrella down beside the plane, and ran away.

"Where the hell are we?" Michael asked.

"It says Angra dos Reis over there," I said, pointing to a tiny ramshackle terminal building. Neither of us had any idea where Angra was. We didn't know if we had flown past Rio or hadn't reached it yet. I was too exhausted to try to find it on the map.

We got out of the plane, grabbed the purple umbrella, and made our way through the rain in the direction we'd seen our welcoming committee disappear. The warm air was permeated with potent tropical smells, a mixture of moist earth, decaying vegetation, sweet flowers, and the slightly acrid scent of wet concrete. At the far end of the runway, a short path through dripping palm branches and tall grass brought us to a run-down, whitewashed shack with blue shutters covering louvered windows. The whole structure was not much bigger than my bedroom.

As soon as we stepped onto the unfinished cement porch, the old man motioned us inside. His name was Aloisio, and he introduced us to his wife. She had a sweet demeanor—very open and warm—as we exchanged hellos, but there was no mistaking her amazement at the appearance of two foreigners arriving in the midst of such a violent storm. She seemed as surprised to have us as uninvited guests as we were to be standing in her living room.

Even if I had no idea where I was, I felt ever so relieved to be out of the airplane and back on firm ground inside a warm and dry house.

Speaking to the couple in Spanish, I tried to explain what had just happened to us, but I wasn't sure if they understood much of what I was saying. Perhaps words weren't that necessary, since they both appeared to comprehend that we'd just been through something terrifying.

When the old woman offered us a drink, I took a taste of a watered-down tropical fruit juice that I could not identify. Though I was concerned it might be contaminated, I continued taking small sips so as not to offend my hostess.

To hear a telephone ring in such a humble dwelling took me by surprise. The old man answered it and spoke briefly with someone before motioning for me to take the call. I wondered who could possibly be phoning me in a shack in the middle of nowhere, especially since even I wasn't aware of my whereabouts. "Hello," I said tentatively, half-expecting to hear God on the other end of the line.

"You flew right over my house," a man said in nearly perfect English. "I wanted to be sure that you made it to the runway okay. You know you are very, very lucky to be alive."

The caller explained that he was a pilot. When we flew so close to his home in the storm, he knew that we were in dire straits. I thanked him for his concern and brought up one of my own: since I wasn't where I was supposed to be, perhaps the authorities would begin searching for me. Before he hung up, the thoughtful pilot offered to translate my worry to my host, who immediately called someone on my behalf. Overhearing parts of the conversation, it sounded as if I could be in some sort of trouble.

When Michael and I finally checked the map, we saw that we were still 65 nautical miles south of our original destination, Galaeão International Airport in Rio de Janeiro. But that was by a direct line of flight that would have taken us inland over mountains. Angra had no fuel for sale and we had only about 20 gallons left— barely over an hour's flight time with no reserves. The map showed that the last hour and twenty minutes of our flight along the tortuous coast should have taken just eight minutes in a direct line of flight across Angra Bay. If we'd missed this runway and managed to keep on flying all the bays along the coastline toward Rio without hitting anything, we would have run out of fuel.

Though the rain had tapered off, neither of us considered hopping right back in the plane and trying to fly on to Rio. We were so exhausted and so low on fuel that it made better sense to get a good night's rest and wait until morning before trying to continue.

We returned to the plane, loaded our small day packs, and began walking away from the airfield along a narrow road strewn with barking dogs, people of all ages on bicycles, and groups of shoeless children playing ball on the wet pavement. We were so turned around that we didn't know on which side of the road to stand to catch a bus into Rio. Spotting a sign that said Escola Municipal, we walked onto the playground and were lucky enough to find a teacher who spoke some English. When she said the bus ride would take nearly three hours, I thought she must be kidding, but we learned that the road to Rio, until it neared the city, followed the same sort of convoluted coastline we'd just flown. We immediately changed our plans and decided to spend the night in the nearby port town of Angra dos Reis. She pointed the way to a bus stop on the main two-lane highway.

We weren't waiting long under the corrugated metal roof of the bus stop when Michael and I heard the whop-whopping sound of helicopter blades not too far away. As we scanned the sky looking for the craft, it flew right overhead, hovered momentarily, then disappeared in the direction of the airport.

"I bet it's the police looking for us, Michael," I said, feeling guilty about the morning's flight. "It's probably against the law to land here without permission. We'd better go to the airport and turn ourselves in."

Michael didn't agree, but said he would accompany me anyway. We jogged back and arrived as the blades of the helicopter were floating to a stop. A blond man in his midthirties dressed in khaki shorts and deck shoes stepped out with a briefcase and spoke to us in formal English.

"Good afternoon, my name is Bill. How do you do?" Bill was a corporate pilot for a bank in Brazil, but he looked more like an angel to me. He offered us a ride in his chauffeur-driven car to his hotel, twenty minutes north in the town center of Angra dos Reis. He said the hotel was nothing to write home about. We told him we didn't care about the quality of the accommodations; we appreciated not having to figure out where to stay. Privately, I felt comforted by spending the night near a pilot who spoke both English and Portuguese, in case we needed him for something.

On the way into town, I pestered Bill with questions about the weather in these parts. He said it often gets very nasty this time of year, but he wouldn't venture a guess about what the weather might be like in the morning.

Michael and I sat in the back of the car as it sped along the narrow road, passing trucks carrying farm animals and old cars brimful of bronzed people. I gazed at the red brick houses with their metal roofs and noticed that most of them were unfinished and had no windows. Everything had a patchwork look. I later learned that Brazilian property taxes are levied only on completed houses, so homes belonging to the poorest people are often held in a permanent state of construction.

With every humble dwelling looking as if it had been just hacked out of the forest, the common perception of Brazil as an ecological war zone was heightened, yet the power of the remaining forest was equally striking. We were driving through one of the last remnants of the Mata Atlantica, the once vast Atlantic coastal rainforest now reduced to less than 5 percent of its original size. Wherever there weren't buildings, the dense vegetation looked as if it were about to strangle the road and bury it beneath the advancing forest.

This sea of green that the Brazilians call Costa Verde appeared anything but uniform. Shafts of dappled sunlight struck innumerable shades of green mixed with vivid colors as they penetrated mist rising out of the forest. The lavender blossoms of jacaranda trees especially stood out from the broad-leaved hardwoods, while mosses, lichens, and bromeliads clung even to the occasional palm, pine, and banana trees. Whenever we stopped or slowed down, we could hear the din of countless birds. Somewhere in those upper branches were monkeys, parrots, and toucans.

I realized that the Costa Verde had been so named for good reason. It looks so profoundly green and tropical because it has no dry season. That is great news for the plants, but not such great news for me. Yet despite the heavy rainfall, the area was far more populated than I had thought during our flight along the edges of Angra Bay. From what little I had seen out the window, we'd entered deep forests like those of Southern Chile, where no man or woman treads. Now, off in the distance, I could

Cobblestone streets of Angra dos Reis (above and right).

see palatial estates dotting the coast above white beaches. I chuckled to myself at the thought that just an hour and a half ago we had been fighting for our lives seemingly in the middle of nowhere, and now we were riding in a chauffeur-driven car in a tropical resort area for rich Brazilians. I'm not a very religious person, but I did begin to wonder if perhaps I had an angel looking out for me.

The gated enclaves ended as we crested a hill above a deep harbor beneath the old town of Angra dos Reis, which rose into the hills and gradually merged with the forest. I read that it was founded in 1502 and lives on as a traditional port town of middle-class fishermen, shipbuilders, and local businessmen.

As we turned off the main road into the oldest part of town along narrow cobblestone streets lined with dreary storefronts, there was little about it that appealed to me. We rounded a corner past a church and stopped beneath a six-story, fifties-style building that seemed somewhat out of character with the older architecture all around it. This was the Caribe Hotel, where Bill was staying. As  he led us into a spacious lobby with floor-to-ceiling windows and helped us check in, I was hoping for the best.

With anticipation of a cozy place to collect myself, I eagerly followed a young dark-haired girl who led us upstairs to our room on the fifth floor. When I opened the door and peeked inside, my heart sank. The room was small, dark, and dismal. I lay on the spongy bed and felt a pang of homesickness. I had the sudden urge to call home, talk to all my friends, and tell them that I was still alive, but Michael, embarrassed by our joint stupidity, didn't think that was such a good idea. He didn't have to explain why he wanted to keep silent about the events of the day. We both recognized that we had only narrowly escaped being statistics in the most common cause of death in small planes: flying VFR into bad weather. That bothered me in a strange way. If I were going die, it would be a shame to have it happen from something so commonplace, so unheroic, and, with hindsight, so avoidable.

When I couldn't stand being in the room any longer, I went down to the hotel lobby and placed a call to John Jauregui, my doctor in California. I told him about the shooting pains in my left arm and the pieces of bone that I could see with my naked eye, sticking out of my upper gum. He interrupted my story. "You've got antibiotics, right? Your arm sounds infected."

I acknowledged that I did have one wide-spectrum antibiotic with me. "Then start the Cipro immediately," he advised. After a long pause, he concluded, "Barbara, I'm more concerned about what you've described in your mouth. Get yourself home as soon as possible."

I hung up the phone, plopped down on a black leather couch in the corner of the hotel lobby, and began to sob uncontrollably. People started to stare at me, and though I felt deeply embarrassed, I couldn't stop the tears. The harder I tried, the

more I cried. A man watching from across the lobby walked over to try to help, but I was crying so hard I couldn't get any words out of my mouth. He insisted on taking me to a hospital and flagged down a cab. I let him escort me to a 24-hour emergency clinic.

On our way there, the good-hearted fellow introduced himself as Gringo, a nickname he'd been given in Brazil because he was foreigner from Costa Rica. For the first time since Michael and I landed, I laughed. His name struck me as hilariously funny because I thought only Americans were ever singled out as gringos.

This Gringo worked in Rio de Janeiro as a television director for one of their prime-time programs. After we arrived at the clinic, he carefully translated my Spanish into Portuguese for a doctor who removed a forgotten and infected stitch, cleansed my wound, and sent me on my way with several prescriptions that I never intended to fill.

After I paid about $20 for the medical visit, Gringo and I slowly wandered back on foot toward the hotel. I told him my story about the day's flight, about the river rafting accident, and how everything was going poorly in Brazil, where I couldn't understand Portuguese. I was still tearful and clearly feeling sorry for myself. Gringo listened intently and then asked me to sit down on a dimly lit bench in one of the tiny town squares. He began to relate an anecdote in Spanish that had a universal message: don't cry over spilt milk. His story helped me regain my calm and begin thinking about the days ahead.

Due to facial injuries from the rafting accident, I lost my smile (above).

I felt very motivated to get out of Brazil. Having relied on my Spanish in every Latin country until Brazil, I felt handicapped not to be able to speak Portuguese. Not understanding the native language seemed especially dangerous in the air. On the ground, getting the food I ordered was a game of roulette. Asking for help in the event of another serious problem was a real fear.

Though English is the official international flight language, most Brazilian controllers couldn't speak it well enough for us to understand each other beyond a few memorized phrases and responses. That certainly had compounded our problems today. Getting weather information in English would have made all the difference. We would have put down well before getting into the severe rainstorms.

However, not speaking Portuguese seemed like a minor concern compared to the physical discomfort I felt in my mouth, lip, and left elbow. My lower lip was so sensitive where the stitches had just been removed that I couldn't drink anything hot without using a straw, and paper straws were not always easy to come by. Both my lips had become so unbearably chapped that none of the over-the-counter lip protectors I had with me eased the itchy puffiness. With some of the bone broken out of my upper jaw, I felt self-conscious about letting anyone see my false teeth with a visible gap above my temporary bridge. To complicate things further, the laceration that had split my lower lip made it extremely painful to smile. Grinning was out of the question.

Not until I lost my smile did I begin to realize how often I used it. I was like a sharpshooter without a gun. In my newly disarmed state I felt like some unwilling volunteer in a feminist study—both horrified and amused at myself for feeling so compromised by not being able to use a flirtatious smile to get my way. It was becoming ever apparent that all my life I'd been using my smile to open doors and smooth over difficult situations. But just as I'd used my smile on others, I had also used it on myself. The act of smiling made me feel happier right down to a cellular level. Now that my smile was gone, something was missing all the way to my toes. When I looked in the mirror, the scarred face of a stranger stared back.

Though I felt lucky to be alive, I wasn't feeling all that lucky otherwise. As I tossed and turned all night long, my tongue would inadvertently find its way to the hole above my front teeth, and I'd flash back to crashing into the rock wall in the Bio Bio River. Then rocks along the rugged Angra coast would appear, blurred by rain, and I'd fly all around the bay searching for a beach to land on, until I'd finally wake up, wondering if my luck had run out.

RIO AT LAST

XIX

*I*n the morning, I felt reluctant to get out of bed, but the room was so dark and small that I forced myself to get up and prepare for another day of flying. At breakfast the sky was clear, but by the time we took a cab to the airport, many low clouds had already appeared. As I preflighted the plane, I kept glancing at the sky. It seemed that puffy white clouds were mystically multiplying. According to my earlier conversation with Bill, this was normal. I didn't like how it looked, but we didn't have far to go and it was still early enough that we could reach Rio before the heavy rains would begin.

At the airport there was no paperwork to do, no flight-service office for filing a flight plan, just Alisio and his wife to bid us farewell. I took the controls and flew out over the ocean to follow the shoreline toward Rio. When I rounded the corner into the next bay, Michael and I both went speechless at the sight of shipping cranes towering up to 200 feet. They were higher than we had been able to fly beneath the clouds the previous day. Had we missed the little runway at Angra, we never would have survived flying through this bay.

It took over an hour to reach Jacarepagua, the first airport south of Rio where I could refuel. The relief of touching down safely, knowing we were nearly out of fuel, was immediately replaced with gloom after I checked in at the flight desk. They asked me to pay an outrageous landing fee of more than $150 for just a few minutes' stop to refuel. I had expected to pay some sort of landing fee, but when I was also presented with a gas bill for $60 over what the pump read, I balked. The cost of fuel was already close to a dollar a gallon higher than I'd paid in any country so far.

After a messy debate that I was unable to really understand, I called the U.S. Consulate in Rio. The weekend duty officer spoke with the line attendant, then explained to me that selling fuel to a U.S.–registered airplane was an international

Rugged terrain surrounds Rio de Janeiro (left).

transaction and all American aircraft have to pay 17 percent more than Brazilian planes. I wasn't being singled out.

"This is a very poor country," he said. "The government wants U.S. dollars. Just be glad you aren't conducting business here. Why don't you come on into town and have a good time?"

I couldn't imagine having a good time in Rio. I wanted out of Brazil more than ever. I'd heard too much about Rio being unsafe, with literally hundreds of thousands of abandoned children on the streets supporting themselves by theft and violent crime. Locals no longer dared to stop at red lights at night or roll down their window when a smiling child approached them with a flower or a newspaper during the day. I didn't have the energy left to even think about submitting myself to this kind of environment. I was afraid that if I stopped for a day, I'd lose what momentum I had left to continue.

Seen from above, Rio appeared absolutely fascinating. The gigantic city was surrounded by and intertwined with national parks and ecological preserves created to protect some of the last intact fragments of the Mata Atlantica, which is far more endangered than the more famous and biologically distinct Amazon rainforest.

*Tijuca National Park preserves a section of
Brazil's endangered Atlantic Forest (above).*

236

Through a government boondoggle, the Jacarepagua airport where I had just landed had been constructed in the heart of one of these protected areas. I was standing in the middle of tons of pavement that had only recently been home to many exotic birds and critters.

Beyond the runway were new apartment houses, stores, and a conference center. The irony was that environmentalists from all around the world were being invited to this very spot to attend the 1992 United Nations Earth Summit, a conference on the state of the global environment. But even if Galen were invited to participate, which was likely because of his service on the boards of several environmental organizations, I wouldn't consider returning. Again, I felt like Dorothy in the *Wizard of Oz,* trying to click the heels of her red shoes together to trigger the magic that would take her home.

Within the hour, Michael and I took off again bound for Salvador, almost 800 miles to the north. As we made our way past Rio, its expansive beauty from the air amazed me. Long, white beaches lined the twisted coast. Granite domes rivaling those of Yosemite rose out of lush, green forests that blanketed their flanks and encircled the city. Most of the wildlands were within Barra da Tijuca National Park. Somewhere down there were the sands of Copacabana, the heart and soul of Brazilian beach culture, where locals go before, after, or instead of, work.

I'd expected the familiar postcard view of Rio to stand out from high over the city, but at first I couldn't find it. I kept looking for the huge statue of Christ the Redeemer looming directly over the city, with the bald dome of Sugarloaf in the distance. As I focused most of my attention on flying into an area with lots of air traffic, I never figured out which of the many domes was Sugarloaf and only spotted the statue after Michael pointed it out and asked me to lean forward so he could snap a photograph out of my window.

From above, Rio appeared to be a whole series of separate cities, each with its own beach and forest, linked by roads and tunnels, but divided by towering rock walls draped with dense greenery. The merger of wild and urban landscapes looked exquisitely elegant, like a giant garden with just the right balance between natural growth and cultivation, but I felt very glad to be sightseeing "The Marvelous City" high above it. I had no desire to enter the expanding concrete jungle that had diminished Rio's reputation as a dream destination and the world's most beautiful city.

As Michael and I flew farther north, the weather worsened. Another rain shower hit when we had been in the air a mere 55 minutes. I couldn't bear the thought of repeating yesterday's experience, so I turned back and landed at the nearest airport beside Macaé, a bustling town of 100,000 split between servicing the beach culture and the offshore oil industry. On the ground again so soon, I felt defeated. I had to face the fact that perhaps I was in over my head.

This time I walked into the weather office with a dictionary in hand. A man behind the counter went upstairs to get the tower controller to help translate. After spending the next hour trying to learn how to interpret their weather code, I resorted to drawing pictures of clouds and rain showers for the controller to point out the one that best described what to anticipate. In the end, I came up with a reasonable idea of what to expect: light rain, heavy rain, and more rain. The rainy season would last three more months. We were in a tropical region where thunderstorms were a daily occurrence.

I didn't own any of the expensive devices specially designed to tell if there's a thunderstorm nearby. Flying in bad weather without one, I could easily penetrate an embedded cell without knowing it and tangle with winds so fierce they could snap off my wings. Most commercial aircraft have some version of a stormscope that depicts areas of precipitation and electricity in front of the aircraft. These devices cost many thousands of dollars and take up more room than I have to spare on the limited cockpit panel of my small plane. Besides, I couldn't justify spending that kind of money on something that I would rarely use. At home, I simply don't fly IFR in severe weather, so I don't have a valid use for one. Here, where thunderstorms are more common than not, I was wishing I had invested the money.

Though I've always loved watching lightning flash from cloud to cloud and cloud to ground from the safety of my home, I began to see thunderstorms differently in the late seventies after flying into one in a commercial jet. The first sign of trouble was severe turbulence followed by a blinding flash of light, then a deafening boom. The plane began shaking violently. Some of the passengers screamed. A few minutes later, the captain came on the radio and explained in a Top Gun casual drawl that we'd been struck by lightning, but not to worry. It happens all the time. The captain's cool demeanor didn't stop some of the passengers from crying. Immediately after the lightning strike, a young man asked me to sit next to him for the remainder of the flight. He acted extremely nervous, though he said he flew biweekly between San Francisco and New York. He said he was certain that the pilot must be fibbing because he had never been through anything like that in all the years he'd been traveling coast to coast.

Since some thunderstorms top out above 40,000 feet, flying over one is out of the question. In reality, it is quite rare for jets to experience lightning strikes because they give thunderstorms a wide berth, often going far out of their way to avoid the towering monsters. But what about me? It was clear that neither Michael nor I could chance being bounced in the air like a chew toy for a rottweiler. Beyond that, lightning strikes can cause a temporary loss of vision and permanent damage to navigational equipment.

The best I could do to avoid flying into an electrical storm was to use what pilots call a "poor man's stormscope," where you turn up the volume on your ADF (automatic direction finder), an old-style navigational system with a needle that points toward a radio beacon as the device continuously broadcasts an audible signal in Morse code that spells out the station's two- or three-letter radio identifier. If we were to hear crackling over the radio with the ADF turned up, then we were probably nearing an electrical storm. It was certainly better than nothing, but it wouldn't tell me where a cell was, only that one was nearby.

Staying clear of thunderstorms was no guarantee of keeping out of trouble. Many famous explorers had commented on the legendary power of the rain along the Atlantic Coast of South America that had already chipped paint off the leading edges of my wings and struts. Antoine de Saint-Exupéry described being blown out to sea by the notorious winds of Patagonia as he flew full-throttle toward land. Charles Darwin sailed around the world for four years and singled out the rain on the Brazilian coast as like that of nowhere else on earth. When he stepped off his ship in Salvador in February, 1832, he took a short walk into the Mata Atlantica and was caught by rain so severe that it stopped him in his tracks before he could make it back to the harbor. "I tried to find shelter under a tree, which was so thick that it never would have been penetrated by common English rain," he wrote in *The Voyage of the Beagle*.

Knowing that it was already raining hard along the route to Salvador, Michael and I could agree on one thing: we weren't ready to fly. We went into a small café at the base of the tower and ordered hamburgers and colas. I began making out two lists: problems and options. "I'm sorry," Michael said yet again. "I don't think I am the right co-pilot for you in this situation. Even though I have more IFR hours, I'm not confident enough in myself to encourage you to go IFR."

"Maybe we could call Hernán and hire one of his pilots to fly home with us," I suggested.

"In that case I wouldn't stay," Michael admitted. I had touched a sore spot, and I was surprised at his reaction. I thought bringing in a more experienced pilot was a good option for our joint safety, as well as for the learning experience. If I chose another one of the options on my list—to leave the plane in Brazil until the rainy season was over—exorbitant tie-down fees charged by the hour would have the Brazilians soon owning my beautiful Cessna 206.

One of my goals for this journey before I left home was to return a better pilot through actual experience. I never imagined that so many of the flight hazards that I'd studied in textbooks would become realities. I felt trapped. I didn't want to disappoint Michael but I didn't want to die either. Every time I tried to imagine flying into clouds, I kept having visions of the instrument gauges bouncing around and becoming impossible to read in severe turbulence. If I were to stumble inadvertently into one of those cloud monsters, flying out of it by instruments would be a challenge for even the most experienced pilot. In flight terminology, severe turbulence describes air so rough that for moments, minutes, or eternity, controlling the plane becomes impossible.

Michael and I were no longer seeing eye to eye. Feeling very much alone, I wanted to confer with Galen, but he was climbing with Doug somewhere in Patagonia. I'd stopped relying on Michael after he'd said, "I think I can see, I think I can see," and kept on flying into weather that almost killed us. I wasn't angry with him, but I had grown distinctly leery of his ability to evaluate our situation. Nor was I confident about my abilities; I still had trouble trusting my instincts.

The vacuum-pump failure in Peru had also taken a huge toll on my psyche. Having several of my instruments suddenly stop working and flying partial panel was no longer a textbook notion. I'd learned from experience just how dangerous it could be. Even before we'd entered Brazil, I was feeling more intimidated than ever about instrument flight after experiencing what it's like to lose my most important gauges and fly into the clouds.

After yesterday's flight to Angra, nothing about flying seemed safe. I'd lost whatever remaining innocence I had. I no longer trusted any system or any person, including myself. I felt more than scared; I felt broken and paralyzed about making what could be my last decision. I wasn't about to fly VFR under pregnant rain clouds, nor was I ready to fly IFR into them.

After I went back to concentrating on my short list of options, I stopped after scrawling, "Leave keys in the plane." It just slipped out of somewhere in my subconscious. Until the words were on paper, I'd never really toyed with the thought of letting my plane be stolen, but I was feeling so desperate that, for the moment, I was willing to consider anything that would get me home and out of this miserable situation alive. But not being a quitter, I quickly eliminated the thought and went back to trying to envision more sensible ways of getting myself out of this pickle. None came to mind.

Sitting there in the café, with Michael despondent and me spouting tears when anyone glanced my way, we must have looked like a pair of escaped mental patients whose last dose of medication had just worn off. Michael finally admitted that he had kept on flying VFR toward Rio because he was afraid of flying my plane on instruments in such awful weather. He revealed that the kind of instrument flying he'd done before had been as a copilot, not as the pilot-in-command.

While Michael's revelation instantly made me understand his actions and empathize with him, it also reinforced my commitment to put my trust in myself instead of others. Throughout my life, I'd had reason to believe that I could overcome anything if I applied myself. I remembered how I had almost failed a statistics course in my senior year of college. Mathematics had been my Achilles' heel since the fourth grade, when I did poorly on an exam designed to fast-track students according to their scores. I was transferred to a remedial math class and my grades plummeted.

At UC Davis, I was required to take at least one math class that I foolishly put off until the very end. The statistics class that I entered baffled me. Working my way through school and riding a bike to class, I managed to scrape together enough money to hire a math tutor. After testing me, he said that helping me get anything above a C was out of the question. I fired him and hired another tutor who was equally discouraging. Enough of dream squashers! I fired him, too, and began attacking statistics as if my life depended on it. There were days I studied so hard that my brain felt like it was blinded by a white light. I was certain that I was attempting the impossible.

I remembered how there had been times when answers to clothing-production problems would come to me like flashes in the night, always after many hours of pondering a solution. With that in mind, I plodded on until the night before my midterm exam. Finally, in what felt like an instant, my muddy brain turned crystal clear. I closed my statistics textbook.

My then-boyfriend Don asked, "Why are you putting your book away so soon?

"I got it!"

"You got what?"

"I got statistics! I understand it and I don't need to study anymore!"

He didn't believe me. He still didn't believe me even after I returned from school saying that I passed my midterm with flying colors. He only believed I'd had a complete turnaround months later when a postcard arrived with my final-exam score: 400 out of 400.

I would not have graduated with highest honors if I had accepted other people's opinions about my statistics aptitude. Keeping that lesson in the back of my mind and using it to bolster myself for everyday challenges, I came to believe that there wasn't anything I couldn't do if I really wanted to. That's what had enabled me to take my first flying lesson. I knew deep inside that if I fully committed myself, I could master all the skilled maneuvers and technical knowledge required to operate an aircraft reliably. And I did just that.

Now that confidence was melting away. I'd met my match and I was losing. In the past, time had been on my side to turn overwhelming challenges into successes through my ability to focus my mind. If I concentrated on a problem long enough, I eventually came up with a good solution. But gnawing at me was the fact that while I was sitting here at this airport trying to make a decision, I was being charged for every minute that Five Lima Yankee was sitting on the ground. The pressure to leave was intense. I felt foolish feeling so scared just sitting in an airport, but it seemed more like hovering inside an ever-darkening grave as dirt was being shoveled into the few remaining airholes.

After lunch, Michael and I wandered back out to the plane. Just when everything seemed completely hopeless, a pilot stepped out of a twin-engine plane and came over to admire my 206. He introduced himself to me in English as Benito and said, "I've got over 6,000 hours in 206s. I love these planes. Where are you two headed next?"

I told him we were bound for the coastal city of Salvador. He said that he had just come from there and that it was an easy IFR flight over low terrain. When I said I was concerned about encountering thunderstorms, he told me that his plane was equipped with weather radar, and it hadn't shown anything electrical along his route of flight.

"You'll be solid in the clouds for hours, but there's nothing embedded in the clouds to worry about," Benito added.

The desperation that had been burdening my every thought began to vanish. Even so, I wasn't quite ready to let my spirits soar just yet and rush into something based solely on a brief conversation with a perfect stranger. I asked everything I could think of and listened to his answers with the ear of a detective until I came to the conclusion that I would be hard-pressed to find anyone more qualified to give me information about flying to Salvador.

Benito had just flown from there. He was a local charter pilot who flew the same route frequently. That he had so much flight time in my kind of airplane was a rare bonus. It also spoke volumes about the depth of his experience. The weather radar in his plane gave me more information about what was actually happening in the area than I had been able to ascertain from the official weather briefing, just minutes earlier. And the best part was that he spoke perfect English. There was no mistaking what he'd just said.

The time had come for me to make my own decision. Nobody but me was going to fly us out of this. Nobody but me was going to make the final judgment of whether to set off again into clouds that could easily end our lives.

I dug deeper within myself than ever before. All of my instincts began to come together. Hearing my inner voice so loud and clear felt astoundingly satisfying after having listened to others for so much of my life. I realized that I was ready to go for it. The time to fly was now.

OVER THE AMAZON

XX

*E*ven though I was committed to flying 5 more hours on to Salvador, I reminded myself to keep an open mind and stop short of my destination, if necessary. If something didn't feel right, I'd consider all my options, including returning to this airport soon after takeoff. Though landing again immediately would be expensive, I'd decided not to let money dictate my decision. Life was worth so much more than any amount of fees the Brazilians could possibly levy. If I had to put down every 30 minutes to stay alive, I would do just that.

It would be close to four before I could be in the air. Darkness would descend rapidly over the tropics just after six. Flying at night on instruments would intensify the risk, but with two pilots on board, I felt it was a risk worth taking.

From here on out, I would fly and Michael would navigate. I folded up my lists, stuffed them in my pocket, and dashed back into the flight operations office to file an IFR flight plan. For better or for worse, I had made a decision. It felt far better to attempt the flight than to continue vacillating on the ground like a gutless goose.

Flying day after day made the routine of hopping into the plane feel much like getting into a trusty old car on a long road trip. After so many days of traveling, sitting in the cockpit felt comfortable and right. I slipped into my seat and patted the instrument panel the way I used to pat my horse, Copilot, when we were on the trail. I felt a deep affection for my plane. My sense of comradeship with her was growing daily as she carried me safely from place to place, sharing my ups and downs. After this trip, I promised we'd never part. We would be partners for life.

When ground control cleared me to taxi, I quickly made my way to the run-up area and checked the engine. Meanwhile, Michael refolded the Jeppesen instrument maps to display our route. As he called out the VOR frequencies that I needed for the departure procedure, I dialed in each one with our primary course fixed into

Rain clouds over the Amazon Basin (left).

the number-one radio unit. We briefed the clearance with each other, and once he confirmed that he was ready to go, too, I radioed the tower for an IFR release and waited to be cleared for takeoff.

My veins pulsed with excitement at finally getting back in the saddle and distancing myself from the anguish and hopelessness I'd been feeling in the café. Though the mere thought of hours of instrument flight through tropical rainstorms gave me sweaty palms, something felt different now. My apprehension seemed suddenly contained and manageable. Once I'd made the decision to go, the ritualized process of setting up for the flight busied my mind and stripped much of the anxiety away. Now my attention was completely focused on a series of structured procedures that were apart from my personal world and fears. I was no longer thinking about towering cumulus, nor reliving yesterday's horrendous flight. Even my frequent flashbacks of the Bio Bio had ceased for the moment. I wasn't living in the past or thinking very far into the future. My mind was centered in the present.

The words "just do it" kept coming to my lips. The idea of simply putting one foot in front of the other took on a power all its own. It gave me a newfound sense of confidence. I could feel myself rise above my free-floating anxiety and see it for

Misty sunrise over the Amazon rainforest (above).

what it was: valuable as a warning signal, but nothing more. I would not let my anxiety rule my decisions.

Tower cleared me for takeoff. I started the timer clipped to my control yoke as we began to speed down the runway. The second the tires left the ground, I looked up at the overcast sky with anticipation. The ground rapidly dropped away and the clouds moved ever closer as one minute ticked by. Toward the end of the second minute, I climbed through 1,000 feet and the visual world below me vanished. We had suddenly entered a whiteout of swirling mists, which swiftly turned to solid rain.

My ability to control the airplane by visual reference to the earth's horizon was over. I had to change to guiding my plane entirely by the readouts of multiple gauges. It was quite a rush to switch abruptly from a natural, seat-of-the-pants way of steering and avoiding obstacles easily seen to putting my total faith in what the instruments read as I flew into a featureless void at 150 mph.

My eyes darted from the attitude indicator, which said my wings were level and we were still climbing, to the vertical speed indicator, to the airspeed indicator, and then to the directional gyro, always returning back to the attitude indicator as my base. The combination confirmed that I was indeed climbing on course. With the plane clearly under control, I glanced at my engine gauges. All systems were in the green. At last, I could feel the muscles in my neck and spine relax. I let myself settle into my seat.

As we motored forward through pure whiteness, it dawned on me how safe I felt being up in the clouds, as if I were wrapped in a child's warm blanket. Now I was a true believer in instrument flight. Getting back on the horse made me glad that I had committed to fly on to Salvador. If rain were all I'd encounter, I'd be in great shape.

At 5,000 feet, I leveled out the airplane and trimmed the elevator for a slight nose-down position. Though I was on constant alert for any sign that something wasn't right, it was different from the kind of fear that had kept me on the ground. Everything seemed so much easier, as if my mind had sped up or the world had slowed down.

Minutes turned to hours as I continued on, ever more at ease with my relationship between the outside whiteness and the world inside my cockpit. I reflected on how that master writer about flight, Antoine de Saint-Exupéry, compared the whirring of his motor in the air to the beating of his heart. He saw both as machines so perfect that he became unconscious about their existence and thus more aware of the realities of the natural world outside his being or his cockpit. "He who uses this instrument should be able to forget that it is a machine," Saint-Exupéry wrote in *Wind, Sand and Stars*. "It is not with the metal that the pilot is in contact. . . . It is thanks to the metal, and by virtue of it that the pilot rediscovers nature. . . . The machine which at first blush seems a means of isolating man from the great problems of nature, actually plunges him more deeply into them."

When I called a flight controller to ask for an update on weather at my destination, no one replied. I tried again. Still no answer. Seconds later, I overheard a Brazilian pilot on the radio speaking Portuguese to a flight controller about an "American female pilot speaking English." After a long silence, someone from Flight Center replied to me in my own language and asked me what I wanted. I wondered where the controller had to go to find someone who could communicate with me in English. For once, I got a weather report that I could fully understand. For that I was thankful to the nameless pilot who had been conscientious enough to get someone to help me. It seemed as if another angel had appeared out of nowhere.

As the plane droned on, I asked Michael to take the controls while I found something to put on my chapped lips. The blisters and scabs over where my lip had been severed had started itching so badly that I couldn't take it any longer. When I didn't find any Chapstick or other moisturizers, I dug deeper in my toiletry kit and came up with a tube of Preparation H. The ingredients listed on the label were petroleum, mineral oil, shark liver oil, beeswax, and lanolin. When I unscrewed the top and took a sniff, the pungent smell of shark liver oil dominated everything else. I next checked the indications, which read: "temporarily shrinks hemorrhoidal tissue and gives temporary relief of itching." That cinched it. I had to do something to relieve the pain, so I smeared the awful-smelling, amber-colored goo over my lower lip and instantly felt relief. A tube of Preparation H would never look the same again.

As day turned to night, I switched on the instrument panel lights. Even when I dimmed them in the gathering blue darkness, they glowed more brightly than anything in my field of view, heightening their importance as my only source of reference other than Michael's navigation. He was following our position using a tiny map light under the control yoke on his side, remaining focused on his task with a casual, yet professional manner that inspired my confidence. But no pilot sitting in the right seat was going to fly my plane again on this journey, no matter how experienced. Michael could be Chuck Yeager for all I cared. Being at the controls of my own plane here and now felt safer and more comfortable than letting anyone else fly.

It was nearly nine o'clock by the time I finally broke out of the clouds and was welcomed to the airport at Salvador by a neat row of runway lights glistening out of the darkness like the proverbial diamond necklace against black velvet. The lights of the distant city, 20 miles away on the coast, glowed with that special clarity that comes right after a rain.

As we took a taxi to a small inn near the airport, I mentally added up the day's total flight time: 7.2 hours. Nearly 5 of those had been in the clouds, 2 in the dark, and additional time had been spent in four different airports—a good day all in all, now that my feet were firmly planted on the ground.

For many days I'd been fighting off fatigue. Now, after a day of hard flying, I could let myself give into it. I slumped into the backseat of our taxicab as we rode into town. From somewhere deep inside me came a warm glow that felt strangely energizing. There was no hiding that I was proud of myself for finally going for it. Today, it had worked out in my favor. I'd see about tomorrow.

From the small inn we walked to a local restaurant, seeking only a quiet meal after a long day. Though I wasn't in a festive mood, the sound of live Brazilian music accented by a powerful African beat of drums and tambourines lifted my soul. I watched with delight at the couples all around us having a great time.

As I looked at the local people, something seemed different here. It took a little while before it dawned on me that as I flew north toward the equator, the color of people's skin darkened. Now, the region's nickname, "Africa in exile," made more sense to me. The area around Salvador had taken on that name because of the huge number of slaves brought in over three centuries from West Africa to work on sugar plantations. Their free labor had also supported Brazil's exclusive rubber industry, until the British smuggled out saplings to plant in Southeast Asia and slavery was finally abolished in 1888, well after the Civil War in the United States.

If it could be said that anything good evolved from that era of human abuse, it would be the way the slaves of Brazil used music and dance as an elixir for their souls. The most famous music festival in the world, Carnaval, may have been born out of pagan spring festivals and structured around Portuguese Catholicism, but its special brand of frenzied energy and wild rhythms was infused by African slaves and their descendants. As a result, Carnaval in Salvador remains distinctly more participatory, more musical, and more African than in Rio, where it has evolved into more of an elite commercial dance event and tourist spectacle.

Immediately after Christmas, the people of Salvador begin thinking about Carnaval. They practice their music, make costumes, rehearse dances, and generally work themselves into a state of excitement for the real event that comes in February. That's the energy that Michael and I found ourselves surrounded by when we stepped into the restaurant.

The very rich and the very poor in Brazil share a love for their native music, though according to a United Nations study quoted in my guidebook, they don't share much more. In 1990, Brazil had the most unequal distribution of wealth on the planet, exceeding that of India and every Arab nation. Despite Salvador's reputation as a tough city, the evening I spent there listening to music was an antidote for my bruised soul. It seemed that any country so infused with music could not be such a bad place after all. Back in my hotel room, I wrote down my second thoughts about Brazil in my diary, summing up the country as "a nation of music, color, fruit, and sweat."

The next morning, we were out at the airport early. By 7:30 we were in the air. The weather was basically clear as we left the coast and headed inland to begin a major shortcut across the hump of Brazil over flat, arid terrain. Some of it was desert, which meant minimal rainfall even at the height of the rainy season. Compared to what we'd been through, both the weather and the flight were easy to negotiate. Perhaps the worst of Brazil was over.

After a long, but uneventful flight, the terrain became quite moist again as we neared São Luís on the coast. Before reaching the somewhat impoverished old colonial city of 700,000 crowded onto an island just offshore, we flew over extensive palm plantations. They were created long ago by clearcutting what had once been a region of deep forest watered by heavy tropical rains.

I had been warned repeatedly by Brazilian pilots to beware of theft in northern Brazil, but the airport at São Luís was unguarded. I'd been emphatically advised not to trust anyone and to be especially careful within a day's flight of the border because of rampant drug smuggling and theft of desirable aircraft, such as mine. In order to prevent my airplane from being stolen, I considered disconnecting the battery, then debated over whether I should just sleep inside the plane. In the end, I concluded that I'd rather lose my trusty bird than my life. I chose a good hotel from my guidebook, but before opening the door of the plane I had to deal with another potential hazard.

According to flight advisories I'd read before leaving home, we had entered a serious malarial area, with strains that are resistant to standard medications. I had chosen not to take Larium, the preferred preventive drug for these resistant strains, because of my history of adverse reactions to medications. Once, when I began taking Larium before a trip to Asia, I could barely drive my car over the bridge across the bay to get home just a few hours after swallowing the first tablet. I felt so delirious that the idea of ever flying on it was clearly out of the question. Later, I read that a major international airline had banned their pilots from taking Larium because it had caused psychotic breakdowns. When I mentioned this to an adventure travel agency in Africa, they told me that they had yet to evacuate a client for malaria, but had recently done an emergency evacuation for a reaction to Larium.

Before getting out of the plane, I resorted to the old-fashioned method of malarial protection by covering myself from head to toe. Even though it was extremely hot and muggy outside, I kept the windows closed while I put on a long-sleeved shirt, buttoned it at the wrists and neck, and sprayed my clothing and all remaining exposed skin with a strong mosquito repellent, which I passed on to Michael. By the time we finished, I felt as stinky as a head of garlic inside a pressure cooker.

On our way into town, we let the chatty cab driver take us on a short tour of the old part of the city. I felt bad about not spending more time in each new city, but in my mental state, just moving on was more appealing than playing tourist. Even when healthy, to me being a tourist meant challenging myself as I traveled through a country, rather than passively visiting places.

In the morning, I still had an airplane, along with a mixed weather report. As I contemplated flying toward the Amazon Basin, I felt a renewed sense of adventure. I went to the terminal building in search of a cup of coffee and found myself conversing with a good-looking guy, draped in gold chains, who spoke Spanish as well as Portuguese. I appreciated his company as I sat down to sip my coffee through a straw so as not to sting my lip. He was a pilot, too, and wanted to know where I was going next. "Macapa," I said, explaining that it was the last major airport before I crossed the border into Suriname on a very long leg to Georgetown in Guyana.

"That's great! That's where I'm going too," he said. "What time are you taking off?"

After I told him my entire flight plan all the way to Venezuela, he said that he would be flying right behind me and would call on the radio so that we could stay in touch. We bid each other adiós.

When I returned to the plane, Michael seemed flustered. "Let's get out of here," he said, but before he could tell me why, a second dark-haired man in his twenties walked up and flirtatiously said hello. He, too, was a pilot. As he fingered his set of gold chains, I was amused by how much he looked like the other man I'd just met.

I wondered if wearing gold chains was customary for pilots in this region.

"What kind of flying do you do?" I asked.

"I ferry airplanes between Brazil and New York," he replied. I tried to get a glimpse of his eyes through his oversized dark glasses, to judge who he really was, but I couldn't. Something about the way he hovered around me started to give me a strange feeling, so I said good-bye, hopped in the plane, and quickly closed the door.

"I don't feel good about that guy," Michael said. "He asked me all kinds of questions about your radios and long-range tanks. I also caught him checking our oil."

"He checked our oil? That's really weird!" I said. It was hard to believe that a complete stranger would check someone else's oil. I glanced back at the guy and was startled to see him engaged in a very serious conversation with the man I'd met while I was having coffee. When the two of them spotted me looking at them, they lit up with identical plastic smiles. My entire body shivered. Something was really wrong. Feeling a surge of panic, I started the engine without looking at my checklist and immediately called for clearance to taxi. I wanted to put as much time as possible between these shady characters and me.

Though the weather was clear at takeoff, the typical cauliflowerlike cloud formations soon began building on the horizon. While we were still within radio range,

Typical morning cloud buildup over the Amazon Basin (above); a wildly colored toucan stands out from the dull hues of a Brazilian rainforest (right).

I kept our number-two radio dialed into the airport at São Luís, but didn't hear either of the guys I'd met call for a takeoff clearance. Nonetheless, I mentally replayed my conversation with the first man and chastised myself for telling him everything about my future flight plans. I didn't blame Michael for showing off the plane—I would have done the same. If those two guys were teamed up to steal my aircraft, it would be simple. All they needed to do was follow me to Macapa.

As I continued my scan from instrument to instrument, I could not get the faces of those two men out of my mind. They looked so evil, so transparent. But then I must have looked transparent to them in my vulnerability. This trip had stripped

away any masks I'd ever worn that might have fooled someone into thinking that I was anything other than who I am. In the past, I'd been accused of wearing my emotions on my sleeve, but now I was certainly wearing them on my face. Though I certainly still had my secrets, most of me burst through for public viewing.

"How does the weather look to you?" I asked Michael, as we neared the Río do Pará on the edge of the vast Amazon Delta.

"It looks okay to me," he replied.

I didn't agree. A wall of darkened sky lined the distant horizon in the direction we were heading. "Can you get me the tower frequency?" I said. "I'm diverting to Belém."

Michael seemed a little surprised at my quick change of plans. I was a little surprised, too, more because I wasn't asking him to sanction my decision. I knew that if I landed at the great Amazon port town beside the southern channel of the river, we wouldn't have to worry about the weather getting worse in the afternoon. We'd also put down at a well-guarded major airport far away from Macapa, where I'd told our smiling new friends we'd be. The expense would be worth it.

Once we were on the ground, I headed to the flight service office. Since this was a major international airport, it had a very large and sophisticated weather department for briefing pilots who fly in and out of one of the rainiest cities in the world. I discussed our options with an English-speaking briefer, who looked me in the eye and gave me some firm advice: "In these parts, get off the ground before sunrise and land before noon; otherwise, you can expect imbedded thunder-storms."

That warning sounded familiar. The only part that was different was how early he thought I should get started. I don't mind getting up at the crack of dawn, but the mounds of required red tape meant I'd have to be out of the hotel by 4:30 A.M. If I were going to take a shower and have a cup of coffee before leaving, I'd be getting up no later than four. I cringed at the thought, but there would be only a few more days of flying in weather like this. I decided to get a good night's rest and go for the most comfortable and secure night's stay in Belém. From the list of hotels at the airport, I chose the five-star Belém Hilton. If I had to spend all the rest of our savings to be comfortable while I worked at getting myself home alive, so be it.

Soon we were in a taxi. I spoke to our driver in Spanish, and he replied in Portuguese. Somehow, we managed to understand each other. We wound our way down streets lined with mango trees and colonial buildings into the thriving city of over a million people. Our hotel was situated in the heart of the city, just a block from the main plaza. In the comfort of my room, I laid my maps out on the floor and considered my options. I would file a flight plan to Georgetown in Guyana, with Cayenne in French Guiana as an alternate. In between the two countries lies Suriname. I didn't get a visa or prior permission to land there before leaving home because it required a police report from my country. It seemed like such a hassle that I thought I would simply overfly the tiny country with my long-range tanks. But that was before I'd experienced flying in the tropics. Now I wasn't so sure.

Just in case I ran into bad weather tomorrow, I telephoned my office in California and asked our assistant to call the Suriname Embassy in Washington, D.C., and request permission to land at Paramaribo in the event of a weather emergency. She called back with a name to contact if I needed to land there. With a backup plan in place, I lay down for a restless night's sleep.

At four in the morning we got up. As we headed to the airport, there were far more people on the street than I expected at this ungodly hour before dawn. The region was so hot and humid that I could see why people wanted to get an early start on the day, as I was doing.

As we took off into the purple predawn haze, I could still see towering clouds on the distant horizon, left over from the previous day's buildup. Some of the biggest ones were occasionally lit up like battleships by bolts of lightning.

The world below us abruptly shifted to a monotonous brown as the morning sun struck open water below. I would have thought we were flying over the ocean, or at the very least a big lake, were it not for the color of the water and what I knew from studying my maps and guidebooks. Strangely enough, though Belém is the major port city of the Amazon, it is not situated on the river itself or on the ocean. It's 75 miles up river from the Atlantic on the banks of the Río do Pará, a giant tributary more than big enough for any ocean-going vessel. The town was built where the Portuguese happened to land in 1616 to establish their first Brazilian colony.

After about 30 miles over water, a green line of palms and mangroves marked the edge of the Ilha de Marajo, an island in the Amazon Delta larger than Switzerland. No words or pictures had come close to preparing me for the true immensity of the Amazon landscape, yet I hadn't even come to the main river. The island seemed to go on forever as we flew nearly 200 miles across the equator over flat country that gradually gave way to jungle, mangrove swamps, and twisting waterways before finally merging into an expanse of water so wide that I had trouble seeing the opposite shore through the humid haze.

Living in California, where it usually doesn't much rain from May to October, it's hard to imagine how a river could ever get so big. Vast areas of the Amazon Basin remain submerged 30 feet deep for long parts of the year. Here, where the days are never long or short, but always hot and humid, it rains almost every day. Massive amounts of water vapor rise into the sky with the morning sun. Massive amounts fall back into a basin that drains one-third of South America, creating a river 4,000 miles long with a flow sixty times greater than the Nile. The tropical biodiversity is so extreme that biologists can't identify one out of three fish for sale in Belém's markets.

Even the terrain itself has defied normal classification and mapping. Beyond Macapa, we encountered the ominous monotony of dense jungle as far as we could see. The U.S. Department of Defense ONC (operational navigation charts) showed my route—and 300,000 other square miles of the Amazon Basin—as white squares devoid of contour lines, with the bold warning: "RELIEF DATA INCOMPLETE." I was within a vast, white area on the map demarked only by a maze of river channels and the words "MINIMUM ELEVATION FIGURES ARE BELIEVED NOT TO EXCEED 5300 FEET."

As clouds began to build, we turned on the ADF receiver to listen for possible electrical static, but I thought I heard something else.

"Does the engine sound funny?" I asked.

"Not now, but I thought the same thing earlier," Michael replied. We hoped that we were both experiencing a phenomenon known to pilots as "auto-rough," in which long flights with constant engine sound, especially over water, provoke imagined mechanical failures.

If my engine were to quit over the Amazon rainforest and we survived, we'd most likely be trapped in the treetop canopy 100 feet or so above the ground. I didn't have any rope on board, so we wouldn't be able to lower ourselves. No one would find us. The high temperatures alone would be unbearable.

Even if we managed to get down, survival on the jungle floor would be tenuous. I'm afraid of poisonous ants, anacondas, and alligators. I have no idea which plants are edible and which the Indians use to make poison arrows. I wouldn't want to try to kill monkeys, or any of the other rich forest life that could keep a person alive in the wild jungle. Flying over the opaque brown waters of the Amazon had looked positively inviting compared to this thick jungle canopy. I vowed never to fly here again.

The Amazon got its name from a legend about women who were far more independent and committed to an adventurous life than I have ever been. Early Spanish explorers named the region Amazonia after they claimed to have seen female warriors on a riverbank. In ancient Greek, the word *Amazon* meant "without breast," and Greek mythology describes the land of the Amazons as a nation of powerful warrior women who occasionally bore children from unions with strong men of other tribes, whom they conquered. Sons were shipped off or killed. Daughters were hardened into warriors by martial discipline and by burning off their right breasts so that they could shoot bows and throw javelins as well as any man.

As we approached the border of French Guiana, my first concern was still getting accurate weather reports. Once I crossed the international border, I would only be allowed to land at major international airports, which were few and far between. My options were narrowing.

By the time I crossed into French Guiana, the clouds had built up into spectacular white castles all around us. It wasn't raining yet, so we hadn't had to divert from our straight route of flight. Armed with frequent weather updates, I felt comfortable continuing on. I was so vigilant about contacting flight controllers about weather that I imagined they might be somewhat fed up with my frequent calls. But I didn't care much what they thought.

Even though some of the clouds were growing ever higher, I decided to continue on with my plan to overfly both French Guiana and Suriname. If I could reach Georgetown today, then I'd be in good shape to make it to Venezuela in a single flight tomorrow. Kike, a Venezuelan adventurer who'd climbed with Galen and worked for us for two years in the Bay Area, had invited me to stay with him in Caracas.

In Belém, I'd phoned Kike with my itinerary and mentioned my concerns about the bone that was still protruding from my upper gum. He promised to make arrangements for me to see a highly qualified dentist upon my arrival. From Caracas, Michael could fly home commercial in time to go back to college.

Two hours later, I was over Suriname. A weather update informed us that the cloud level in Georgetown had dropped down to 200 feet above VOR minimums. That was too close for comfort. If the clouds lowered more, I would not be able to land, and the map showed no nearby alternate international airport that I could safely reach with the amount of fuel I had aboard. The odds of having to land in Georgetown on instruments in the midst of a serious rainstorm seemed high enough for me to chicken out, declare an emergency due to weather, and land at Suriname. I'd just have to take my chances with the officials of a country that I knew was politically volatile. I kept the name of our contact at their embassy safely tucked away in my shirt pocket.

Dropping into the clouds, I flew an IFR approach into Paramaribo, landing just before an American helicopter touched down. When I struck up a conversation with the pilot, who was ferrying the helicopter from the United States to Brazil, the first thing he told me was that it was a good thing I hadn't tried to continue on to Georgetown; the VOR had been out of service for three days. A twin-engine plane carrying passengers had just crashed trying to get into Georgetown without navigational aids. All aboard had perished.

Georgetown had experienced massive power failures due to an oil shortage. Even the emergency generators had been turned off at the airport. This kind of story made me appreciate how fortunate pilots are in the United States. I was thankful I'd made the emergency landing when I had.

The terminal building seemed like something out of the old movie *African Queen*. The humidity was palpable in an empty and drab beige room that smelled of sweat. I felt a little uneasy as Michael and I walked through the terminal, looking for someone to check us into the country.

Toward the back of the building, a gentleman asked me to step into a tiny room. As he watched me fill out the forms, he leaned way back in his seat and puffed on a cigarette. When he realized that I did not have a visa, he appeared to be licking his chops as he explained that I could be in big trouble. His English was perfect, and we understood each other completely.

If I'd expected to clear immigration without delay, I was wrong. Soon, another taller and thinner man joined in interrogating me nonstop. The two of them bounced comments back and forth in English, giving me the strong impression that a bribe was expected. They were leading me toward believing that I had done a very bad thing arriving without a visa, but instead of cash, I handed over the name of the man at the embassy who had given me verbal permission to land. The immigration officers grumbled and left the room.

During the interrogation, we learned that in the weeks since I'd left the United States, the country had undergone a coup. The military had taken over, but guerrilla rebels were roaming the countryside along with supporters of the opposite cause—reestablishing ties with the Dutch, who had ruled Suriname off and on until 1975 and given the struggling country substantial economic aid.

As I wandered back toward the main room, I was busying myself looking at what was on the walls and closed doors when I happened on one that was wide open. Inside, two men appeared to be exchanging a large sum of money. When they saw me staring at them, they hurriedly closed the door.

If only we'd cleared immigration before I'd spotted the men and the money, I thought to myself. Even though I'd just avoided disaster by not flying on to Georgetown, I had the feeling that my timing wasn't working out so well today. Just two hours ago I was up there in the air, wishing I were down here. Now that I was down here, part of me wished to be up there again, bound for a more stable political and geographical climate, but the other part was clearly telling me, "Not today." I had no intention of getting back into the air until tomorrow, and then only after confirming good enough weather at Caracas, our final destination before leaving South America.

When the immigration officers returned, they said we could not go into the town of Paramaribo without visas. Then they disappeared with our passports. After locating a fax record of my request through the Suriname Embassy in Washington to make an emergency landing anywhere in Suriname, they came back and eventually granted me permission to remain in the country for only 24 hours. We would have to stay in the vicinity of the airport and agree to spend the night in accommodations of their choosing.

After the airport officials were finished with us, Michael and I headed out to park the plane for the night and collect our things. To my surprise, the tower controller directed me to taxi to the far side of the field, out of sight of both the terminal and the tower. Since the airport was encased by dense, green jungle and appeared emptier than any place I'd ever landed, the request to park so far away didn't make any sense. After several attempts to persuade the controller to let me leave my plane where it was, I reluctantly taxied to the dark and lonely designated spot, where I didn't dare leave anything of value in the plane.

There was nothing in sight to tie the plane to, so I set the brakes and secured the control surfaces from the inside, while Michael checked the oil. When he reported that the dipstick showed below 9 quarts, I wasn't worried, since I'd brought along extra oil. The plane normally blew off a quart or two after a couple of long flights. Deciding to see for myself, I wiped the dipstick clean and checked it again. I normally filled it to 11 quarts, and the stick now showed between 9 and 10, which was not as bad as Michael's reading, but still low.

The airplane was still hot and oil could continue to trickle down and increase the reading after it cooled down. Only if the reading stayed below 10, would I feel the need to add oil before launching off on the 6-hour flight to Venezuela. Then Michael threw me a curve ball. He sheepishly admitted that he had already used up the extra quarts of oil that I had stored in the rear of the plane and hadn't told me when we were still in Belém, where I could have easily purchased more. By the looks of this airport, I'd be lucky to get a pint of Coca-Cola, much less a quart of 50-weight Aeroshell aviation oil.

The humid air sizzled under a bright, cloudy sky, and I'd wanted to get inside the shady guesthouse as soon as possible. Now I'd have to stay out and search for oil. Though the mosquitoes weren't out in the midafternoon, once it began to cool down, they'd appear. I could hear the sounds of countless birds in the rainforest just beyond the runway, and I decided that before going any farther, I would spray myself from head to toe with "jungle juice" and button up my long-sleeve cotton shirt at the wrists.

I tracked down the man in charge of the fuel truck, who said they did not have oil for small aircraft. If I needed some, I would have to fly or drive to the domestic airport in a distant suburb. When I explained that neither of these options was possible without a visa, he said that since the coup, cabs weren't coming to the airport regularly, and if I ordered one and sent someone else to pick up oil for me, it would probably cost over $100. That would be expensive for oil, but cheap if it kept me from burning up my engine.

While I was out on the tarmac, still trying to conjure up a plan, a local pilot arrived in a small Cessna. I dashed over, introduced myself, and explained my predicament to the stately gentleman, who looked inside his plane but didn't turn up any spare oil. Michael suggested using automobile oil, but there was something about putting anything other than the specified aviation oil in my turbo-charged airplane engine that didn't seem right. When I asked the local pilot for his opinion, he said it wasn't a good idea and could harm my engine. He casually walked over to my plane, checked the oil for himself, and announced a reading just over 10 quarts.

As soon as the pilot walked off, Michael became agitated.

"What's up, Michael?" I queried.

"You don't seem to believe anything I say," he snapped, sounding insulted.

"It's not that I don't believe you, it's just that I want to get as much information as possible before I decide what to do next," I said, hoping to explain away my actions. But he was right that I didn't believe him. And it wasn't just Michael that I didn't believe. I didn't believe anybody anymore without obtaining some sort of personal verification. I'd reached the point where I wasn't about to take one person's word for anything. After I asked those who had some expertise what they thought, I would digest it, compare it to what I knew, and keep on asking if I needed more information before making a final decision.

Charles Lindbergh once said that for a pilot, "life itself depends on accuracy . . . It's vital to my sense of values. I've learned not to trust people who are inaccurate." The stakes were too high for me simply to shoot from the hip anymore. Not until something felt right in my gut was I about to budge. Somewhere along the coast of Brazil I'd truly discovered the positive power of the word *no*.

Before we had a chance to leave the airfield, crowds of people began arriving. The ghost-town atmosphere in the terminal turned lively with bustling energy as it filled with men, women, and children of all ages, colors, and ethnic backgrounds. My new pilot friend explained that he'd come to meet a KLM flight that was about to arrive from Amsterdam. I stayed and watched as the jumbo jet touched down smoothly, screeched to a halt, and taxied to the terminal, stopping near the spot where I had originally parked. Now I understood why I had been requested to move my plane, but I still didn't like being parked so far away. Someone could leisurely tamper with the plane, and nobody would notice.

No sooner had the jet off-loaded its passengers and boarded new ones, than it prepared to depart by a route sure to blast Five Lima Yankee with its engines as it taxied for takeoff. My plane wasn't tied down and could easily be flipped over.

Michael and I raced back and stood at attention under each wing, ready to hang on the struts if necessary. As the KLM jet taxied by, we were hit by a sudden gust of hot air and an ear-piercing roar. We both hung onto the plane as it pitched and shook, trying to take off on its own. As soon as the jet was out of range, we relaxed our hold. Within minutes the airport slipped back into its sleepy state.

Since Michael and I had done all we could do, we headed off by foot to find the guesthouse. As we walked along the dirt road, sounds of other human beings were conspicuously missing. The noises of nature stood out as birds sung in tropical trees and insects hummed in the background.

At the guesthouse a friendly young man greeted us and offered us something to eat and drink before showing us to our rooms. I sipped Coca-Cola with a straw and told stories of my adventures as we sat at the counter of a clean and simple dining room that smelled of fresh paint. By the undivided attention showered on us, I suspected we might be the first guests to grace this place. After dark, we were still the only guests. It felt so isolated that I wondered why anyone would stay here if they weren't forced to, as we had been. Perhaps we were in a glorified prison for errant tourists. Nonetheless, it was good to have a bed to sleep in.

The following morning we were up early for coffee and toast, but I knew something odd was about to occur when the friendly young man turned cold. After he handed me our hotel bill, my heart nearly stopped. We were being charged over $100 for food, though we'd only consumed a couple of hamburgers and Cokes.

When I asked to see a menu, price list, or some itemization of the meals, nothing of the sort was available. After a brief standoff, he disappeared and came back to say that the food was all-inclusive and the bill reflected the fixed price. I knew we were being ripped off but there wasn't much I could do. I was nearly certain that this guesthouse was in cahoots with the guys at the airport because they had insisted that we stay here, but I decided to pay the bill and get out of Dodge.

We walked back to the airport, managed a fairly speedy checkout, and then dashed over to the plane. Everything about the morning looked good: my plane had not been touched, the dipstick read over 10 quarts, and the weather was much improved.

We departed visually and soon turned on course toward Michael's final destination: Maiquetia, the international airport near Caracas. We sat quietly, side by side, listening intently to the motor as it chugged us on a northward course that briefly sent us out over the Atlantic Ocean.

We chose an approach course to Caracas following the shoreline of the Cordillera de la Costa, which turned out to be so spectacular that I asked Michael to write the word *beautiful* on the map. After more than six hours in the air, we landed at 3:30 P.M.

Clearing immigration was a comparative breeze. We didn't have to wait long before my friend, Kike, met us at the airport. The following day, Michael departed on a commercial jet to Colorado, while I stayed on to spend a little more time in Venezuela with Kike and another friend. He took me to see his dentist, who found and removed more fragments of bone that had worked their way to the surface of my gums. Again, I was advised to return home to the United States as soon as possible to see a specialist.

I made arrangements to catch a commercial flight home to see my own dentist and called Galen in California. He agreed to accompany me back to Caracas, from where we would turn the flight from Venezuela to Miami into a two-week, island-hopping vacation.

Before departing, I left Five Lima Yankee safely tucked away inside a hangar, under the care of a highly recommended mechanic and his sister. They promised to take good care of Lima Yankee, change her oil, do a 100-hour inspection, and touch up the paint on her rain-chipped body. We both needed some healing time from encounters with wild waters. In a few weeks, we would have a fresh start for our final journey back to California.

Tropical coast of Venezuela (right).

OFF THE TOP

XXI

The day after I arrived back in Berkeley, I went from one dentist to the next in a series of appointments, suffering through root canals in my broken teeth. Galen had already given our RSVP to a formal dinner that night at the home of a Nobel laureate in honor of a Chinese intellectual who had been imprisoned after the riots at Tiananmen Square, so I agreed to attend.

High as a kite on pain pills, the first I'd taken since the accident, I managed to hold my own through some fascinating cocktail conversation with a group of well-known people that included Linda Ronstadt, Jerry Brown, Peter Coyote, and Doug's ex-wife, Susie.

Susie came over to offer some warm words after learning from Galen what had happened to me on the Bio Bio. When I told her that I went along on the raft trip partly because Doug had told me that she had rafted it with her daughters, she chuckled. She said she knew what I was going through trying to keep up with men like Galen and Doug.

"I got so tired of the macho," she said, before launching into a description of a scuba-diving vacation she took with Doug and Peter Buckley off the coast of Australia. She had been about to dive without a buddy, but as she started to lower herself into the ocean, she thought the skies looked extremely menacing. She asked the boat captain if black skies were normal for the season. He explained that the weather was quite normal, but scuba diving during hurricane season wasn't. Susie stopped the story there and gave me a knowing look before adding, "Be careful and take good care of yourself. If you need any help, please call me."

It wasn't until I later asked Peter about the scuba trip that I learned Susie was knocked off the yacht by a gigantic wave. She was washed back onto the deck when another wave returned her. Peter concurred that the trip had been organized for the worst possible time of the year.

My favorite beaches were on the lazy island of Anguilla, where turquoise waters lapped coral sands for miles (left).

I came away from the party feeling better after hearing Susie's story and realizing that someone out there had had experiences similar to mine and understood what I had just gone through. But it wasn't over yet. I was planning to return to Caracas to fly the plane home and was determined to make the rest of the trip a very different experience, applying all that I had learned so far to make it safe, enjoyable, and just plain fun.

Two weeks later, I returned to Caracas with Galen to complete my adventure. We planned to take off across the Caribbean the morning after arrival, but something seemed peculiar when we crossed from the terminal to the general aviation side of the field to check in with the mechanic about my airplane. Not until I went to pay the departure fee did I realize that there were no longer any U.S–registered aircraft with tail numbers beginning with N parked on the field. All of them read YV for Venezuela. During my two-week absence, the airport authorities had changed the tie-down fees for foreigners and slapped me with an $800 bill for parking, even though my plane had been left with a mechanic for repairs and service.

My mechanic said Venezuelan bureaucrats had oil on the brain and knew they could get away with charging American companies exorbitant fees for arriving in private jets. After concocting a plan, he made out a bill for the work he had done on my plane and itemized parking into the statement. It wasn't the truth, but he wanted to prevent his government from gouging me. He accompanied me to the main terminal and spoke on my behalf to the authorities, explaining that I should be exempt from the new parking charges for three reasons: first, I'd paid him for parking; second, my plane had been parked in his hangar, not out on the tarmac, the entire time I was gone; third, the parking fees were many times lower when I first arrived, and no one had advised me of any upcoming change. The government official argued loudly and would not budge. I finally resorted to pleading. When nothing worked, I paid the bill and bid South America good-bye and farewell.

We departed in clear skies, hugged the rugged shoreline, and headed east toward Trinidad—back in the general direction from which Michael and I had originally come. Towering hotels, skyscrapers, and clear skies gave way to virgin forests, vertical cliffs, and clouds, reminding me of flying through Brazil. As I came abeam Isla Margarita, just off the coast, I was surprised to hear a Venezuelan pilot call out my tail number over the radio. Once he established contact, he introduced himself as a friend of Kike's and asked me a few questions about my flight through South America and my stay in Caracas. He said he was flying a jet for a small airline. (Much later, back in the States, Kike gave me the sad news that this pilot and his copilot were shot and killed while doing a mail run to a remote Venezuelan airstrip.)

As the flight minutes ticked by, the cloud layer thickened, bringing rain showers to the nearby coastal mountains. Their ominous dark cast caused me to think twice about finally cutting my umbilical cord with the mainland of South America and flying out over the ocean. In similar weather, I never would have taken off from Angra dos Reis to fly the coast of Brazil, but something felt very different here, and it was more than just the terrain. The difference was in me and in how I imagined the world outside my windscreen, for flying is done more with the mind than with hands and feet on stick and rudder.

As I was feeling slightly anxious on my first over-water stretch just a few miles to Trinidad, breaking away from the top of the continent I thought about how pilots had flown single-engine planes solo all the way across the Atlantic Ocean almost three-quarters of a century before my day of relative puddle jumping. Charles Lindbergh once said that through flying he "learned that danger is relative, and that inexperience can be a magnifying glass."

My magnifying glass was finally losing the constant focus on danger it held for me as I flew across a foreign continent, injured and in pain, along a flight path chosen for me by a much bolder pilot who had already led me into several life-threatening situations. Today, I was a much more experienced and confident pilot than the one who had secretly hoped her plane might be stolen in Brazil so she wouldn't have to continue on the next morning. I was north of the equator now, flying entirely on my own terms with no fixed schedule, bound for the United States. The next two weeks would finally be a flight of my own timing.

The first channel crossing was so short that Trinidad didn't seem to be an island at all, but rather a continuation of Venezuela. The tiny Republic of Trinidad and Tobago consists of two islands situated 22 miles apart. The southernmost of the two, Trinidad, was discovered by Christopher Columbus in 1498 and begins the chain of islands that swoop northwest through the Caribbean. Tobago, much the smaller and less populated, appealed to us because our guidebook described it as a more laid-back, "Robinson Crusoe island." The only modern pirates in its quiet bays are its frigate birds made famous in a documentary by David Attenborough for mid-ocean thievery of fish from red-billed tropic birds.

Along the northern shoreline of Trinidad, forested mountains climb steeply to 3,000 feet, and then drop off into a flat valley brimming with the high-rise build-

*We sought out the wilder parts of the Caribbean, such
as the Pitons of St. Lucia that drop vertically into the
sea (above) and Dominica, "The Nature Island," where
I landed on a short runway set into the hills (right).*

ings of the capital city of Port-of-Spain. The weather was just as bad as on the mainland, probably due to wet clouds being lifted over the rugged island. Once I turned
northeast on course for the relatively flat island of Tobago, sunnier skies graced my
path. As I neared the tiny Crown Point Airport on the southern tip of Tobago, blinding rays of sunshine bounced off the ocean, reflecting back every conceivable hue
of blue.

After our arrival, Tobagonians greeted us, beaming big smiles and offering warm
hellos. The guidebook description of the island being more laid-back proved absolutely correct. We were required to wait for four hours until a customs agent came
to the airport and cleared us into the country. Meanwhile, I kept myself busy organizing maps, updating my logbook, and repacking the plane.

Once we were free to go, we rented a car and toured the pint-size island for an
hour before checking into our hotel, dropping our bags, and making a beeline for
the beach. Galen and I held hands and played in the surf. For the first time in a long
time, we were finally alone and without impending responsibilities. The Andes and
the Amazon were behind us and we had no schedule, no reservations, and no traveling companions. I stretched out on the sand, rested my head on Galen's firm chest,
and delighted in simply being here.

I thought about how far we'd come as a couple from when we'd first gotten together, and how much more confidence I had gained in myself. Not long after we met, he took me hiking up a narrow jeep road in a steep Eastern Sierra canyon. At one point I gripped his hand so hard that he asked, "What are you afraid of?"

"I'm going to fall," I said.

"Then what?"

"I'll die."

"No you won't. Watch me," Galen said as he ran toward the edge of the steep drop-off, jumped, and disappeared from view.

"Please don't do that!" I screamed.

Galen answered calmly, "Look over here. I'm perfectly okay!"

I opened my eyes and saw him standing in wildflowers 10 feet down the mountain slope, beaming with both hands held high, looking like a storybook character.

That same summer, he took me on a hike to Cathedral Peak in the high country of Yosemite National Park. Along the way I asked him what was in his backpack. He said he was carrying a water bottle and climbing rope in case I got scared near the summit. I trotted along behind him, naively unaware of what was coming. When the hiking trail faded into a scramble up rocks, fear began welling up inside me. I asked Galen to tie me to the rope. After he firmly tied the rope around my waist and began leading me along, I felt much more secure with the nylon umbilical cord connecting me to him.

Because his adventures had been so widely published, several hikers coming down the peak recognized him and smiled when they saw him leading me across easy terrain on a long leash. Not until we got to a vertical rock wall that led to the final summit spire did I understand his true intentions for bringing along a rope. As Galen climbed to the top, I froze in place at the base of the climb. My legs, no longer under my control, began quivering. Galen waited for me to follow, holding the rope in one hand and his camera in another.

"I can't do this," I said.

"Sure you can," Galen said confidently.

"No, I can't!" I screamed. Now I was not only losing control of my legs, but also panting for breath and beginning to feel light-headed.

"Put the camera down and hold the rope with two hands," I begged.

"Trust me. Everything is okay. I have lots of experience doing this," he replied with a grin.

As I stood on the ledge and saw the granite wall dropping away over a thousand feet beneath me, my stomach felt as if it was in my throat and I feared that I might faint, although I had never done that before.

I could not bear to look back down, so I looked up at Galen and asked, "Can you please pull me up?" We'd been together for a mere three months, and I was still trying to impress him, but the terror I felt standing on such narrow footing was too great to ignore. What he thought about me was becoming less important as time passed.

"You can climb it by yourself with the rope for safety. Just give it a try," Galen said firmly.

I thought that he was absolutely crazy and even wondered if this was a method climbers used to get rid of unwanted girlfriends. To calm my wild thoughts, I reflected back to an hour before, when Galen had last said that he loved me. Perhaps this was just a test or a practical joke. But the look on his face said it was neither. With unwavering patience, he sat there on top, waiting for me to climb the spire.

My life was in Galen's hands, and there was something right about that, for although I was a grown woman, I still believed in fairy tales. Galen was my knight in shining armor, my Prince Charming. I trusted him to take care of me as my father had taken care of my mother.

My mother met my father, a sailor in the United States Navy, when she was in her early thirties and they were both living in the Hawaiian Islands. As soon as they married, my mother stopped working and gave birth to me the following year. Around the time my brother was born, she had a near accident in her car and stopped driving altogether. From then on she depended on my father to take care of her. My parents remained madly in love to my father's dying day.

When I met Galen, somewhere deep in my unconscious I believed that he would take care of me and fill my life and my soul as my father had done for my mother. But my fantasy of being taken care of was mine alone; Galen did not believe in fairy tales. He believed in the intelligence and independence of women. His mother was a well-loved and famous concert cellist, who was also a women's rights activist and blood relative of Susan B. Anthony, the famous suffragette at the turn of the twentieth century. Though Galen wasn't perfect in his respect for women's autonomy, I'd never met anyone who believed in women more than he did.

On that first "hike" up Cathedral Peak, Galen made it clear that the longer I clung to the cold rock wall and avoided climbing the final granite chimney, the more time I would spend stuck on a tiny ledge alone. I took another deep breath and gave my serious predicament a little more thought. How could Galen refuse to haul me up as I had asked? My father would never have left my mother dangling on a rock ledge. He would have protected her from being exposed to such danger in the first place. What, I asked myself, had happened to chivalry?

Galen just stood there on the summit looking down with firm resolve. I was beginning to feel tired, hungry, and on the verge of wetting my pants. If I were going to die, I wanted to get it over with quickly, so I began clawing at the granite and pulling myself upward, scraping my knees as I pressed them against the hard rock. Once I had set my mind to it, I climbed at lightning speed and crested over the top, where Galen greeted me with a big smile and said, "See? That wasn't so bad after all."

The actual climb wasn't so terrible; Galen was right. But being exposed for my emotional weakness made me feel deeply embarrassed. I was afraid that Galen saw me for what I was: a coward, plain and simple. Unconsciously, I had set a somewhat deceptive, yet attractive trap by portraying myself to be more independent and self-reliant than I really was. And before Cathedral Peak, I had really believed myself to be the confident person I presented to the world.

Though Galen had been willing to hold a rope for safety, he was not about to pull me up to the top. And throughout our years together, he had insisted that I do that under my own power by myself. Now, lying on the beach on the last leg of my own adventure, I felt the joy of having gained that power in a world more of my own choosing.

Though Galen and I had been at odds, I still recognized all the wonderful ways that our marriage was worth the difficult times. Galen's brilliant mind keeps me challenged; his love of the natural world connects me to it as well; his constant creative drive encourages me to be creative, too; his energy invigorates me; and his unconditional love heals my heart. No one is perfect, and I'm certainly no exception, yet I have found a partner who accepts me as I am and, even more important, accepts me as I change. We have become so much more together than either of us would have been had we gone our separate ways. Marriage to Galen has been much like being on this trip: a true adventure.

Before long, the sunset painted the distant cumulus a deep salmon color. To the west, towering anvil clouds reached toward the heavens. As we strolled lazily along the shore with the gentle sound of water lapping at our bare feet, we watched the tallest clouds flash with lightning.

By now, I had a good sense of what many of the classic wild places of Latin America looked like from the air—how the Amazon River edged its way into the jungle during the rainy season, and how the snows of the Andes floated like clouds high above the distant horizon. What I was about to see and do was something entirely new for me: flying over ocean from one tiny island to another. It had a mystery all its own.

Unlike following the coastline of South America, there is no obvious route to fly through the Caribbean. It's the most politically and geographically complex part of the Americas. Perhaps Saint-Exupéry best described how it felt to be flying in the Caribbean when he wrote: "The hours during which a man flies over this mirror are hours in which there is no assurance of the possession of anything in the world. These palms beneath the plane are so many poisoned flowers. And even when the flight is an easy one, made under a shining sun, the pilot navigating at some point on the line is not gazing upon a scene. These colors of earth and sky, these traces of wind over the face of the sea, these clouds golden in the afterglow are not objects of the pilot's admiration, but of his cogitation. He looks to them to tell him the direction of the wind or the progress of the storm, and the quality of the night to come."

Flying my own airplane gave me the freedom to follow my whims as well as those of the weather. Galen and I decided not to make any reservations ahead. If we liked a place, we'd stay two or three nights. If it were not inspiring, we'd move on. We charted a tentative course from Tobago to St. Lucia, Dominica, Barbuda, Anguilla, North Caicos, and finally the Bahamas.

Early the next morning, we departed into mostly sunny skies and flew on to St. Lucia, where before landing I circled the Pitons, twin forested rock spires that rise over 2,000 feet out of the sea. I made several arcs near the tree-covered cliffs. In the middle of a good weather pattern, we decided to fly early in the morning past Martinique to Dominica, called "The Nature Island." Instead of landing and asking airport personnel their opinion about the best lodge to stay at, I continued on past the airport for a couple of minutes and checked out the hotels from the air.

The runway was quite short and surrounded by mountainous terrain on all but the ocean side. It was obviously necessary to fly very close to the terrain to put down on the runway in time to get stopped before the end of an airfield I would have chosen to bypass before this trip. After flying for the better part of two months, I was finally feeling as comfortable with my plane as I did with my bicycle after riding it solo down the California coast for a month.

We spent our first morning on Dominica's beaches, and planned a jungle hike to the island's main attraction for the second morning. The "Boiling Lake," one of only two in the world, is the result of rain-fed torrents pouring into an active volcanic steam vent.

The next day we flew to Barbuda, where I put down on one of the shortest strips on which I'd ever landed. During the final phase of flight, the stall-warning buzzer blared continuously. The only other time I'd landed on a runway almost as short as 1,680 feet was with an instructor.

"You had lots of room left over," Galen said teasingly, as I stopped near the end and turned around on the runway to taxi back.

"Yeah, right!" I said, beaming from ear to ear. When I got to the ramp, we spotted a twin-engine aircraft with two badly bent propellers. The locals said the pilot had run off the end of the airstrip.

The island was devoid of tourists and we had an 8-mile-long coral beach almost to ourselves. At dawn, we visited the Barbuda Frigate Bird Sanctuary, where 5,000 huge birds nest and breed in a dense mangrove swamp. A local guide poled us through some shallows that he had personally trenched out in order to get people within an arm's reach of active nests. Galen was able to take much better photos than in the Galápagos Islands, and the birds didn't seem the least bit disturbed.

Strong ocean breezes facilitated my short-field takeoff as I quickly climbed out into clear skies bound for Anguilla, which our guidebook described as "the best-kept secret in the Caribbean." The flat little island just 5 miles beyond the discos and golf courses of "thoroughly discovered" St. Martin is geographically nondescript, except for its shoreline, where just before landing we flew low over the most beautiful coral beach either of us had ever seen. Miles of white coral sands dropped into the sea so gently that all the adjoining waters had a stunning transparent turquoise look that reminded me of the very best of Hawaii or Mexico.

We spotted a small hotel on the beach from the air, and, immediately after landing, went to see if they had a room. The desk clerk told us that the Shoal Bay Resort only took advance bookings of full weeks, but after meeting with the manager and

explaining that we would be writing about and photographing our travels, we were given a suite that would be empty for the next three days.

We spent the next day wandering up and down an absolutely white beach beneath cerulean skies that matched my image of paradise as it curved out of sight beside parallel arcs of aquamarine waters. We were absolutely content to swim, snorkel, sunbathe, sip lemonade on the veranda, write in our diaries, read books, and generally relax. As evening came, locals informed us that all the action and nightlife were happening on St. Martin, just a few minutes away by boat. We decided to stay put where we were for two more full days.

When it came time to leave, I felt sad. I loved the simplicity of island life—walking on the beach, reading, and hanging out with Galen. I hoped to come back again soon, but suspected that once this trip was over, the likelihood of ever coming back was slight. Our life at home would fill with other types of adventures. I wanted to make the most of every moment while I had the chance.

Not long after departure, we encountered a gradually thickening cloud layer over the ocean. I chose to go on top instead of underneath, even though I was fly-

Waterfalls on Dominica (left); magnificent frigate birds took flight as we floated through a mangrove swamp on Barbuda Island (above).

ing on a visual flight plan by way of the Virgin Islands. It was actually easier to stay above the clouds and navigate off of my instrument flight maps. With blue above and white below, the only way I knew I had begun to fly over Puerto Rico was by my instruments and maps, one of which had "U.S.A." written in parentheses beside the island.

Growing up in the western United States, Puerto Rico had always seemed like some tiny, distant, not-very-American spot in the Caribbean, but flying over an island more than 150 times larger than Manhattan and knowing there were more than 3 million American citizens living down there was another matter. When I first heard the voice of an American flight controller contacting me on the radio, a sharp pang of homesickness hit me. I realized how much I missed my country, and what it meant to be returning there with my airplane.

After overflying Puerto Rico, I let down over the north side of far larger Hispaniola Island, which is divided into Haiti and the Dominican Republic. The hilly terrain was dark, cloudy, and lush, reminding me of pictures I'd seen of Vietnam. The 10,000-foot runway at Puerto Plata in the Dominican Republic was so long that I chose to land more than halfway down to avoid having to taxi so far to get fuel and go through customs. I wanted to depart as soon as possible to complete another leg of 105 miles over water to the Turks and Caicos Islands. We would be leaving the Caribbean proper and heading north over the Atlantic Ocean, where for the first time, I would be out of sight of land. Flight service said many VFR pilots had gotten into trouble flying over these open waters.

Water and sky merged to become one as I flew over an endless string of islands in the Bahamas and landed at Nassau, where Liz and Larry Roberts greeted us. I'd met Liz some years before while attending language school in Costa Rica. We stayed in their plantation-style home and took a moonlight tour in their little Boston Whaler through a harbor filled with giant cruise ships.

As I prepared my paperwork for arrival in the United States, Liz and Larry related a story about U.S. Customs boarding a yacht in Bahamian waters and cutting it up with a chainsaw to look for drugs. When the agents didn't find any, they left the boat destroyed with no legal responsibility to put it back together again. I'd heard similar stories about aircraft being dismantled on the tarmac and left that way. When I went to my room to pack my bags, I let Galen know how worried I was about clearing customs in Miami, especially after having flown through most of the major drug-smuggling countries in the world.

Galen looked me in the eye and deadpanned, "Right now, all the customs agents in Miami, all the sheriff's deputies from the surrounding counties, and 87 U.S. Marshals are preparing to meet your flight tomorrow morning. As for that form that asks you to list, in the little box, the countries you've traveled through, just write 'see attached,' and enclose a list of all the Latin countries we've traveled through with the dates in your logbook."

Before going to bed, I called flight service, filed an instrument flight plan to Miami International, and asked them to advise customs of my arrival. Knowing that I could be liable for more than $5,000 in fines if I didn't advise customs more than an hour prior to arriving, I took the secondary precaution of calling U.S. Customs myself, giving them my tail number and estimated time of arrival, and taking down the names of everyone with whom I spoke. I fell asleep dreaming about all those agents Galen mentioned being there when I arrived in the United States.

Not long after departing the Bahamas, an American controller vectored me around other air traffic, and then into sequence to shoot the ILS at Miami International. My assigned route popped me in and out of gigantic towering cumulus, which tossed us around a little, but much less than I expected. When cleared for the approach, I dropped out of the clouds and had my first view of the United States: Florida beaches shadowed by towering high-rises.

"Hoorah, we're home!" I shouted to Galen.

An overwhelmingly patriotic feeling pulsed through me. I almost blurted out, "I love you!" to the tower controller. Such simple things as being able to listen to automated weather reports in English and being able to understand every other pilot made me so glad to be back in the States.

A storm front rapidly approaching Miami had already brought 50-knot winds with higher gusts to the airport. Knowing this in advance, both Galen and I had cinched our seatbelts before entering the clouds. As I closed in on the runway numbers, I caught a glimpse of a jumbo jet waiting for takeoff. I chuckled out loud at how funny I must have looked to the passengers, bouncing around in the air like a party balloon. The winds were by far the worst of the entire trip, with a gusty cross-wind component, but I felt the same kind of comfort that I'd gained after years of skiing when I could finally start down a steep hill of huge moguls and feel totally in control, if only for the moment.

When my wheels were just about to kiss the ground, the tower controller asked me to expedite getting off the runway so an airliner could land behind me, but I

was still too busy landing and hanging on to respond. The winds were whipping me about so wildly that I was going to take whatever time I needed to remain safe. The jet would just have to wait its turn.

I taxied fast and exited the runway in plenty of time for the airliner to touch down. Ground Control directed me to customs, where I parked near a private jet arriving from Venezuela. As I started for the door, a customs agent came out and told me to remain in the plane until the people in front of us were finished. When it was my turn, I handed my paperwork over to a uniformed officer, who quickly scrutinized my form with the attached list of every country I'd visited. After a long pause, he looked up and said, "Wow, what a great trip!"

"It was a trip of a lifetime!" I beamed back.

The officer walked out as if he were going to search the plane, but barely glanced inside at the contents before signing off our paperwork and saying, "You kids get out of here! Have a nice day."

Seeing the surf break over coral reefs surrounding the Grenadine Islands made me want to be down there on the beaches rather than up in the air (right); the sculpted reefs of Road Bay were beautiful, but less inviting (above).

Oakland Bound

XXII

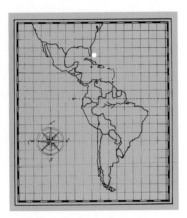

Our timing was perfect for Galen to catch the next flight to Bloomington, Indiana, where he had been invited by the brother of the Dalai Lama to give a lecture on Tibet. From there, he would fly home commercial. After he was safely on his way, I roamed the airport for a few hours until Phil Ayers, our bookkeeper's husband, who had recently gotten his pilot's license, arrived on a flight from California. As arranged before I left in November, I had called him from the Caribbean, and he came out to join me for the experience of a single-engine flight across the United States. I thought that having another pilot beside me to help navigate in winter IFR conditions would make flying into inclement weather much safer.

The winds aloft had worsened, registering 60 knots directly on my nose. I decided to wait an extra day in Miami. When I called Flight Service the next morning, the winds were still bad, but the briefer said I wouldn't encounter much in the way of turbulence, just a very slow ride. I decided to try flying north, up the Florida Panhandle, and see how it went.

As lunchtime approached and I had made much slower progress than anticipated, I landed in Panama City for food and fuel. When I pulled up to the pumps, I learned that the airport had just run out of fuel. Luckily, I'd filled my tip tanks in Miami and still had enough to make it safely to New Orleans. Another pilot flying an underpowered little Piper Tomahawk wasn't so lucky; he had been blown out to sea in the high winds. Not until after he made a 180-degree turn back toward shore did he realize the seriousness of his situation, as he slowed to a crawl flying head-on into the wind. He nearly ran out of fuel trying to make it to the closest airport and arrived beside me on fumes.

As Phil and I prepared to head off to the little airport café to grab a bite of lunch, we learned that the pilot had failed to get more than a few cups of fuel by draining the last drops out of the pump hoses. He sent someone out to buy automobile gas, which he thought would run well enough to get him home.

Passing a sailboat en route to Miami (left).

After we finished eating, I could barely tear myself away from the counter as we listened to locals spin stories with such a drawl that they made me believe every cliché I'd ever heard about the South. According to them, alligators breaking into homes and brothers marrying sisters were everyday occurrences.

The contrast between the slow-talking locals and the urgent tone of an air traffic controller after we had continued on toward New Orleans could hardly have been more dramatic. "Five Lima Yankee. Traffic twelve o'clock. Five miles. Four F-14s."

Several dark fighter jets appeared, arced around to my left, and disappeared. Minutes later, I sensed that I might not be alone and swiveled in my seat just in time to spot two jets closing in on us. "Look who's here!" I exclaimed to Phil as they aimed straight at us and broke away only at the very last moment, banking steeply to the left. While I had been out of the country, we had gone to war with Iraq. My plane provided a perfect moving target for military pilots on training missions. I thought to myself that if I were a young fighter pilot, I'd want to do the same thing. It looked like they were having a lot more fun than me.

We slipped into New Orleans just before a major winter storm hit. A line of thunderstorms blocked my ongoing route, and it looked like we wouldn't be going anywhere in the morning.

Phil and I spent the next day sightseeing around town, but our experience was very different from that of other tourists who had chosen New Orleans as their destination. While they ambled the streets and shops in slow-moving, chatty packs, Phil and I felt a strong sense of urgency. Both of us missed traveling with our spouses and were most anxious to get on with the flight. Even my driving was making Phil jumpy. He mentioned that I'd picked up some bad habits in Latin America as I decisively navigated the streets like a Buenos Aires taxi driver, rolling through stop signs and changing lanes to save seconds. He alternated calling home with my frequent calls to Flight Service to keep tabs on how the storm was progressing. Phil's wife had an office at their local airport and told him that their pilot friends were betting on how many days we'd have to wait out the big storm. From TV coverage and FAA flight information, a retired airline pilot guessed one week.

When I called home, Galen gave me some bad news. Hugh Swift, his frequent running partner and close friend of many years, had just fainted leaving a local doctor's office, hit his head falling backward onto a curb, and died instantly. Hugh was a mild-mannered adventurer who spent his winters in Berkeley writing guidebooks and his summers in the Himalaya, once walking the entire length of the range.

Hugh's death was a powerful reminder of life's fragile and fleeting nature. I would have accepted it better if he had been killed during one of his remote adventures to Tibet or Nepal. But to die so young doing something so mundane underscored my views on death, risk, and living life to its fullest. At least Hugh had managed to lead a full life, no matter how short, of exploring the far corners of the world and sharing his experiences with others through his writings. I reflected on how another close friend, Janine Jackson, had been less lucky. She died of liver cancer at 37, just two years before I left for South America. A selfless and dedicated mother of two teenagers, she was putting off doing things for herself until after her kids left home. She never realized some of her private desires, such as getting a sports car when she turned 40. When she died, I was already 40, and I began viewing each year that I lived on as a bonus. My desire to challenge myself by doing things that I dreamed of doing before it was too late was partly a result of contemplating her untimely death. I wasn't about to expose myself needlessly to danger, but neither did I want to look back on my life and wonder, "What if I had . . . ?"

Yet another unforeseen death took Phil and me totally by surprise. As we watched television to kill time, I commented, "Isn't that *our* parking lot on the news?" pointing to the screen. We both raced to the window and looked out to see if indeed it was. Sure enough, our hotel parking lot was the scene of the featured story about a hotel guest who had just been murdered in front of his wife and friends while walking into our hotel. He died in the elevator.

After all I'd been through, the thought of dying in some common hotel shocked me into calling Flight Service one last time before going to sleep.

"Could you be ready to go right away?" the briefer asked me after I explained that I was hanging out in a hotel waiting for improving weather.

"You bet!" I said.

He explained that there was a brief lull in the storm, and if I could depart immediately, I would get past the worst of it; if not, I'd be stuck for days. I filed an instrument flight plan for San Antonio, asked Phil to pack his things, and raced downstairs to pay the hotel bill.

Shortly before midnight, we lifted off in pitch-black skies that would have been a formless blanket of whiteness by daylight. Once I leveled out at my assigned altitude, I requested a weather update along my route. For the moment, there were no thunderstorms ahead, only rain.

Phil did not have any instrument training, so he didn't want to fly for even a minute in the clouds. Since my autopilot had failed somewhere over Chile, it was hard to really focus on my maps for more than a few seconds while flying the plane by hand, but it felt relatively easy now, compared to before this trip, when I never would have considered a single-pilot IFR night flight through a storm.

After 90 minutes in the air, a weather briefer reported bad news: a moving line of thunderstorms had developed over Texas and active cells were reported all around my westward heading. After a few moments of trying to locate the reported weather on my maps, I called Houston Center and asked for a vector to the nearest airport with an instrument approach. Lake Charles, Louisiana, was off to my right, 30 nautical miles north, and about the same distance from the Texas border.

I pulled out my approach charts and prepared for landing. The tower was closed, and after Approach Control cleared me for the ILS approach, I was completely on my own. The winds were fierce as I fought to maintain control of the plane.

During my descent on the ILS, I asked Phil to call out my airspeed. At times the wind shear was so intense that it took full throttle to maintain my altitude on the glide slope. When I finally dropped below the clouds, the runway lights were turned off, something for which I was unprepared. I quickly remembered the procedure and clicked my radio transmitter several times until two of the most beautiful rows of white lights I'd ever seen appeared out of the black void. Just before my wheels touched down, I glimpsed an orange windsock blowing wildly every which way.

"Nice landing!" Phil exclaimed, as we rolled safely and softly to a stop.

It was two in the morning, but after landing at night in such weather, my heart was pumping like I'd just drunk two double lattes. As I shut down the engine, I could feel the plane rocking in the wind. A gust nearly ripped the door off its hinges when I opened it. We quickly jumped out and tied the plane down before the winds could carry it away. By the time we checked into a hotel, it was nearly 3 A.M. and I fell asleep the minute my head hit the pillow.

The morning news focused on coverage of heavy flooding in New Orleans, but according to my FAA weather briefer, I had nothing but multiple layers of clouds all the way across Texas. The line of thunderstorms I had avoided by diverting to Lake Charles had passed overhead in the night.

We returned to the airport in a leisurely manner, but my heart nearly stopped when I stepped out of the taxicab and saw that my airplane was gone. I spun around in circles looking every which way for my plane, to no avail. As I was about to report the theft, a young man working at the airport explained that tornadoes had passed by in the night and my plane had been put into a hangar. Though it took a while for my plane to be untangled from all the others, having had it protected was well worth the wait.

Once we reached Texas, I continued flying on instruments between wispy clouds that looked like layers of cotton candy. For three hours and thirty minutes, I never saw another plane, nor much of Texas. Somewhere east of San Angelo we flew out from under the weather front into winter blue skies. Exhausted, I decided to call it a day and land at San Angelo, which would put me in a perfect position to make it to Las Vegas the next day.

Phil and I grabbed a ride on an airline crew van to a nearby hotel. Before leaving the airport, the van driver also picked up three neatly uniformed airline pilots, each carrying a leather flight bag. After we exchanged hellos, I joined in with small talk about how the bad weather was and how hard it had been trying to fly home. One of the pilots sarcastically responded, "Yeah, it's a bitch being a passenger, isn't it?"

Riding in a crew van with my leather Jeppesen flight chart binder on my lap in plain sight, I was surprised at his assumption. I decided to clear the up matter.

"No. I'm not a passenger. I'm flying my *own* plane home."

"Really? Where's home?" the handsome pilot asked, still sounding smug.

"Oakland," I answered.

"Where did you start from?" he inquired.

"Today? Or in the beginning?" I asked.

"In the beginning, of course," he said, sounding amused.

"Well . . . I started in Oakland," I said pausing to gather my thoughts on how best to sum up my flight, "and now I'm returning to Oakland via Chile and Argentina."

"Jesus Christ!" the guy exclaimed as his eyes lit up. He turned to the other two pilots, who had been listening closely, and despaired, "*What* in the *hell* am I doing with *my* life?"

Phil and I couldn't help bursting out laughing.

For the remainder of our ride to the hotel, the pilot asked me questions with awe and respect. Once we were alone, Phil admitted everyone on this trip had treated him as if he were my flight instructor. He hadn't told me sooner for fear of hurting my feelings.

I replied that today was the first time someone at an airport had talked down to me as if I was a commercial passenger. Most people assume I'm at least a flight attendant.

*When I landed at Las Vegas, jumbo jets dwarfed
my plane (above); when Doug landed in a field below
Fitz Roy, he tied down to a fence post (right).*

In the morning Phil and I flew on to Tucson for lunch and Las Vegas for the night, where I had agreed to meet Galen at a photographic convention. When I decided to stay an extra night to be with Galen, Phil caught a commercial flight home.

That evening, I joined Galen for dinner with Werner Publishing's Steve Werner and Deb Levine. Galen had been writing a monthly column for their *Outdoor Photographer* magazine for several years. During dinner, I tentatively began sharing my story about my flight to South America. They wanted to hear everything about the rafting accident in the Bio Bio, and flying myself to an oral surgeon, as well as my travels on the coast of Brazil. When I finished, Steve asked me if I would

write a feature article for their magazine *Plane&Pilot,* illustrated with Galen's photographs. I hadn't given any thought to writing about my trip for publication, but agreed to give it a try.

Before the night was over, I told Steve how he had inspired me six years earlier, when I was about to get my pilot's license, by answering "It's just one runway to the next," after I'd asked him what it was like for him to fly his Cessna all the way from Los Angeles to Jackson Hole, Wyoming. Little did he know that his words would end up being my daily mantra as I worked my way from California to Argentina and back.

Back at the hotel, I asked Galen if he'd heard anything about Doug's trip home. He pulled out a postcard that had just arrived in Berkeley, sent to both of us weeks before from Southern Chile. It was made from a photo Doug had taken of his plane on a dirt runway at Fundo Renihue, a huge forested *estancia* he had decided to buy after spotting it from the air with Galen. He wanted to save its temperate rainforests from being cut and exported to Japan, but he also wanted to move out of San Francisco and live permanently on the land. Parts of his message were addressed to me:

> *Barbara, I hope you had a good trip back. You're probably lounging on beaches, living the life in Venezuela about now! . . . It was a great trip with you guys! See you in SF!*
> *Ciao—D.T.*

When it was time to leave Las Vegas, I went to the airport and quickly readied Five Lima Yankee and my maps for departure from McCarran International. I chose the same route that Galen would be driving when the convention was over—crossing Death Valley to Mount Whitney, then flying up the wide-open Owens Valley, alongside the Eastern Sierra. Though I had always thought of this as Galen's favorite place in the world, it was now becoming mine as well.

I'd flown this same route a number of times, and nothing on the horizon looked different, but something felt changed. As I sailed along in smooth winter air, my heart soaked in the familiar landscape below my wings with renewed passion. I felt a sense of perfection flying alone on the last leg of my journey. Effortlessly, I glided by rows of snow-covered granite peaks above the deepest valley in America and marveled at their noble and rugged beauty. After I crossed Mammoth Pass and came abeam Yosemite Valley, Half Dome reflected its glory in the cold winter sun. Occasional puffy clouds were forming in the distance, but now I viewed them as friends, not foes.

Over the Central Valley, I monitored other pilots communicating on 122.8, a common frequency for airports. I could hear pilots from Truckee to Turlock, coming and going just like always, and I wanted to call out to them and say, "Hello everyone. I'm back!"

Homeward bound to Oakland Airport, my mind, my body, and my soul felt freshly stretched and nourished. When Bay Approach handed me off to Oakland Tower and I was cleared to land like a thousand times before, something was different—my tires, which had touched down on so many lands, now seemed to have taken on some sort of intangible spirit, as if they were directly connected to the confidence that I'd gained. They touched down gently, and almost as softly as my hands guided the control stick.

The ground controller's voice sounded like family, but I didn't think she had missed me in the months that I had been gone. She had no idea that I'd flown nearly 25,000 miles and 165 hours of flight since we last spoke, and that I had been privileged to fly low over the ruins of Palenque, the sands of the Atacama, the snows of the Andes, and the beaches of Brazil. Perhaps she noted a change in my voice, the ease with which I now spoke. But if she didn't, it didn't matter. I knew where I'd been and where I'd come from.

Across the bay, the skyscrapers of San Francisco sparkled in the morning sun, and ships sailed under the tall bridges. I reflected on our friend Hugh dying practically on his own doorstep, and thought about those well-meaning friends who had warned me not to go on my trip for fear I'd perish somewhere in Colombia or Peru.

Though many of these friends say that I'm brave, I never think of myself that way. Once I became a pilot, it amused me that people started jumping to the conclusion that I must be bold or daring, otherwise I wouldn't be flying. They see boldness as acting fearless in the face of danger, a sentiment that is echoed in the famous saying, "There are old pilots and there are bold pilots, but there are no old, bold pilots." I prefer to think of boldness in the way that Goethe expressed it when he wrote: "Whatever you can do, or dream you can, begin it! Boldness has genius, power, and magic in it."

Flying does not come naturally to me the way I've heard other pilots say it does for them. Even though I pushed beyond layers of fear to learn to fly, I've never gotten completely over being afraid. The more I know, the more there is to worry about. Nonetheless, I still love flying.

There was a time when I was first learning to fly that I naively believed my fears were temporary, and that after enough hours in an airplane I would eventually be set free forever from such lowly human feelings. During this sophomoric stage, I innocently asked a female flight instructor when the butterflies in my stomach would go away.

"Maybe never," she replied.

I thought she was joking, but time has proven how right she was. There's rarely a day that I fly when I don't feel a tinge of fear in the pit of my belly. So far, I've not personally met a single pilot who doesn't admit to feeling afraid some of the time. Even when a flight is going well, without a wisp of wind or a cloud in the sky—even when I'm having a great day and there is nowhere else I'd rather be than in the air in my own plane—I feel a little anxious and constantly on the alert for anything that might go wrong.

When my fear gets the better of me, I sometimes get stomach cramps. They normally go away once I ask myself what is really so scary. The answer is often simple. I might feel rusty on crosswind landings. Or the weather looks worse than the flight controller predicted. Or I'm flying into a new airport and don't know what exactly to expect. Once I'm armed with the reason I'm feeling anxious, I set out to get more information or sometimes sign up with an instructor for additional training.

Fear isn't a reason not to fly. I know now that fear is my biological warning system that I can tune into to keep from blundering on into disaster. I see fear of flying as a beam of light through the fog radiating from a lighthouse: it lets me know that something on the horizon could wreak havoc if ignored. A veteran bush pilot once said to me, "The day you're not afraid is the day I don't want to fly with you."

I could have found plenty of reasons not to fly my single-engine airplane to Patagonia—but I would have missed the greatest adventure of my life. Even though I may have slain my fears one by one this time, I know they'll be back. And when they return, I'll fight them off again. Anything truly worth doing in this life comes with risk, and risk is never without fear.

*I'll never forget the feeling of flying down
the spine of the Patagonian Andes (above).
Beside N735LY at our new home airport
in Bishop, California (right).*

EPILOGUE

Though the outer journey of my adventure ended when I returned home from Patagonia, much of my inner journey had just begun. During the next twenty-two months, I made nearly one hundred visits to dental specialists, including six surgeries to replace lost bone, gum, and teeth. Each new experience of pain in my mouth triggered intense flashbacks of the rafting accident.

I began avoiding activities that held even the slightest hint of risk, including such simple joys as riding my bike in the park behind our home. All the insight I had gained toward the end of my flight adventure seemed to have vanished. A friend referred me to Molly Sterling, a wise and wonderful psychologist who guided me on an inner journey to recognize how my relationships and my belief systems had played into bringing me so close to death so many times during the trip. Molly gently helped me discover that I had, in fact, been better informed than anyone to come up with my own solutions, and set me on the path to truly putting faith in my intuition.

I wasn't alone in having positive life changes in the wake of our Latin American flight adventure. All six people, pilots and passengers alike, went through major personal transitions for the better in the years that followed.

Doug Tompkins made special note of a remote *estancia* on the edge of Renihue Fjord in Southern Chile and purchased it soon after his return. He flew home by way of the Pacific Coast of South America after hearing about the conditions I had encountered on the coast of Brazil. Even so, bad weather delayed him once he crossed back into the United States, and he arrived in San Francisco on a commercial flight, returning some weeks later for his plane.

Over dinner one night, Doug told us his grand plan. His purchase included a large area of southern temperate rainforest, which was threatened by timber exports to Japan. While American environmentalists were asking him to contribute up to $50 an acre toward saving public lands at home, he could use the interest on the money from the sale of his company to buy threatened forests in Patagonia in better condition for $12 an acre.

Within the year, Doug was living full-time in Southern Chile. He was able to purchase private forest that extended from Argentina to the Pacific Ocean before the government realized what had happened. National newspapers carried front-page stories about the gringo who had bisected the nation, along with quotes from politicians who disbelieved Doug's rhetoric about saving their forests. Rumors circulated about secret American missile bases and plots to undermine the Catholic Church's policies on birth control (based on nefarious references to the Foundation for Deep Ecology, which Doug had founded to seek broad-based solutions to global environmental problems, including overpopulation).

Doug soon married a mutual friend of ours, Kris McDivitt, who gave up her job as CEO of the clothing company, Patagonia, to move onto the roadless Renihue *estancia*. Friends who visited Doug told us that his life was in danger, but when we spent a Christmas with him and Kris at Renihue, he scoffed at the veiled threats and had a positive twist to his scathing national media coverage. He expressed gratitude to Chilean newspapers and magazines for bringing the controversy over the destruction of the nation's native forests into every home. He said that all of his money invested in advocacy advertisements could not have brought about as great an awareness.

Only after he and Kris had worked together to amass a wild area larger than Yosemite National Park did he enter into negotiations with the Chilean government about giving the land to Chile if it could promise better environmental protection than in the nation's existing national parks. In 1997, Pumalin Natural Park was established as a new kind of wholly natural preserve. In March 2002, Kris appeared on the *Today Show* to pitch their newest vision of a Patagonia Land Trust dedicated to acquiring wildlands in Argentina as well as Chile.

On Doug's recommendation, I began volunteering my flying skills to LightHawk,

The ranch Doug flew over and purchased at Renihue
Fjord (top); a fraction of the southern temperate rainforest
Doug has saved through subsequent purchases (bottom).

a nonprofit organization that called itself an environmental air force. Taking politicians, scientists, and televisions crews up in the air allowed them to directly observe areas of special concern from a unique perspective. I participated in flights from the Yukon to Costa Rica and became the first volunteer pilot to serve on the organization's board of directors. Today, I no longer fly for LightHawk, but I continue to volunteer my services and my airplane for environmental issues in which I believe.

Peter Buckley, Doug's business partner in the European franchises of Esprit, followed his lead in environmental philanthropy. He currently serves as president of the David Brower Center, a huge "green" building complex that will occupy a full a city block in Berkeley by 2006, thanks in part to the $2 million financial commitment Peter arranged to launch the project. The center is named for the legendary environmental advocate and native son who passed away in 2000.

Michael Craig decided to give up his career in commercial aviation after his experiences on the Brazilian coast. He returned to college, and after graduation went to work for the city of Aspen, his hometown.

Robert Cushman, my brother, returned home to a rude awakening: his girlfriend of seventeen years left him for someone she met at her fortieth birthday party. But within the year, he fell in love with a teacher who proved to be his true soul mate. They soon married and now live happily, with their two daughters, in a home he built for them in the mountains outside Truckee, California. He received a promotion and is now the director of ski patrol for Squaw Valley, USA.

Soon after I returned from my flight, I began writing the article requested by *Plane&Pilot*, basically ignoring that the publisher told me the magazine's features ran no more than two thousand words. I had never written anything more than bits and pieces for catalogs and promotion, and after paring the story down to what I thought was the bare bones, I turned in eleven thousand words. When Galen learned what I had done, he replied, "In thirty years of writing, I have never violated a word count like that."

"That's what it took to tell the story," I said, with newfound confidence.

Galen was dumbfounded when an editor called to say my story was being serialized at almost its full length. My growing realization that it was best to trust my own intuitions was confirmed when the story received so much attention that all the back issues quickly sold out. That's when I decided to write this book.

I began writing by relying on a combination of my memory, diary, and flight log, plus hours of video, thousands of still photographs, and conversations with my traveling companions. It wasn't enough. In December 2000, Galen and I took a commercial flight to Rio de Janeiro, where we rented a helicopter and returned the route of my stormy flight into Angra dos Reis. Landforms along the tortuous coastline seen for the first time on a clear day matched my memory and the times I'd scrawled on the flight map. Before returning home, we took a long flight over the

Amazon Basin, and then spent some ground time along the river. The experience gave me a better feel for these tropical wilds than I had gained from flying over them the first time.

As I opened myself up to my inner journey, my life continued to unfold in unexpected ways. By the late nineties, our lives in the city appeared splendidly ordered with ample opportunity "to get away from it all" in N735LY to distant continents. But despite the powerful cultural draws and friendships in the San Francisco Bay Area that had been Galen's lifetime home, we were finding peace of mind ever more elusive in a world of gridlock and greedlock.

We decided to pick up our stakes and move to the little town of Bishop in the Eastern Sierra. Here amid the wildlands we most love, we opened a new gallery and offices in the town's historic bank building and purchased a home just minutes away with views of 14,000-foot mountain ranges in both directions.

On the other side of town is a broad, 7,000-foot former military airstrip, where N735LY sits ready at a moment's notice. Still my flying partner after eighteen years, she's been fully overhauled with a 1999 Cessna paint scheme, new upholstery, and a new engine. Though I haven't flown her to South America again, I have made several trips to Mexico and around the American West, as well as numerous flights for aerial photography, assignments, lectures—and just plain fun. ‡

Home again with Galen (above).

Flight Log

Date	From	To	Total flight hours
11/30/90	Oakland, CA	Palm Springs, CA	3.1
11/30/90	Palm Springs, CA	Mexicali, Mexico	1.1
11/30/90	Mexicali, Mexico	Mazatlán, Mexico	6.2
12/1/90	Mazatlán, Mexico	Zihuatenajo, Mexico	4.2
12/1/90	Zihuatenajo, Mexico	Puerto Escondido, Mexico	2.5
12/3/90	Puerto Escondido, Mexico	Palenque, Mexico	3.1
12/3/90	Palenque, Mexico	Campeche, Mexico	1.5
12/3/90	Campeche, Mexico	Chichén Itzá, Mexico	1.3
12/4/90	Chichén Itzá, Mexico	Chetumal, Mexico	1.8
12/4/90	Chetumal, Mexico	Belize City, Belize	.5
12/4/90	Belize City, Belize	San Pedro Island, Belize	.4
12/5/90	San Pedro Island, Belize	Belize City, Belize	.4
12/5/90	Belize City, Belize	San José, Costa Rica	5.7
12/6/90	San José, Costa Rica	Panama City, Panama	2.9
12/6/90	Panama City, Panama	Cali, Colombia	4.0
12/7/90	Cali, Colombia	Quito, Ecuador	2.3
12/8/90	Quito, Ecuador	Talara, Peru	3.7
12/8/90	Talara, Peru	Lima, Peru	4.2
12/9/90	Lima, Peru	Juliaca, Peru	3.9
12/10/90	Juliaca, Peru	Arica, Chile	1.7
12/10/90	Arica, Chile	Antofagasta, Chile	2.4
12/11/90	Antofagasta, Chile	Santiago, Chile	4.9
12/13/90	Santiago, Chile	Temuco, Chile	3.0
12/13/90	Temuco, Chile	Coihaique, Chile	4.6
12/14/90	Coihaique, Chile	Balmaceda, Chile	.4
12/15/90	Balmaceda, Chile	Balmaceda, Chile	2.9
12/15/90	Balmaceda, Chile	Bariloche, Argentina	3.4
12/18/90	Bariloche, Argentina	Puerto Montt, Chile	.9
12/23/90	Puerto Montt, Chile	Temuco, Chile	2.2

Date	From	To	Total flight hours
12/28/90	Temuco, Chile	Santiago, Chile	2.9
1/02/91	Santiago, Chile	Buenos Aires, Argentina	5.5
1/03/91	Buenos Aires, Argentina	Porto Alegre, Brazil	4.3
1/04/91	Porto Alegre, Brazil	Angra dos Reis, Brazil	5.7
1/05/91	Angra dos Reis, Brazil	Rio de Janeiro, Brazil	1.2
1/05/91	Rio de Janeiro, Brazil	Macaé, Brazil	1.3
1/05/91	Macaé, Brazil	Salvador, Brazil	4.7
1/06/91	Salvador, Brazil	São Luís, Brazil	5.9
1/07/91	São Luís, Brazil	Belém, Brazil	2.2
1/08/91	Belém, Brazil	Paramaribo, Suriname	4.7
1/09/91	Paramaribo, Suriname	Caracas, Venezuela	5.9
1/16/91	Caracas, Venezuela	Caracas, Venezuela (local flight)	1.3
2/05/91	Caracas, Venezuela	Tobago, West Indies	3.6
2/06/91	Tobago, West Indies	St. Lucia, West Indies	1.8
2/07/91	St. Lucia, West Indies	Dominica, West Indies	1.7
2/09/91	Dominica, West Indies	Antigua, West Indies	.9
2/09/91	Antigua, West Indies	Barbuda, West Indies	.4
2/10/91	Barbuda, West Indies	Anguilla, West Indies	.8
2/12/91	Anguilla, West Indies	Dominican Republic, West Indies	4.2
2/12/91	Dominican Republic, West Indies	North Caicos, West Indies	1.8
2/13/91	North Caicos, West Indies	Nassau, Bahamas	2.9
2/14/91	Nassau, Bahamas	Miami, FL	.8
2/16/91	Miami, FL	Panama City, FL	4.3
2/16/91	Panama City, FL	New Orleans, LA	2.0
2/18/91	New Orleans, LA	Lake Charles, LA	1.9
2/19/91	Lake Charles, LA	San Angelo, TX	3.3
2/20/91	San Angelo, TX	Tucson, AZ	4.1
2/20/91	Tucson, AZ	Las Vegas, NV	2.8
2/23/91	Las Vegas, NV	Oakland, CA	2.8

GLOSSARY

ATIS (automatic terminal information service): The recorded weather information available at most airports with control towers.

ADF (automatic direction-finder): An old-style navigational system with a needle that points toward a radio beacon as the device continuously broadcasts an audible signal in Morse code that spells out the station's two- or three-letter radio identifier.

AGL (above ground level): Altitude in feet above ground level.

ADCUS (advise customs): The abbreviation used when filing an international flight plan to request customs be advised of an aircraft's time of arrival.

DG (directional gyro): A gyroscopically controlled instrument that indicates heading.

DME (distance measuring equipment): A gauge that measures distance to a navigational radio beacon on the ground.

FBO (fixed base operator): An aircraft support operation based on an airfield.

GPS (Global Positioning System): A satellite-based navigation system.

IFR (instrument flight rules): Rules that govern flight in weather conditions below VFR weather minimums. Also used to define the weather conditions and the type of flight plan under which an aircraft is operating.

ILS (instrument landing system): A sophisticated system that guides instrument-equipped airplanes vertically and laterally to a precise landing. In the event of bad weather, it provides the most accurate and desirable method of navigating into an unfamiliar airport.

IMC (instrument meteorological conditions): Weather conditions below VFR weather minimums.

Loran (long range aid to navigation): A system for measuring distance and position from a ground-based navigational aid.

MOA (military operations area): Special-use airspace designated for military activity.

OBS (omni-bearing selector): The part of an airplane's VOR indicator that allows a pilot to dial in a chosen course.

ONC (operational navigation charts): World-wide flight charts created by the U.S. Department of Defense.

partial panel: A phrase used to indicate the failure of primary flight instruments used for IFR flight.

STOL (short takeoff and landing): Special aircraft equipment that enables shorter takeoffs and landings.

Vector: A compass heading given to a pilot by an air controller based on radar position information.

Victor airway: A federally established system of airways 8 miles wide and up to 18,000 feet, based on radio beacons.

VFR (visual flight rules): Rules specifying minimum cloud clearance and visibility requirements for flight by visual reference. Also used to define the weather conditions and type of flight plan under which an aircraft can operate by visual reference.

VOR (very high frequency omnidirectional radio): A ground-based navigation system using fixed onmidirectional radio beacons.

WAC, WACs (world aeronautical charts): Flight charts at 1:1,000,000 scale covering large geographical areas.

ACKNOWLEDGMENTS

I would like to thank my husband and best friend, Galen Rowell, for his unwavering support. Without his constant editorial help and consent to write about events that involved both of us the way I saw them, this book would never have seen print. My thanks go to Doug Tompkins for his invitation to fly to Patagonia—an adventure that changed my life for the better in so many ways—and for his vision and courage, especially evident in his bold methods of saving wildlands. I thank my brother, Robert Cushman, for his loving friendship and support. Michael Craig for joining me my on the Atlantic Coast and sticking it out when the going got more than difficult.

My thanks for sharing stories go to Peter Buckley, Dick Dorworth, Pat O'Donnell, Lito Tejada-Flores, and Susie Tompkins. I am deeply grateful to all who offered food, shelter, and companionship during the flight, including Juan and Patti Abadi, Kike Arnal, Cado Avenali, Phil Ayers, and Hernán Boher.

After I returned home from my flight, many people influenced the course of this book. Molly Sterling pointed me inwards during rough times of self-doubt. Steve Werner published my story in *Plane&Pilot* and allowed me to break the rules. Debra Levine of *Plane&Pilot* gave her unwavering enthusiasm.

Kirsty Melville took a chance by asking me to tackle a more difficult path than the breezy picture book about my flight that we had proposed. Melissa Stein provided the superb editorial guidance and vision to keep my message on course. Lorena Jones for her editorial dedication to the project. Sharon Silva contributed a highly skillful proofread. Jenny Barry brought it all together with her brilliant sense of design.

In a broader sense, my thanks go to Barry Lopez for sharing his insights with me about the importance of storytelling. My special thanks go to Sue Clark, Bob Dye, and Peter Gaylord for teaching me to fly, and last but not least to all those wonderful people who helped me at sometime during the process: Pat Anderson, Justin Black, Nenelle Bunnin, Sheila Canavan, Peter and Karine Croft, Chris Eckstrom, Phil and Sue Esdaile, Nancy Finch, Eddie and Tim Ford, Nancy Hult Ganis, Joelle Green, Joel Hancock, Linda Jenkins, Paul and Charissa McDonald, Marcelo Miller, Matthew and Susan Naythons, Linda Lee Nikolaus, Vivian Patterson, Liz and Larry Roberts, Skip Slyfield, Dean Stevens, Kathy Taft, Kris Tompkins, Lyla Wolden, and Kristen Wurz.

A Mountain Light Press Book

A Kirsty Melville Book

Ten Speed Press
P.O. Box 7123
Berkeley, California 94707
www.tenspeed.com

Distributed in Australia by Simon and Schuster Australia, in Canada
by Ten Speed Press Canada, in New Zealand by Southern Publishers Group,
in South Africa by Real Books, in Southeast Asia by Berkeley Books, and
in the United Kingdom and Europe by Airlift Book Company.

Cover and interior design by
Jennifer Barry Design, Sausalito, CA
Layout production, Kristen Wurz
Maps by Kirk Caldwell

Library of Congress Cataloging-in-Publication Data

Rowell, Barbara Cushman.
Flying south : a pilot's inner journey / by Barbara Cushman Rowell.
     p.   cm.
ISBN 1-58008-282-3 -- 1-58008-471-0 (pbk.)
1. Latin America--Description and travel. 2. Cessna aircraft--Piloting.
3. Air travel--Latin America. 4. Rowell, Barbara Cushman--Journeys--Latin America.
I. Title.
F1409.3 .R69 2002
918.04'33--dc21   2002066202

First printing, 2002   Printed in Hong Kong

1 2 3 4 5 6 7 8 9 10 — 05 04 03 02

AFTERWORD

Barbara had just finished *Flying South* when the four of us flew to Nome, Alaska, in July 2002. We spent three weeks circumnavigating the Bering Sea on the *World Discoverer,* as Galen and Frans conducted a joint photographic workshop onboard. We had been close friends for years, but our busy lives never gave us enough opportunities to be together. Galen had just returned from a grueling *National Geographic* assignment in Tibet, where he hauled 275 pounds of gear through thin air for seven weeks. Barbara was excited about sharing her book and her journey with the world. They were as at ease with themselves as we had seen them in years.

Moving to Bishop had been good for them. "I'm walking on clouds," Barbara wrote to Chris after they found their new home. They had come full-circle, back to a place that had nurtured Galen as a mountaineer and photographer; a place that made Barbara feel free. She called it "paradise." They had found their real home.

At the end of the trip we flew back together to San Francisco and parted with embraces at the airport. We drove home to Santa Cruz and Barbara and Galen went to Oakland, where a pilot from Bishop picked them up in a charter plane. They were eager to make it home that same night. The next day we learned that during their final approach to Bishop airport, something had gone terribly wrong. The plane had crashed in the desert. There were no survivors.

Now, in the aftermath of an event that will never seem real, we can only take comfort from remembering the people they were and the memories they left behind. Barbara and Galen were larger than life. They affected the aspirations of many people who were touched by their photographs, their stories, and their spirits. They lived every moment with a sense of risk and adventure. They dreamed big dreams. They never saw obstacles, only opportunities. May they continue to inspire us all.

—Frans Lanting and Christine Eckstrom
Santa Cruz, California, August 2002